Synkrētic

The Journal of Indo-Pacific
Philosophy, Literature & Cultures

2022 / № 1

Synkrētic
The Journal of Indo-Pacific Philosophy, Literature & Cultures

ISSN 2653-4029

Editor: Daryl Morini
Deputy Editor: Christian Romuss
Associate Editor: Devon Turner

www.synkretic.com

General enquiries: editor@synkretic.com

Correspondence should be addressed to

The Editor, Synkrētic Journal
c/o Irukandji Media Pty Ltd
Unit 9 204 Alice St
Brisbane City Qld 4000
AUSTRALIA

Synkrētic acknowledges the traditional custodians of the lands of Brisbane on which we work, the Turrbal and Jagera peoples.

Published in Australia by Irukandji Press, Brisbane.

Irukandji Press is a trade name of Irukandji Media Pty Ltd, an ASIC-registered, special purpose not-for-profit company.

ISBN 978-0-646-85574-5

Layout and editorial matter: © Irukandji Media Pty Ltd, 2022

Cover design and typesetting: Arthur Arek

Contributors

Georges Baudoux · Elsdon Best

Claro R. Ceniza · Brian Chung · A.P. Elkin

Roque J. Ferriols · Jerry Flexer · Alex François

Arthur Grimble · Rolando M. Gripaldo · A.C. Haddon

Ferry Hidayat · Te Rangi Hīroa · Daya Krishna

Aporo Te Kumeroa · Rubenson Lono

Kaspa Niu Maketi · Emele Mamuli · Te Mātorohanga

Daryl Mendoza · Leonardo N. Mercado

George Mombi · Daryl Morini · Stephen Muecke

Āpirana Ngata · Noel S. Pariñas · Nēpia Pōhūhū

Anne Quito · Emerita Quito · Byron Rangiwai

Mary Rokonadravu · Hu Shih · Percy Smith

Nei Tearia · Teliki Thomas · Florentino T. Timbreza

David Unaipon · Willy Usao · Voltaire

H.T. Whatahoro · Anshi Zhou

Acknowledgments

Synkrētic №1 (Feb. 2022) was a collaborative enterprise involving 41 past and current writers and oral history sources from 15 countries across the region.

Contributors to this issue are from the Indo-Pacific countries of the Philippines (9 writers), New Zealand (9), Solomon Islands (5), Australia (4), China (2), and from Indonesia, India, Fiji, Papua New Guinea, New Caledonia, and Kiribati (1 each). The remaining 6 writers in this issue are from the US, Canada, France, and the UK.

Synkrētic thanks all rights holders whose support made this issue possible, and especially the people and organisations listed below.

Institutions, estates and individuals

Claro Rafols Ceniza Estate
Professor Daniel Raveh
Ma. Dreena Quito del Mundo
Ms Judy Kropinyieri
Mitchell Library
Professor Shail Mayaram
State Library of New South Wales

Publications and publishers

adda (Commonwealth Writers)
Ateneo de Manila University
Council for Research in Values and Philosophy
De La Salle University Press
Editions de Conti (MkF éditions)
Journal of the Polynesian Society
Folklore journal (The Folklore Society)
Nouvelles Éditions Latines
Oceania journal
Philippine Studies: Historical and Ethnographic Viewpoints
Philosophia: International Journal of Philosophy
Quartz news

For

Ben, Geoff, Jean-Louis, Marianne, Roger,
Seb, Simon, Stephan and *Tim*

with gratitude.

Contents

The Indo-Pacific origins of philosophy

Synkrētic is a new journal devoted to Indo-Pacific philosophy, literature, and cultures.

The Indo-Pacific is that vast expanse of sea, islands, and continents which converge on maritime southeast Asia, then ripple out into its hyphenated oceans. In short, it is made up of the Asia-Pacific region plus that minor added detail of South Asia, which was cut out when its boundaries were drawn up by diplomats in the 1990s.

Though it is a 19th century European construct, the concept *Indo-Pacific* has only gained widespread currency in recent years. Many sound arguments for why this frame better fits our remarkably diverse region have identified political, strategic, and economic grounds. The Indo-Pacific has been called the new centre of global economic growth. While true, to reduce it to 60% of global GDP or US $50 trillion is to sell it short. It is also called the world's geopolitical centre of gravity. This is typically a bad place to be. In physics, the centre of gravity tends to attract large, heavy objects. *On War*, the West's military classic, says that the centre of gravity is where the 'most effective blow is struck' to an enemy force.[1] Gravity is at work when half the world's 470 submarines patrol six cramped chokepoints in one Southeast Asian archipelago.

But few arguments have identified culture, which in silent and subtle ways threads this otherwise disparate group of countries together. The Indo-Pacific region is more than the central nervous system of world trade, guarded and threatened by rival networks of military bases. It is also a superhighway of ideas which, over millennia, gradually connected the inestimably diverse civilisations of East, South, Southeast Asia, and Oceania into an ever-closer union.

While Europe was a Roman province, the Indo-Pacific's overland Silk Road and maritime trade routes were great conveyor belts of ideas, which sailed down the South China Sea and through the Malacca Strait.

Thus, an Indian prince closes his eyes under a tree for a week. Just a few centuries later, Buddhism has spread to China, Japan, and Southeast Asia. Some of its roots reach as far away as Greece. By the 19th century, 'Indian wisdom flows back to Europe' at a rate of knots, which some philosophers hope will fundamentally change European thought for the better.[2] The philosophy born in Nepal soon sails into San Francisco harbour in the hearts of Chinese migrants. In the present day, millions of Westerners close their eyes like the Buddha to meditate. The Indo-Pacific did fundamentally change the West's thought, ethics, and spirituality, entangling both regions as a result.

For millennia, Indo-Pacific thinkers have created, innovated, and refined philosophical thought on the deepest problems of metaphysics, epistemology, logic, ethics, and science in the context of their own cultures. But to understand and sometimes even see *Indo-Pacific philosophy*, three common assumptions need to be let go.

The first assumption to discard is that philosophy is done either by: i) an academic alone in their cold office reading an angry genius; or ii) an angry genius alone in their Swiss summer house denouncing their academic readers. This cliché of modern Western philosophical practice reduces the 'wisdom lover' (*philosophos*) to an individual writer. After all, we only think as individuals and only think clearly in writing.

Nothing can be learned without letting go of this idea. The Indo-Pacific's 4.3 billion people belong to twenty-odd countries. Each one is a microcosm of sub-national cultures, clans, and tribes. China counts 56 cultures, Indonesia has 300, the Philippines lists 181. Australia is made up of 278 cultural groups, two of them comprising 250 Indigenous cultures. 1,652 languages are spoken in India and 1,300 in the Pacific. Of the latter, half are spoken in Papua New Guinea alone, the most linguistically diverse country in the world. Each one of these cultures birthed religious, philosophical, and scientific traditions worthy of consideration. Few focus on the individual, a fundamentally Western idea.[3] In many, wisdom lives in speech and not books.

The second assumption to discard is that the Greek tradition is the *alpha* and *omega* of philosophy. The myth of a so-called 'Greek miracle', popularised by French philosopher Ernest Renan in 1899, exerted a powerful influence on how Western philosophers interpreted Indo-Pacific thought.[4] The term is recent but the story old. Since the Enlightenment, it has been taught that the historical mission of Greece, and therefore its heir Europe, was 'to detect and emphasize the reason or the reasonableness of the universe.'[5] While the world was wrapped in a veil of gloom and superstition, a few Greek geniuses received the Promethean flame and brought its light—logic, reason, science, philosophy—to the nations. 'And their eyes were opened, and they knew…'[6]

Hegel elevated Western philosophy's creation story to a theology. His famous remark, 'what is real is rational', was a *Sanctus* to the Greek miracle, the 'pivot upon which the world-wide revolution then in process turned.'[7] Hegel saw the Greek Spirit as special for being practically 'free from superstition'.[8] The Greeks ushered in the 'dawn of Thought'.[9] Even their myth was better, presumably their honey sweeter.[10] Their 'metaphysical miracle', as Nietzsche called it, was unparalleled.[11] Central to it was the claimed ability of thinkers from Thales to Aristotle to tear reason (*logos*) out of the clutches of myth (*mythos*).[12] This criterion would be applied to Indo-Pacific cultures.

Among others, Western colonies misapplied the myth of this Greek miracle as a lens through which to understand local cultures. When this failed, force was often used to impose the West's secular and religious myths onto colonised cultures. The reflexive use of European philosophy to explain local conceptual universes, on which there were initially scant and linguistically uninformed data, created an enormous distortion field guaranteeing misperceptions and conflict even before politics interfered.

In Australia, the rich traditions of Aboriginal philosophy were often dismissed as meaningless superstition. Dreamtime stories were collected and analysed, but marketed and sold as mythology, *i.e.* pre-philosophical. Into the 1960s, a dead French philosopher still convinced anthropologists that Aboriginal people lacked logic.[13] In other words, they had not yet read Aristotle, whose famed thought travelled everywhere Catholic missionaries went in the Indo-Pacific, like the Philippines.[14] In this context, it would be unsurprising if Aristotle sounded more like a mythical figure to First Australians. In the Middle Ages, the West's own holy men had called him *precursor Christi in naturalibus*, God's precursor in nature.[15] And to this day, Australian 'philosophers are mostly only telling the stories of the Greeks.'[16]

If we have learned anything from past attempts in the last few centuries, let it be that Indo-Pacific philosophies will not be best explained by Aristotle, Locke, or Kant. They must be understood in their own endogenous categories, as developed by those who think in them, in respectful collaboration with other qualified experts thinking in different traditions. But to truly appreciate the wisdoms of the Indo-Pacific, they must also be read as an overarching, contiguous story being constantly and messily overwritten, as a living palimpsest. No single culture writes or owns the whole book. It is anonymous, collective, like a sacred text.

A final assumption best set aside is that cultures, like oil and water, don't mix and are best bottled separately. People have attempted to draw sharp dividing lines between philosophical traditions for centuries. Often, the motive was to protect the West's elixir of life, philosophy, from contamination by so-called 'wisdom traditions', collective forms of cultural knowledge which generations pass down 'uncritically'.[17] Is this distinction valid?

In Europe, the philosopher strips universals of cultural particulars, knits old ideas into a new conceptual net, presents it at a conference: a wisdom tradition lives on. In the Pacific, a philosopher infuses cultural particulars with universals, weaves old ideas into a new tapa cloth, offers it at a gathering: a wisdom tradition lives on. The substantive difference, if there is one, is one of style and cultural context.

To hermetically seal philosophical traditions would be to starve them of the oxygen on which thought lives. Indo-Pacific ideas don't belong in empty museums and under glass display cases, unintelligible but at least untouched. They belong in the world from which each draws breath. 'Philosophy,' Emerita Quito writes, 'is ultimately human before it is Eastern or Western.'[18] No culture has copyrighted *filosofía*, the love of wisdom, least of all the Greeks. Even Greek philosophy, on closer inspection, is a lot less Western than it is claimed to be.

The West, Daya Krishna argues, distorted its cultural self-image by selectively identifying it with Aristotle. Greece worshipped as many gods as India; the West keeps only its 'goddess of Reason'.[19] Did not Thales, who they say first reasoned aright,[20] say 'everything is full of gods'?[21] Just like Laozi, the Chinese founder of Taoism who is still worshipped today, Greek philosophers too were gods, like the volcano-jumping Empedocles and Pythagoras of the golden thigh.[22] Socrates, that great reasoner, reveals in the *Apology* that he is literally a 'gift from God'.[23] Not even Aristotle rejected myth. In a sense, he says, philosophy is the same thing since both arise from wonder.[24]

Indo-Pacific and Western philosophies can enlighten one another too. Pre-Socratic philosopher Anaximander taught that death is an 'atonement' for the 'injustice' of life.[25] Yakili, the sky god of the Kewa people in Papua New Guinea's southern highlands, taught a remarkably similar doctrine.[26] Anaximander taught that humans had to claw their way out of the belly of scaly fish to survive. Melanesians taught that humans had to shed their skins like a snake to survive.[27] Indonesian and Pacific traditions tend to agree with Thales that nature is full of gods.[28]

Indo-Pacific philosophy is not always a story of clashing ideas. It is also one of cross-cultural cooperation, imitation, and replication for ours is a *syncretic* region. The concept of syncretism still arouses horror among religious and philosophical thinkers with orthodox inclinations. It refers to the habit cultures have of stealing each other's values, ideas, practices and symbols; of keeping parts they like, discarding those they dislike, and merging the rest. What emerges is syncretic. It is strange that this habit should still be so vilified when every orthodoxy was once such a gnarled, sorry-looking creature.

What feeling can Karel Kupka's *Aboriginal Madonna* painting, displayed in Darwin, inspire if not that wonder in which philosophy is said to start? If a protest must be lodged, let it be addressed to Jesus, a Jewish syncretist. Or to the founder of Buddhism, who was a Hindu. Much as three Greeks fill all of Europe with their thoughts, so three Germans still influence communism in Asia. Indian migrants mesh Hinduism with Indigenous cultures in Indonesia, Malaysia, Singapore, and Fiji.[29] Indonesia is Islamised by Chinese ships.[30] A Chinese philosopher recruits Aristotle to settle a dispute with Confucius.[31]

Some might call this all rather eclectic. We call it home. We call it *Synkrētic*.

Daryl Morini

Notes

1 Carl von Clausewitz, *On War*, Vol I, Book 6, transl. J.J. Graham (London: Kegan Paul, Trench, Trübner, 1908), 354.

2 Arthur Schopenhauer, *The World as Will and Presentation*, Volume I, ed. Daniel Kolak, transl. Richard E. Aquila (London: Routledge, 2016), 415.

3 In *Synkrētic* №1: Emerita Quito, 'On Asian and Western minds', 58-72.

4 Guy G. Stroumsa, *The Idea of Semitic Monotheism: The Rise and Fall of a Scholarly Myth* (Oxford: Oxford University Press, 2021), 122.

5 George P. Conger, 'Did India Influence Early Greek Philosophies?', in *Philosophy East and West*, Vol. 2, No. 2 (Jul. 1952): 126.

6 Luke 24:31.

7 Georg Wilhelm Friedrich Hegel, *Philosophy of Right*, transl. S.W. Dyde (New York: Cosimo Classics, 2008), xix.

8 Hegel, *Philosophy of Right*, 255.

9 Hegel, *Philosophy of Right*, 287.

10 Hegel, *Philosophy of Right*, 298-299.

11 Saverio Clemente, Bryan J. Cocchiara, *misReading Nietzsche* (Eugene, OR: Pickwick Publications, 2018), 12.

12 Robert L. Fowler, '*Mythos* and *Logos*', Robert L. Fowler, *The Journal of Hellenic Studies*, Vol. 131 (2011): 45.

13 In *Synkrētic* №1: A.P. Elkin, 'Leibniz and the Dreaming', 12.

14 In *Synkrētic* №1: Daya Krishna, 'The West's goddess of reason', 46-57; Emerita Quito, 'On Asian and Western minds', 58-72; Florentino T. Timbreza, 'Filipino logic', 107-110; Leonardo N. Mercado, 'On snow and the Filipino mind', 99-102; Rolando M. Gripaldo, 'How to outgrow Kant', 123-126.

15 Andrea Oppo, *Lev Shestov: The Philosophy and Works of a Tragic Thinker* (Boston: Academic Studies Press, 2020), 130.

16 Lauren Gower, *What do you need a whitefella's education for? A yarn about Aboriginal philosophy*, Thesis for a Bachelor of Arts with Honours in Philosophy, School of Philosophy, University of Tasmania, 2012, 20.

17 This author's useful distinction is used for illustrative purposes. There is no implication that its author agrees with the motives discussed in this piece. William J. Gavin, *In Dewey's Wake: Unfinished Work of Pragmatic Reconstruction* (New York: State University of New York Press, 2003), 150.

18 In *Synkrētic* №1: Emerita Quito, 'On Asian and Western minds', 68.

19 In *Synkrētic* №1: Daya Krishna, 'The West's goddess of reason', 46-57.

20 'Thales said goodbye to myth!' wrote Nietzsche. See Laurence Lampert, *What a Philosopher Is: Becoming Nietzsche* (Chicago: University of Chicago Press, 2017), 99-100; Anthony Gottlieb, *The Dream of Reason: A History of Western Philosophy from the Greeks to the Renaissance* (London: Penguin Books, 2000).

21 This fragment is found in Aristotle, *De Anime* 411a 18, in Angus Nicholls, *Myth and the Human Sciences: Hans Blumberg's Theory of Myth* (New York: Routledge, 2014), 227.

22 In *Synkrētic* №1: Voltaire, 'Pythagoras in India', 218-221.

23 Plato, 'Apology', in *The Last Days of Socrates*, transl. Hugh Tredennick and Harold Tarrant (London: Penguin, 2003), 70.

24 A.P. Bos, 'Aristotle on Myth and Philosophy', *Philosophia Reformata*, Vol. 48, No. 1 (1983): 1-18.

25 Cited in Frank N. Magill, *The Ancient World*, Volume 1 (Chicago: Fitzroy Dearborn Publishers, 1998), 69.

26 Mary N. MacDonald, 'Thinking and teaching with the indigenous traditions of Melanesia', in *Beyond Primitivism: Indigenous Religious Traditions and Modernity*, ed. Jacob Kehinde Olupona (New York: Routledge, 2004), 316.

27 In *Synkrētic* №1: George Mombi, 'The Melanesian concept of *gutpela sindaun*', 36.

28 In *Synkrētic* №1: Byron Rangiwai, 'The mystery of the god Io', 73-85; H.T. Whatahoro, Te Mātorohanga, Nēpia Pōhūhū, Aporo Te Kumeroa, Percy Smith, *et al.*, 'Io of the hidden face', 189-204; Ferry Hidayat, 'What is Indonesian philosophy?', 24-33.

29 In *Synkrētic* №1: Mary Rokonadravu, 'The brief, insignificant history of Peter Abraham Stanhope', 145-155.

30 Tan Ta Sen, *Cheng Ho and Islam in Southeast Asia* (Singapore: Institute of Southeast Asian Studies, 2009).

31 In *Synkrētic* №1: Hu Shih, 'Logic as rectification of thought', 86-96.

ESSAYS

Leibniz and the Dreaming*

A.P. Elkin†

Compared with the philosophical systems of Plato and Aristotle, of Aquinas and Kant, of Berkeley and Bertrand Russell, the inherent and implied cosmologies and metaphysics of such preliterate peoples as the American Indians, the Polynesians, and the Australian Aboriginal people may not seem appropriately termed philosophical.

But if we were to compare the latter with the earliest recorded philosophical essays, such as those of Thales and Heraclitus, who found the first principle in water and fire respectively, we would realise that they were doing no more than what our so-called "primitive" philosophers do: they were looking for 'some one kind of existence out of which the diversity of the universe sprang, and some permanent ground at the back of the never-ending process of change.'[1]

From our point of view, the "primitive" attitudes towards existence were and are pre-scientific, and may not have been built into

---

*   This is an edited extract of A.P. Elkin's 'Elements of Australian Aboriginal Philosophy', first published in *Oceania*, Vol. 40, No. 2 (Dec. 1969): 85-98. Elkin's piece was based on a paper he read to the Anthropology Section of the Adelaide meeting of the Australian and New Zealand Association for the Advancement of Science in August 1969. This edited extract is reproduced with the gracious permission of *Oceania*'s editors.

†   Adolphus Peter Elkin (1891-1979) was an Anglican priest, Professor of Anthropology at the University of Sydney, and the founder of *Oceania* journal. He held a PhD in anthropology from University College London. He lived in Sydney, Australia.

coherent systems of thought. Where, however, we have sufficient material, we recognise that primitive philosophy, though rudiment-ary, was the product of man's intellectual need for a system of some kind in his thought about things. We should remember that, just as the world about which modern thinkers philosophise is the world of human experience, so too the thought-world of Australian Ab-original people is the world of their experience as they have seen it and as it has become intelligible to them. For philosophy 'begins in doubt and wonder, which disturb the peace of ignorance, and its goal is the peace of knowledge.'[2]

Philosophy, however, implies logical thought and the ability to think in general and abstract terms, and serious doubts have been expressed in the past about Aboriginal people's capacity in this re-gard. For example, the view was widespread that while they had words for countless varieties of trees, fish, snakes, birds and so on, they had no general term for tree, fish, snake and other creatures and objects. But in the first few weeks of my field work in the Kim-berleys in 1927 I was recording such general terms, and none of my probing shook my informants. Actually, such terms had been pub-lished much earlier, in 1901 and 1903, for two north Queensland languages.[3] Likewise Aboriginal people use abstract terms, al-though, as it may seem to us, sparingly. They have linguistic mechanisms for making them, *e.g.* by using adjectives as such, or by adding suffixes to other word-forms, even as we say 'the good' or 'goodness'.[4]

As for their method of thinking, it seldom, if ever, seemed logical to settlers and pastoralists, for the background, the major premises, of Aboriginal thought was hidden from them. Moreover, few an-thropologists were not influenced in some degree by the well-argued thesis of Lévy-Bruhl[5] that Aboriginal people, like other primitive peoples, were not only preliterate, but also prelogical. Mystical participation, not logical process as we know it, was the basis and tenor of their thinking.

But here again, I very quickly realised in my fieldwork that Abori-ginal people explained and argued points by what were to me quite logical methods. I could and did disagree with their major premise,

Synkrētic

but not with the inferences drawn from it. Indeed, a fieldworker must arrive at and appreciate their major premises if he is to gain their full cooperation and an understanding of their philosophy of life. Thus, granted a basic theory or doctrine of pre-existence of the souls or life-cells, or existence-potentials of all creatures and phenomena, beliefs and actions regarding human conception, the increase of natural species and phenomena, and the return of the soul after burial ritual to spirit-homes are quite logical inferences.

However deeply philosophical thought probes or scientific research takes us, we do not reach a stage when our world did not exist in some form. It was not preceded by nothing. So, too, Aboriginal thinkers take the world, including the earth beneath, and its counterpart—the sky above—as given. They have no myths recording its ultimate origin. It existed, but "without form and void", that is, without its present geographical form of hills and plains, rivers and springs, and void of living creatures.

Into this "waste" came heroes, the pioneering migrants, some in human form, some in animal form, and some with power of appearing in either form. Moreover, all, especially their leaders, had power to transform the landscape, and even to be transformed themselves into natural phenomena such as rocks and trees, which then became and remained the sacramental repository of pre-existent spirits and "life-cells" associated with the particular heroic figures.

Thus, myths and chants tell of heroes making country, making sandhills, trees, and living creatures, and making wells of water (by plunging sacred poles into the ground). But this making is not a creation out of nothing; the concept should be compared to the "making of man" in initiation. It is a transformation and a revealing of what already exists. Every sacred ritual is the lifting of 'the impenetrable veil of the non-appearing which lies behind the appearance which is the individual's own experience.' As Ashley-Montagu pointed out long ago, in initiation 'the essence of the non-appearing is made available' to the initiate.[6] It is this 'essence of the non-appearing', the *noumena* to use a Kantian term, which is summed up in the concept of the "Dreaming". This may be likened to the ἀρχή (*archē*), the sustaining ground of man and his universe.

13

The Aboriginal thinker tells me that a great snake moved across the country "making" the river, that is, leaving it as its track, and that out of the snake came people and other creatures. He adds quickly, "that Dreaming". By this, he does not mean that his narrative is just a story; nor is the Dreaming for him just a long-past period in a time series when landscape took on its present form and when life filled the void. It is rather the ever-present, unseen, ground of being—of existence. But it appears symbolically and becomes operative sacramentally in ritual.

This brings us to cosmology. The Aboriginal concept of their world is not a foreshadowing of a Leibnizian concept of a harmony pre-established at creation by God. According to Leibniz, the consistent development of everything is determined by preceding or efficient causes—a kind of chain reaction, but determined also by a final cause. For the Aboriginal philosopher or simple believer, the cosmos is the appearance in phenomena, inorganic and organic, of the Dreaming, which in itself does not become phenomena, but without which the latter would not be. Like the dreaming of sleep, it is not limited by considerations of space and time, for all space is here and all time is now. This of course reflects the urgency and immediacy of the food-gathering and hunting economy. Life consists not in building for a future, but revealing what is present, obtaining it, and coming to grips with it. Knowledge and technical skill are essential to do this, but even more so is ritual. Through this the presence of the Dreaming is realised, and its potency, such as was inherent in the cult-heroes, becomes operative and is revealed in the continuity of man, natural species, and phenomena.

The aspect of non-limitation by space or distance is illustrated by the doctrine that every part of a Dreaming being's body, be it human or animal, even if dismembered and scattered, is sacramentally that Dreaming with all its potency. We may see one limb here, another there, the head elsewhere, and so on, all changed to stone or earth or wood; but it is one and the same Dreaming or cult-being present fully in each case; not three or more beings, nor the same being, now here, now there.

Synkrētic

Herein we see Aboriginal man coping with the problem of the one and the many, the particular and the universal. The Dreaming is universal, being the ground of every particular. Thus, every ritual, every particular Dreaming, every symbol, and indeed every situation is a part or expression of the whole; for as in Indian philosophy, 'every bit is filled with the same essential whole'.[7] As the Brihadaranyaka Upanishad reads: 'That is complete, this is complete; from the complete comes out the complete.'[8] So for the Aboriginal expositor, a certain site is Dreaming; the actors in the ritual are Dreaming; and so, too, are the sacred symbols. The Dreaming, however, is not divided into sub-Dreamings, few or many. Conversely, the Dreaming is not the total sum of all particular Dreamings added together, any more than time is the addition sum of all the yesterdays, nows and tomorrows. This is similar to the problem Bergson sought to solve by his concepts of time and duration.[9]

I am not trying to equate Aboriginal thinkers (and there are such) to Indian and Western philosophers, but I am suggesting that they have caught a glimpse of, and attempted to grapple with, similar, fundamental philosophical problems.

Thus, the Dreaming is not just a concept of time or of duration of the Eternal Now. It includes also that which occurs and the beings which exist. These particulars, however, exist in, and because of, the Dreaming. The latter is both the conditioning and the conditioned. The Dreaming also implies a unitary principle with an aspect of determinism. We may compare *Rta*, which in Indian scriptures is the unitary principle and 'the life force', not so much of particular phenomena in nature and in man, as of things in general. Moreover, it compels every creature and everything 'to follow the law of its own existence'. Thus arises the doctrine of Karma.[10] This aspect of determinism is accepted by Aboriginal people. In one region it is referred to as *djarp*. This is the road the individual must follow from birth to death. From it there is no escape. The important thing is to know it, for 'he who has no Dreaming is lost.'

The "particular" in Aboriginal religion is expressed in the many totemic, sky-hero and fertility-mother cults; and also in the doctrine of emanations and of the pre-existence of life-entities or souls, to-

15

gether with reincarnation. Here is an attempt to pose and answer the problem of the individual existence of living creatures and natural phenomena, not only in the beginning but in every generation and period. The answer seems to go deeper than animism with its ascription of dream-souls to all that is; deeper too than Lucretius' atomistic interpretation: 'The seeds of things in solid singleness, and each a single whole.'[11] The Aboriginal philosophers are rather on the Leibnizian track; for while Leibniz spoke of the self-sufficiency and isolation of every monad, *he added*: 'The ultimate ground of the monad's existence lies in Him who created it—in God.' The Aboriginal thinker would say that the ultimate ground of the existence of everything that is, lies in the Dreaming.[12]

Cosmology, however, is not only an exercise of thought; it bears on life and living. The food-gatherer and hunter depends intelligently on what nature provides. He is aware of the relationship in space and time, as we would say, of natural phenomena and happenings to the availability of foods and objects which he needs. Thus, the flowering of a tree in one place is the sign that yams are ready to be gathered elsewhere.

Over the generations, Aboriginal people have built up a systematic body of knowledge about the when and where of food sources and of the normal cycling of the seasons. But this knowledge is systematic because the world, the tribe's universe of thought and action, is a cosmos; that is, it is a system which can be taken for granted, while contingencies are a challenge which can be explained within the system.

A very significant aspect of this everyday cosmology is the way in which man and natural species and phenomena are considered parts of the one and same social, moral, and psychological order or structural system. Two observers, last century, recorded that in their regions Aboriginal people divided everything in heaven and earth between the two moieties of the tribe, and in 1928 I noted a similar, all-inclusive division in the Northern Kimberley. But that is not all: one function of totemism is to classify together in clans, in cult-groups, and in some areas in sections, both man and natural species and objects. Thus, one clan, named for example "kangaroo", includes a descent line of human beings and also some natural species and phenomena. All are kangaroo. This, however, is not merely a matter of structure and classification; it brings man and nature into one moral and psychological system. As man acts and reacts to man, so he acts and reacts towards natural species and phenomena of his own group and of other groups (or classes). Likewise, he interprets on similar lines the behaviour of natural species and objects as being directed towards himself.

According to the philosophy of totemism, man and all that exists not only have a common source in the Dreaming but also constitute a personalised system. Therefore, contingencies can be interpreted and met, and even forestalled, that is, through behaviour of a ritual or formalised pattern.

This leads to some consideration of Aboriginal categories of thought, starting with causation, for causation is inherent in problems raised by contingencies and by change. For *us*, causation implies a linkage of preceding events together with the total context of situations. Aboriginal people, however, look to personal and spiritistic and magical causes, seen or unseen, nearby or at a distance. And these causes are put in operation or are countered by ritual, *i.e.* by patterned, personal activity.

The pointing bone is a simple example: it is the transfer to the invisible of a visible missile, while this invisible object can be removed from the victim and made visible in ritual fashion by the "clever man". But the best illustration is that of totemic ritual which releases life-cells from a spirit-centre, a Dreaming, so that they may go forth and be born 'each after his kind'.[13] Thus, in this context causation is making the way (the road) for the unseen *noumena* to become visible. Similarly, the Aboriginal rainmaker never claims to make rain from a clear sky, but only releases the water from rain clouds, as do Council for Scientific and Industrial Research rainmakers.[14] Likewise, sexual intercourse is not the cause of conception as in our sense, but a preparing of the way, the road, for the entry of the pre-existing child to be incarnated.

But even more significant, especially from the point of view of assimilation and integration, are the Aboriginal categories of time and space, number, property, and ownership.

For persons of European descent, space and time are *our* space and *our* time, that is, concepts developed in "Western" thought. But we are apt to assume that they are essential features of the cosmos rather than categories of thought which enable us to interpret the world as a system in accord with our experiences and our purposes.

Other peoples with different cultural heritages, with different experiences and purposes, may conceive of space and time differently from ourselves. They do, as can be illustrated from, amongst others, American Indian and Australian Aboriginal thought.[15] This may surprise us, and certainly it can be frustrating in everyday affairs.

For us, time is an aspect of existence, stretching back from the present indefinitely in linear fashion, and similarly extending from the same present forward into a possibly unlimited future. Moreover, the present, however we define it, *e.g.* by the moment, or the year, or the generation, quickly becomes past time. It is but a step on an ever-moving escalator, while time itself is a necessary aspect of change and causation. Change implies a movement from a past, however near, to a present, or from a present to a future which almost immediately, if not simultaneously, is the present.

The most striking feature of *our* time, however, is that it is measured by a process of accurate division and subdivision from millennia to seconds and parts of seconds. The steps of the time escalator are calculated and their speed of movement determined. Mathematics and science use this time scale for interpretation, appreciation and prediction, and the world of everyday affairs is set to it. We are subject to an all-embracing system of chronology. We are born and grow up, work and travel, and eventually die (statistically) according to timetables. And we accept all this as essential for social and economic order, and even for health.

Aboriginal people, however, do not understand our attitude. 'White man…him always worry.' The white man has to get something done or to arrive somewhere in a fixed time, and he frets and fumes if something prevents him from doing so. He fumes all the more if his Aboriginal workers are not on time or do not reach his target of work on time. To the Aboriginal, this is needless 'worry'.

The time to finish a task is when it is finished, and the time to arrive at a place is when he arrives. The workman might have a sleep "on the job", *e.g.* making a spear or wooden dish, as I frequently saw, but that is part of the process. The traveller rests in the shade during the hot midday hours, or spends a day on the way hunting, if opportunity occur, for this is nomadic living. Groups summoned by messengers to a "big meeting" for rituals seem to us to move exasperatingly slowly. They arrive in dribs and drabs, but both they and the "host" group are quite nonchalant about this. No precise date is or could be fixed. The visitors have to hunt for, and to gather, their daily food on the way, probably turning aside here and there in order to do so. The "host" group and the visiting groups who have arrived do not grumble about waiting. They go on living: hunting, food-gathering, rehearsing ritual, and having corroborees. The others will come.

The anthropologist, whose time in the field is limited, may worry about what, to him, is a delay, but no one else worries. There *is* no delay.

Over forty years ago near the tip of Dampier Land Peninsula, north of Broome, a very fine Aboriginal man invited me to meet a group of men at a certain secret place to be shown sacred emblems and to hear the associated chanting. An approximate time was arranged by indicating the position of the sun. He called for me, but when we reached the spot not a soul was there. He was not disturbed. To my enquiries, he said simply that the men would come. They did. They drifted in.

Mrs A.Y. Hassell of Esperance Bay, Western Australia, writing between 1860 and 1880, recognised the difference between ourselves and Aboriginal people concerning the concept of time. A young couple were going off on holiday from her homestead. They said they would return 'before the snakes went to sleep', but she just wondered, because when Aboriginal people start 'to wander it is often two or three years before they return. *For they take no account of the time.*' That is, of course, our chronological time. When they return, they do not consider an explanation necessary for being away two or three years longer than the white person might have expected.

In 1946, I paid an unplanned and completely unexpected visit to the Forrest River Mission, Northern Kimberley, travelling by plane from Darwin to Wyndham and thence by launch up the river. This was 18 years after my period of fieldwork there in 1928. Walking up to the Superintendent's house, I felt a tap on my shoulder and looking around saw to my surprise the "headman" of 1928, aged but still active, as well as several younger men. An hour or so later a message came for me to go that night to the camp outside the mission village as the men had something to show me. I went, joined a small ring of men, and saw an act by one performer. I was then told that I should cross the river next morning to go to a ritual place with a number of companions. On arrival, I saw several "old men" chanting under a storehouse for *maiaɲari*, sacred boards, bull-roarer in shape. About 70 of these were fixed upright mainly in a U-formation. I sat nearby in a "shade", as dancers in turn pulled up a *maiaɲari* and carried it with two hands and running towards me placed it, pointing east, in front of me.[16]

The significance of this episode was the immediate disappearance of the 18 years that had passed since my previous visit. It seemed to me, and they acted as though it were so to them, that that gap did not exist. It was just "next" day. Chronological distance did not exist. I had appeared again, just as one or more of their absent tribesmen do, and we went ahead. 'They take no account of time'—*our* time.

Underlying this attitude to time is the Aboriginal concept of "The Dreaming" to which reference has been made when discussing cosmology. Man and natural phenomena do not exist *now*, and events do not happen *now*, as a result of a chain of causal events and conditions extending back to a long-past period—a "Dreamtime", a beginning. They exist and they happen because that Dreamtime is also here and now. It is the Dreaming, the condition or ground of existence. The concept is not of a "horizontal" line extending back chronologically through a series of "pasts", but rather of a "vertical" line in which *the* past underlies and is within the present. As the top of an iceberg is seen and is powerful because of its great unseen mass moving beneath the surface, so man and nature are sustained by the ever-present, latent power of the Dreaming. And Aboriginal man expresses this concept and this belief in his ritual, mythology, and symbolism, through which the Dreaming becomes sacramentally visible and potent. He believes that through ritual the normal cycles and processes of natural phenomena and of man are assured.

Aboriginal people do recognise a past as distinct from the immediacy of today, but it is not a past which is gone for ever. Indeed, it does not extend back far. Father's father is older and more "learned", but he is present; he is in many tribes classified as elder brother. Further, members of great grandfather's generation do exist for some young persons, possibly as old "fathers", or old "uncles", but no thought is given to generations further back. The individual, still pre-existing in his Dreaming place, could not know those who died before his incarnation. Whoever they were, they are either just gone, or else will be reincarnated. So why worry!

To conclude: A striking, if not the basic, difference in the epistemological concepts of Western and Aboriginal thought lies in the presence or absence respectively of measuring and numbering by units in linear order. In the West, *e.g.* length, size, age, and the time required to do or make something or to go somewhere are factors to be measured in determining the number of monetary units to be involved. But such considerations are absent from the Aboriginal living-by-the-day nomadic, food-gathering economy. To subdivide, subtract, and add numerically are unnecessary and irrelevant.

On the other hand, Aboriginal people find the cause and explanation of all that is in the ontological concept of the Dreaming. Therefore, a series of causal factors and situations is not sought. That something is Dreaming or, as in parts of eastern Australia, that the sky cult hero 'Baiame say so' is sufficient explanation. And there we leave the matter.

Notes

1 A.K. Rogers, *A Student's History of Philosophy* (New York: Macmillan, 1907), 12.

2 *Synkrētic* – Elkin misattributes this to Edward Caird. See Thomas Hill Green, 'Review of Edward Caird, *Philosophy of Kant*', in *Works of Thomas Hill Green*, Vol. 3, ed. R.L. Nettleship (Cambridge: Cambridge University Press, 2011), 131.

3 W.E. Roth, *North Queensland Ethnography Bulletin*, No. 2 ('Kokoyimidir Language', with the help of Missionaries G.H. Schwarz and W. Poland); and No. 6 ('Nggerikudi Language', Missionary N. Hey, revised and edited by W.E. Roth).

4 See, for example, J. Gunther, 'The Wiradhari Dialect', in Appendix (pp. 64-05) to *An Australian Language*, ed. by J. Fraser, Sydney, 1892. T.G.H. Strehlow, *Aranda Phonetics and Grammar*, Oceania Monograph, No. 7 (Sydney: Australian National Research Council, 1944), 61-64, 69-71; and for generic terms in the Aranda language, *idem.* 64.

5 *Synkrētic* – Lucien Lévy-Bruhl, *How Natives Think: Les Fonctions Mentales dans les Sociétés Inférieures* (Abingdon-on-Thames: Routledge, 2018).

6 Ashley Montagu, *Coming into Being among the Australian Aborigines* (London: Routledge, 1937), 336.

7 Shri Krishna Saksena, *Nature of Consciousness in Hindu Philosophy* (Benares: Nand Kishore & Bros., 1944), 14.

8 Saksena, *Nature of Consciousness*, 14.

9 H. Bergson, *Creative Evolution*, transl. A. Mitchell (New York: Henry Holt and Company, 1914). Also, Harald Höffding, *Modern Philosophers*, transl. A.C. Mason (London: Macmillan, 1915).

10 Saksena, *Nature of Consciousness*, 15-16; S. Radhakrishnan, *The Philosophy of the Upanishads* (London: George Allen & Unwin, Ltd., 1924), 120.

11 T. Lucreti Cari, *De Rerum Natura*, Book II, lines 157, 159.

12 I suggested above that Aboriginal cosmology does not foreshadow the Leibnizian concept of 'pre-established harmony' through the working of preceding or efficient causes. Here, I suggest that there is similarity in the Leibnizian concept of an ultimate ground of the monad's existence, and the Aboriginal concept of the Dreaming. A useful exposition of the philosophy of Leibniz is given by John Theodore Merz, *Leibniz* (Edinburgh: Blackwood, 1884), Part II, 148-151, 160-164.

13 *Synkrētic* – Elkin is alluding to Genesis 1:11: 'And God said, Let the earth bring forth grass, the herb yielding seed, and the fruit tree yielding fruit *after his kind*, whose seed is in itself, upon the earth: and it was so.'

14 *Synkrētic* – The Council for Scientific and Industrial Research (CSIR) was the precursor to the Commonwealth Scientific and Industrial Research Organisation (CSIRO), Australia's government-funded scientific research agency.

15 John Collier, *On the Gleaming Way* (Denver: Sage Books, 1962), 15-21; A.P. Elkin, *The Australian Aborigines: How to Understand Them* (Sydney: Angus & Robertson, 1964), 233.

Synkrētic

16 Compare the dancer carrying a ritual pointed board in Kurangara ritual at the Sale
    River, Northern Kimberley, 1938. See Helmut Petri, *Sterbende Welt in Nordwest-
    Australien* (Braunschweig: Albert Limbach, 1954), Tafel XIVa.

What is Indonesian philosophy?

*Ferry Hidayat**

For over two centuries, Western scholars have studied Indonesian wisdom traditions without ever catching a glimpse of Indonesian philosophy itself. They documented the Buginese, Batak, Minangkabau, and Balinese philosophies but made no effort to integrate them into a national tradition, much as historians speak of German, Indian, and Chinese philosophy. It's now high time that these diverse philosophies were integrated into an overarching one called "Indonesian philosophy".

Some readers may be surprised to learn that this philosophy includes elements of Indian, Persian, Arab, and Western descent. Indonesian philosophers welcomed and assimilated most of these foreign influences, which shouldn't surprise us since ours is a richly pluralistic culture.

Indonesia's philosophical tradition is grounded in the stories of its ancestors known as the *leluhur* ('virtuous ones') and the *nenek-moyang* ('clever grandmothers'). We may judge from the earliest records that the *leluhur* understood reality as the unity of composite parts. The habit had not yet formed of separating the signifier from what it signifies, to use Swiss linguist Ferdinand de Saussure's terms.[1] The concept and the reality to which it referred were as one.

---

* Ferry Hidayat lectures on Indonesian philosophy at the *Pondok Modern Tazakka* school's Darul Hikmah philosophy centre. He holds a Bachelor of Islamic Theology from UIN Jakarta. He lives in Pekalongan, Indonesia.

This explains the likely intent behind a 45,000-year-old painting discovered in South Sulawesi in 2017. The painting of a warty pig (*Sus celebensis*) with an arrow through its heart suggests that the artist may have treated the pig as literally real. That is, the painter was not expressing a wish that they would succeed in killing the beast in a future hunt. To this ancestor's mind, the drawing actually created the reality it drew. The drawn pig was truly dead, in other words, because their ink had killed it. In Saussure's terms, the signifier was equal to the signified. The ancestors painted their bodies red for similar reasons, believing that the colour red meant blood and that blood meant life.

The wisdom of the ancestors was also expressed in their metaphysical theories of the universe, traces of which survive three thousand years on. In parts of Indonesia, stone axes used for religious rites were believed to harbour spirits. In Java, for instance, souls were thought to inhabit stone ornaments. In the Mentawai Islands on West Sumatra, the *leluhur* believed that everything—not only living beings but objects like stones, trees, rivers, and stars—possessed a soul. The soul was a brother, a shadow, a counterpart to everything that existed in the world. It was an independent entity, quite capable of detaching itself from its physical half. When a soul left its body, it could travel far and meet other souls along the way, later filling in the owner about its adventures. It could even go wandering while a person was awake. The Mentawai people thought that, when a person was moody, it meant that their soul was encountering difficulties. These worldviews infuse the concepts of soul in Indonesia's indigenous cultures. What the Batak refer to as *tondi*, the Minangkabau as *sumange*, the Torajan as *tanoana*, and the Nias people as *noso* contains such ideas.

Early Indonesian philosophers developed concepts of life and death as inter-penetrating realms, an idea found in other Indo-Pacific traditions. The ancients taught that there were two worlds: those of the living and the dead. We know of this from their paintings on bronze Pejeng drums created in Bali from the 2nd century CE. A ship, not meant for sailing, often adorned these drums. Like the ferry that escorts dead souls across the river Styx in Greek mythology, this ship carried the souls of the departed from our world to that of the dead. This boat is also an architectural motif in some Indonesian homes. On Savu Island, one such house has both a bow and a stern. The image of the dead travelling by ship is found among the Dayak and Lampong people, while the Torajan call a coffin a *prau*, or boat.

These philosophical foundations of early Indonesian societies prepared them to assimilate the systems of new Chinese, Indian, and Persian arrivals. Indian migrants came to Indonesia from around 320 BCE, bringing sophisticated philosophical ideas with them. Hinduism and Buddhism proved as attractive to our ancestors as they remain today.

Early Indonesian philosophers conceived of our universe as filled with spirits. They knew that dead ancestors also became spirits, that these resided in things, that there were two worlds. Each of these beliefs was sharpened by the growing influence of Indian philosophy. Hindus often re-named and gave material forms to what the ancestors had spiritualised. What ancient Indonesians saw as spirits, Hindus personified as gods (*deva*), goddesses (*devi*), and manifestations of Brahman. Indonesians' sacred pyramids were given new names. Their life- and death-worlds were now associated with Shiva and Kali, representing the infinite spiritual and the finite natural worlds. The main concept that ancient Indonesians lacked was that of the supreme spirit that Hindus called Brahman or 'the One'.

Over centuries of gradually integrating foreign philosophies and religions into their own, Indonesian thinkers conceived of the unity of all religious truths. The *leluhurs*' highest intellectual and spiritual achievement was to approach Hinduism and Buddhism as one synthetic whole. The 8th century king Vishnu, for example, was typical of this cultural integration as a devout Buddhist monarch who gave himself a Hindu god's name. Similarly, the 10th century Buddhist writer Sambhara Surya Warama praised the Hindu king Mpu Sindok in his sacred literature. Meanwhile, the *Negarakertagama*, a 14th century Javanese epic poem by Mpu Prapanca, blends elements of Shaivism and Buddhism. The *Kakawin Sutasoma*, written by the 15th century poet Mpu Tantular, also integrates both traditions:

Synkrētic

It is said that the well-known Buddha and Shiva are two different substances,	*Rwâneka dhâtu winuwus Buddha Wiswa,*
They are indeed different, yet how is it possible to recognise their difference in a glance,	*Bhinnêki rakwa ring apan kena parwanosen,*
Since the truth of Jina (Buddha) and of Shiva is one,	*Mangka ng Jinatwa kalawan Siwatatwa tunggal,*
They are indeed different, but they are of the same kind, as there is no duality in Truth.	*Bhinnêka tunggal ika tan hana dharma mangrwa.*[2]

Indonesian culture learned much from Indian civilisation, not least the *kavya*, a Sanskrit tradition that influenced the above Old Javanese *kakawin* poem's form. Their authors typically believed that their poetry was inspired directly by the gods, who they believed could live inside their poems as in temples. So, they prayed to the Indian *devas* Vishnu, Shiva, Kama, Ratih, and Sarasvati before writing their beautiful verse. Little wonder, then, that these should be so divine.

As Indonesians wove newer philosophies into their indigenous worldviews, it became harder to resist the charms of Indian philosophy in particular. Indeed, the latter was so successful that, when a wave of Islamic philosophy swept across Indonesia in the 15th century, only the mystical school of Sufism found widespread acceptance among Indonesians—so much did it resemble Indian spirituality. The *Wali Songo*, nine revered saints who introduced Islam to Indonesia, taught a similar monism to that of Indian philosophy using different terms. The poet Ki Ageng Pengging, a student of Syekh Siti Jenar's Sufistic monism,[3] puts it beautifully:

Buddha and Islam are never different. Their forms are two, their names but one.	*Agama Buda Islami Karonina nora béda Warna roro asmané mung sawiji.*[4]

As with Indian philosophy, Indonesians only took from Islamic civilisations those features which fit in with indigenous thought. They were guided by their faculty of *budi*, which I analyse below.

These virtuous first Indonesian philosophers, the *leluhur*, remained a guiding light in our culture until certain critics scorned them. This began with 19th century Wahhabi-inspired Muslim reformers who criticised the traditional wisdom of the ancestors, known as their *adat*. Their divisive teachings sought to degrade the foundations of Indonesia's indigenous civilisation, inspiring future generations to sacrifice their culture in exchange for the false promise of a Middle Eastern paradise.

The Wahhabi critique of Indonesian philosophy would be repeated, maybe more successfully, in a later wave of rational philosophy originating in Western Europe.

As we saw, the Indonesian philosophical tradition is marked by a powerful integrative impulse. The Indonesian thinker is not beholden to the dichotomy between reason and sense perception typical of Western philosophy, which thinkers including Frithjof Schuon regretted.[5] This is reflected in our language.

Indonesian features the unique word *budi* that integrates both faculties. The *Great Dictionary of the Indonesian Language* defines *budi* as an 'inner faculty which integrates reasoning and feeling to distinguish between good and evil.'[6] The cultural products of *budi* are called *kebudayaan*.[7] In Indonesian, this word contains the concepts of science, spirituality, religion, philosophy, and technology and refers to *budi*'s manifestation in the external world.

The Indonesian philosopher who first popularised this concept, Sutan Takdir Alisjahbana, argued that *budi* could be translated into German as *Geist*. But it didn't correspond, in his view, to the cognate English word "mind". The difference between both words lies in the relation of mind to culture. The English "mind", Sutan thought, had nothing to do with culture, while the German *Geist* did. This was why the human sciences in Germany could be called either *Geisteswissenschaften* ('the sciences of the spirit') or *Kulturwissenschaften* ('the sciences of culture').[8]

Synkrētic

Budi was impossible to translate into English, he argued, because
the word "mind" had a cognitive character with no reference to culture. It was cut off from the faculties of intuition, feeling and
imagination produced by religious, creative, and artistic activities.
For Sutan, the concept of *budi*, which he opposed to base instinct,
was the 'characteristic [trait] of the human psyche'.[9] Sutan was dis-
satisfied with the English language's inability to accurately convey
this Indonesian word, but he went no further in explaining why he
thought this was the case.

What makes *budi* untranslatable into English, in my view, is the
sharp distinction which this language draws between mind and culture. This distinction spawned a series of unending, abstract
philosophical speculation in the West that never needed to result in
concrete things, which is at odds with Indonesian thought. *Budi* is
always indivisible and concrete. In the English-speaking tradition,
the concept of mind is narrowly related to cognition and thinking.
But beyond thought, culture is about the overall human capacity
to reason, feel, imagine, create, even dream a new world.

Budi's integrative character aided Indonesian culture in unifying
disparate philosophies. As a result, Indonesians don't draw sharp
distinctions between philosophy, religion, science, and art. Nor has
their culture been rocked by either hardline materialism or idealism.
Indonesian sciences and philosophy are as deeply affected by æsthetics as are its religions and art. Because *budi* combines thinking
and feeling into one integrated process, the famous Borobudur
Temple, mystical literature, dances, sculptures, music, and architecture are as beautiful as Indonesian philosophy.

Indonesian culture shows this motif time and again. For example, the Islamic-inspired Javanese literary form of *serats* combines
poetics with philosophising. So do the Javanese *kakawin* poems
mentioned earlier, which draw on both Hinduism and Buddhism.
Or take the examples of Hamzah Al-Fansuri, who expressed his
Sufistic faith in Malay poems called *syairs*, while King Visnu of the
Sailendra Dynasty built the Borobudur Temple to worship his holy
ancestors. The poetry of Indonesia's traditional societies, which
contain some of the first-known forms of cosmology and cos-

mogony, are as perfectly rational as the modern essay form. And its early oral mythologies are as beautiful, reasonable, and awe-inspiring as ancient Greek ones. Traditional *pantuns* poems mix beauty and wisdom as well as Homer, but unite them in a single idea.

Budi epistemology balances a thinker's mind and senses, the ideal and material worlds, unlike European philosophy's compartmentalisation of the modern mind. The Indonesian thinker is unafflicted by the war of all against all that has raged in the West between rationalism, empiricism, idealism, and materialism. This attitude even extends into classical Indonesian literature. Writers known as *pujangga* were poet-philosophers, but it was philosophy that always gave 'the legitimising stamp', as Subagio Sastrowardoyo writes.[10] Modern Indonesian literature is also notably philosophical.[11]

To be clear, *budi* epistemology has not gone unchallenged in the history of Indonesian philosophy. In the early 1900s, the philosophical movement of Islamic modernism condemned feeling and its manifestation in culture as idle fantasies (*takhayyul*) and superstition (*khurafât*).[12] It's unclear what they saw in Indonesian culture warranting this, but the rationalism of Dutch thinkers was a likely influence. This was when Indonesian thinkers began accepting the supremacy of reason over feeling.

In the 1920s, philosopher and politician Tan Malaka also condemned feeling and advocated the primacy of reason and logic. Tan thought a conceptual 'steel wall between the past and the future' should be built to prevent returning to the old ways. Rational thought was the 'peak of human civilisation' and the way of the future. Only it could bridle our 'illusory imagination' and find the long-yearned-for truth.[13]

This very debate played out in the Investigating Committee for Preparatory Work for Independence, an organisation set up in the dying days of Japanese occupation in 1945. In one of its sessions, the poet and politician Mohammad Yamin succeeded in establishing rationalism's dominance over feeling, which he called 'irrationalism' and 'pre-modern logic'. Yamin argued his case so strongly that rationalism, which he called by the harmless name of 'wisdom' (*kebijaksanaan*), was later accepted as a core principle of

Indonesia's state philosophy of Pancasila. It is found in the fourth *sila* which begins, '*Kerakyatan yang dipimpin oleh hikmat kebijaksan-aan...*' This is often rendered as 'democracy guided by inner wisdom', but the word *kebijaksanaan* is in fact Yamin's own translation of the concept of rationalism.[14]

So it was that Western epistemology's arid rational thought began replacing *budi*, the beating heart of Indonesian philosophy. From the 1940s, philosophy came to be understood as chiefly an act of reason, including in Sutan Takdir Alisjahbana's metaphysics. He argued that we should philosophise independently of all beliefs, creeds, even science. In philosophy, 'there is nothing holy, nothing sacred, nothing forbidden, nothing tabooed, everything is brought into the examining field of thought.'[15]

Probably no idea was as revolutionary in Indonesian thought as Nurcholish Madjid's method of rational secularism. Though Madjid never claimed to be promoting secularism, it certainly fed on his ideas. In so sharply distinguishing between the divine and the profane, he succeeded in dichotomising religion and culture, once closely interwoven. He hoped to build a new positivist culture thereby, one cut off from Indonesia's spiritual roots.[16] These ideas fell on the sympathetic ears of Western-educated secularists and the Berkeley Mafia, technocrats so called for their influence over Indonesian President Suharto's New Order administration.[17]

On the other hand, the supremacy of feeling over reason that some Indonesian philosophers have promoted can lead to a radical sensism: the doctrine that the senses are the only true sources of knowledge. From the 16th to the 20th centuries, a chain of Indonesian thinkers including Ki Ageng Selo, Pakubuwono IV, and Ki Ageng Suryomentaram had adhered to a philosophical position placing feeling (*rasa*) over reason (*akal*). In a similar manner, Ki Ageng Selo, the great ancestor of Javanese kings who established the 8th century Mataram kingdom, wrote:

I really hope, o my grandchildren,	*Poma-poma anak putu mami,*
That you may never boast of reason,	*Aja sira ngêgungakên akal,*
For the man of reason's beauty fades.	*Wong akal ilang baguse.*[18]

This man of reason may have kept their looks had they known that thought without feeling is empty—and vice versa. Since sense and reason share *budi*'s path to the truth, there can be no loss if none's master or serf.

The traditional wisdom of our ancient philosophers has long been a bulwark against Wahhabi- and Western-inspired efforts to divide the Indonesian mind. Their customs and laws, known as *adat*, resemble the philosophers' *sophia perennis*. These *adat* contain the eternal wisdom that *Tuhan*, as the Malay call God, decrees amid the world's flux. Together, the concepts of *budi* and *adat* are the fruit of an Indonesian philosophy rooted in the wisdom of the ancestors and the worship of the gods.

Notes

1 'The content of a word is determined in the final analysis not by what it contains but by what exists outside it.' Ferdinand de Saussure, *Course in General Linguistics*, eds. Charles Bally and Albert Sechehaye, transl. Roy Harris (London: Duckworth, 1983), 160.

2 Soewito Santoso (ed.), *Sutasoma: A Study in Old Javanese Wajrayana* (New Delhi: International Academy of Indian Culture, 1975), 578.

3 Moelyono Sastronaryatmo (ed.), *Babad Jaka Tingkir: Babad Pajang* (Jakarta: Proyek Penerbitan Buku Sastra Indonesia dan Daerah, Balai Pustaka, 1981), 74.

4 See Ulfa Tursina, Sahid Teguh Widodo, Kundharu Sadhono, 'Syncretism in The Drama Script of Syekh Siti Jenar Written by Martha Vredi Kastam', in eds. Kundharu Sadhono, Deny Tri Ardianto, M. Furqon Hidayatullah, Vita Ratri Cahyani, *Seword Fressh 2019*, Surakarta, Centra Java, Indonesia, 27 April 2019, European Alliance for Innovation, 106.

5 Frithjof Schuon, *The Transfiguration of Man* (Bloomington: World Wisdom Books, 1995).

6 See '*budi*', in *Kamus Besar Bahasa Indonesia*, available at: <https://kbbi.web.id/budi>.

7 See '*budaya*', in *Kamus Besar Bahasa Indonesia*, available at: <https://kbbi.web.id/budaya>.

8 St. Takdir Alisjahbana, *Polemik kebudayaan: Pokok pikiran* (Jakarta: Pustaka Jaya, 1977), 6-7.

9 St. Takdir Alisjahbana, *Kebudayaan sebagai perjuangan: Perkenalan dengan pemikiran* (Jakarta: Dian Rakyat, 1988), 84.

10 Subagio Sastrowardoyo, *Sekilas soal sastra dan budaya* (Jakarta: Balai Pustaka, 1992), 135.

11 See, *inter alia*, contemporary Indonesian writers including Sutardji Calzoum Bachri, Sapardi Djoko Damono, Linus Suryadi AG, Chairil Anwar, and Sitor Situmorang. In Sastrowardoyo, *Sekilas soal sastra dan budaya*, 137.

12 Deliar Noer, *Aku bagian ummat aku bagian bangsa: Otobiografi* (Bandung: Mizan, 1996), xiii.

13 Tan Malaka, *Gerpolek* (Yogyakarta: Jendela, 2000), 171-172.

14 See *Lembaran Negara Republik Indonesia Tahun 1995*, No. 1 – 88 (Jakarta: Sekretariat Negara Republik Indonesia., 1995), 19-20.

15 Sutan Takdir Alisjahbana, *Kalah dan menang fajar menyingsing dibawah mega mendung patahnya pedang Samurai* (Jakarta: Jakarta Dian Rakyat, 1981), 2.

16 Muhammad Kamal Hassan, *Muslim Intellectual Responses to 'New Order' Modernization in Indonesia*, transl. Ahmadie Thaha (Jakarta: Lingkar Studi Indonesia, 1987), 246-247.

17 Hassan, *Muslim Intellectual Responses*, 9-10.

18 Soetardi Soeryohoedoyo, *Pepali Ki Ageng Selo: Puncak-puncak dalam pandangan kesusilaan, kefilsafatan dn ketuhanan dalam kesusastraan Jawa* (Terbitan: Surabaya: Citra Jaya, 1980), 18.

The Melanesian concept of *gutpela sindaun*

*George Mombi**

Many cultural groups in Melanesia aspire to an ideal of *gutpela sindaun*, the perfect life.[1] *Gutpela sindaun* is a state that was lost when the first ancestors committed a great wrong, in a period known as the *taim nambawan tumbuna i mekim asua*. The first ancestors, or *namba wan tumbuna*, are solely responsible for this loss.[2]

How do Melanesians know this? There is no simple answer. Knowledge of the lost *gutpela sindaun* is drawn from diverse myths that vary from tribe to tribe. Despite their many variations, Melanesian myths tend to agree that the good life was terminated on account of the ancestors' wrongdoing, or *asua*, against a folk hero. In response to this idea, Melanesians past and present have fashioned social, economic, and religious practices that actively seek to restore the lost state of *gutpela sindaun*, which is still deeply desired.

In Neo-Melanesian or Tok Pisin, the term *gutpela* means 'good, attractive, fine.'[3] *Gutpela* also connotes the adjectives 'well, decent, perfect, pleasant'. The term *sindaun* literally means 'to sit, sit down, live, stay,'[4] but it also implies the concept 'way of life.' Hence, *gutpela sindaun* means a perfect and a pleasant way of life. Related concepts include *gutpela laip* (good life), *laip is pulap tru* (fullness of life), and *nogat hevi na bagarap* (no problem or calamity). The terms *istap gut*

* George Mombi is Dean of Graduate Studies at the Christian Leaders' Training College, where he teaches theology. He holds a PhD from the University of Otago and is a former Langham Scholar. He is based in Banz, Papua New Guinea.

(keeping a good life), *istap stret* (having an orderly life), and *istap klin* (being clean physically and ritually) are also used to describe the primal concept of *gutpela sindaun*.[5]

While some scholars define this idea in terms of material wholeness,[6] others speak of a relational wellbeing.[7] Others combine both attributes, which is correct in my view.[8] *Gutpela sindaun* implies both bodily and spiritual wholeness.[9] What Ennio Mantovani calls 'the completeness of life' is the key to understanding the Melanesian search for a holistic existence. For this reason, *gutpela sindaun* can also be understood as synonymous with the Melanesian concept of 'life'. It contains the Melanesian values of achieving happy relationships, prestige, security, health, wealth, meaning, success, both on this earthly plane and in relation to the cosmos.[10]

In Melanesian thought, *gutpela sindaun* is not an abstract notion of salvation. Rather, it refers to a pragmatic, concrete, this-worldly salvation that will involve the restoration of the known cosmos to its original state. Traditional Melanesian culture looks to the material world for abundance and fullness of life.[11]

Gutpela sindaun is an understanding of life as corporeal earthly immortality.[12] It is an ideal of immortality lived on earth, in contrast to our current mortal state. It refers to a life that is spiritually and physically complete, balanced, and theistic as well as bio-cosmic, meaning a life that is centred on both God and earthly life.[13] This life is one integral whole with no demarcation between the spiritual and physical realms.

Immortality, in the Melanesian mind, means life without ageing. This notion is depicted in the Grujime myth of the Mundogumur people, among many others. In this story, a woman named Grujime and her two daughters went to pound sago, the starch found in tropical palms. While they were doing so, the occultists or *sanguma* crept up and killed Grujime. She had thankfully hidden her two daughters before the attack. One had climbed a tree and the other hid under sago palm leaves. After the *sanguma* had killed her and disappeared, Grujime came back to life through her blood. She patched up her body using some sago starch. Then she called out to her daughters to come out of hiding. But the one in the tree mistook her mother for a spirit. She took fright, came down and ran home to tell their father what had happened. Her father frantically rounded up the men of the village and, as soon as his wife and their other daughter arrived with a bag of sago, the men chased her out of the village. She fled to another one and tried to settle there. But she couldn't rest, for she could hear the banging of slit-gongs, which meant the villagers were still chasing her. And she kept going until she reached a place far, far away. The location where Grujime was killed and revived is still known today. It lies just on the outskirts of Fudukuang village, in the hinterlands of Biwat village on the Yuat River, my home village. The Mundogumur people believe that if Grujime had been allowed to stay, human beings would not now grow old and die. Instead, at the point of death they would enter fresh new bodies and live on.

Other myths use the analogy of a snake shedding its skin to explain rebirth.[14] In other words, corporeal earthly immortality is understood as the removal of old skin and putting on of new skin like a snake. It is believed that human beings originally possessed the gift of immortality and could shed their bodies and be reborn as youths.[15] The ancestors lost immortality due to their evil ways (*pasin nogut*) and, as a result, were subjected to today's unhappy, spoiled, mortal life (*sindaun nogut*). The desired return to *gutpela sindaun* lies at the heart of Melanesian cultures, religions and the so-called cargo cult movements.

Ancestral myths and Melanesian worldviews are the interrelated background elements to *gutpela sindaun*.

First, ancestral myths or *tumbuna stori* explain what life was like in the beginning, its termination, the present state of life, and its future restoration. The term *tumbuna* means 'grandfather, predecessors [and] ancestors.'[16] It can also be applied to the continuing line of descendants from grandparents down to their grandchildren and posterity. *Stori* means 'story, [narrative], parable, to tell a story.' The term *tumbuna stori* thus implies an ancestral story or history passed down from generation to generation. In oral societies like those of Melanesia, *tumbuna stori* is an oral account of how the world and life came to be, how it is now, and how it will be.[17]

Myths are the basis of socio-religious, -economic and -political practices in Melanesia. People there believe that myths tell the stories of real events that occurred in the past, which in some cases are supported with visible evidence. As Mircea Eliade notes, in primal and archaic societies myth 'happens to be the very foundation of social life and culture... [It] express[es] the *absolute truth*, because it narrates a *sacred history*... Being *real* and *sacred*, the myth becomes exemplary, and consequently *repeatable*, for it serves as a model, and by the same token as a justification, for all human actions.'[18]

This holds true across Melanesian societies, where myths are believed to sacralise the cosmos and explain the world's origins.[19] As Kees Bolle writes, myths are 'an expression of the sacred in words' that reveal the foundations and purpose of the known world.[20] This makes them living realities. According to Malinowski, the myth

expresses, enhances, and codifies belief; it safeguards and enforces morality; it vouches for the efficacy of ritual and contains practical rules for the guidance of man [sic]. Myth is thus a vital ingredient of human civilization; it is not an idle tale, but a hard-worked active force; it is not an intellectual explanation or an artistic imagery, but a pragmatic charter of primitive faith and moral wisdom.[21]

Through such myths, people attempt to explain how life was in the beginning as a physical and spiritual whole.

Melanesian myths often suggest that, in the beginning, life was perfect. The ancestors had fashioned a spiritually and materially integrated, perfect life. But they lost immortality due to a great wrong they committed, called *asua*. The myths variously identify the *asua* as impatience, murder, sexual intercourse, and so on.[22] For the Yangoru people in East Sepik, it was the murder of the god-man Saii-Urin.[23] These were the immediate causes of *gutpela sindaun* being lost. But many myths anticipate that our currently unbalanced state will come to an end when the departed ancestors return. Ancestors like Saii-Urin and Manamakari, the ones who terminated the good life,[24] are the key to restoring it.[25]

Melanesian ancestral myths emphasise themes central to *gutpela sindaun*. Researchers have categorised these myths according to their five over-arching themes.[26]

The first is that of the division of humankind. The second is the separation of the two brothers. Third is the lost paradise. Fourth is the end time or eschaton. And the fifth theme is the advent of the ancestor hero or redeemer. Another scholar has categorised Melanesian myths into the five themes of creation, death, the first human, culture and cargo myths.[27] From a Christian perspective, there is substantive overlap between both lists, which I amalgamate into one. Some of these mythical themes clearly parallel biblical ones, which for many Melanesians provides a bridge between the Christian gospel and their traditions. This is why, historically, Melanesian thought about *gutpela sindaun* was re-read in light of ideas more recently introduced by the Christian faith.

At least four interrelated themes capture the essence of belief in the *gutpela sindaun*. The first is that of the creation of the cosmos and everything therein. Creation myths are found among many Melanesian tribes. As Wendy Flannery observes, although not many of these are detailed cosmogonies, Melanesian myths generally tend to account for the origin of *their* world, people, culture, environment, rituals, etc.[28]

The creation myths of the Ngaing people of Madang, Papua New Guinea, are an example of this. They are one of the cultures whose beliefs illustrate creation as a staged process.

In the first stage, the high god or supreme being Parambik initiated the creation of the cosmos with land, rivers, wild animals, birds, plants, totems and war gods.[29] From the coast to the highlands of the country, people have generally believed in the existence of a high god or supreme being who authors or creates life. Many peoples in Melanesia believe in the existence of a high god, but they rarely invoke them to meet their material needs.[30]

In the second stage, the Ngaing believe that semi-gods, superhumans, and totemic beings[31] created parts of the natural world and human cultures.[32] Customs, rituals, artefacts, social order, and magic generally belong to this second stage. For example, the To Kabinana and To Purgo myths of the Tolai people suggest that these two brothers created certain features of the world including culture, but not the whole cosmos.[33]

We also see this in the Madang people's Manup-Kilibob myth.[34] After a falling out, Manup and Kilibob began creating separate parts of the world. Manup is credited with creating love magic, sorcery and warfare. Meanwhile, his younger brother Kilibob made human beings, pigs, dogs, food plants, artefacts, new islands, reefs, and the peoples of the Rai coast of Madang.[35] He gave them 'the power of speech [languages], plants, bows and arrows, stone axes, rain and ritual formulas.'[36] Many cultures associate such superhuman beings, or culture heroes, with their group.[37] While some treat myths on the origins of culture and humanity separately, they arguably come under the broader theme of creation.[38]

The second theme is that of a lost paradise or *gutpela sindaun*. This myth suggests that an idyllic life was 'spoilt by foolishness, disobedience, or ingratitude'.[39] The Mansren or Manamakari myth of Indonesia's West Papua is one of many such myths.[40] Death myths also depict the same idea. These often portray superhuman beings or sky gods ending the good life to punish humans for their wicked ways.[41]

A third theme is that of the end time or eschaton. Many myths predict a cosmic upheaval when a redeemer will restore the lost golden age. Some speak of natural disasters such as a solar eclipse or a violent earthquake before the final coming of the culture hero.[42] In one case, a native of the Markham Valley, in Papua New Guinea's Morobe province, reportedly had visions of the end of the world during which the ancestors would cause earthquakes and floods.[43]

A fourth theme is the return of the culture hero and dead ancestors who will restore the good life. Departed culture heroes like Manamakari or Saii-Urin who confiscated corporeal earthly immortality will return with this same gift. Immortality and prosperity will be regained on their return.[44] Friedrich Steinbauer's account of a cargo cult myth vividly demonstrates this idea's direct lineage to the *gutpela sindaun*. The story goes that Kilibob, the younger of the two brothers in the Madang myth, initially created the cargo that Europeans brought with them. They only gained technological mastery over Melanesians by a costly mistake that the latter made:

Whites and Blacks were allowed to choose what they wished. Kilibob made firearms and iron ships and placed them beside the traditional weapons and canoes. The Blacks chose the latter because they were familiar with them. Their choice forced them to stagnate. The Whites, however, chose the advanced, technical implements and so became superior to the Blacks. Only when Kilibob returns and shows the Blacks the way to technological mastery over the world will equality between the two be established.[45]

The myth predicts that former relationships will be restored. Melanesians' ancestors will be reunited with their living relatives, and peace and harmony will once more reign in the universe. This will mark a new beginning of the golden age, that is a return to *gutpela sindaun*.[46]

Some scholars see the cargo cult phenomenon as a core theme of Melanesian myths.[47] But the idea of "cargo" is clearly a later development.[48] It is the modern expression of Melanesian beliefs in a corporeal earthly immortality, which culture heroes will bring back for the living. The arrival of Europeans and their material goods was often understood as confirmation of older, established myths. As Glynn Cochrane writes, 'new concepts were not created in a vacuum' but 'had to be linked to old ideas and theories,' making them 'limited by myths which were in existence at the time'.[49] Cargo myths tapped into the pre-existing notion of a lost paradise. They were fuelled by a hankering for its restoration, reuniting the living and the dead. These ideas trace their ancestry to the *gutpela sindaun* myth, pervasive even in Melanesian worldviews.[50]

A worldview is the way in which cultures 'conceive of the world, how they categorize the things in the world and structure their knowledge, and how they interpret life experience so as to live fulfilling lives.'[51] Often taken for granted, a group's worldview is the very heart of its culture and shapes every part of it.[52] It provides a framework for interpreting the world, while religion reflects a people's view of transcendent reality.[53] Melanesian worldviews are often religious worldviews dominated by ancestors and spirits.[54] Tribal people in general tend to fashion an encapsulated cosmology which 'embraces the divine, the human and the natural in one interlocked, working system, usually with a hierarchical arrangement.'[55] This interweaving of worldview and religion links nature, human beings and supernatural beings. The heart of Melanesian worldviews beats with the same concern for *gutpela sindaun*.[56]

Melanesian understandings of the cosmos are not as divided as in the West.[57] They tend to see the spiritual and material worlds as two sides of the same coin. Theirs are 'unitive worldviews',[58] meaning that they view the world as an inclusive system embracing the whole of reality, including transcendent powers such as gods and culture heroes, which the latter created and bequeathed to humans.[59] This frames the cosmos as a 'finite and almost exclusively physical realm', as Peter Lawrence writes.[60] Human beings are the locus of both systems. These are so interwoven in Melanesia that religious consciousness tends to influence social values and relationships. The latter gives spiritual and religious meaning to everything in one's earthly life.[61] In turn, such worldviews inevitably also shape Melanesian belief systems, religions, and cultures.

The interconnectedness of the material and immaterial realms depicts a cosmic-centric *gutpela sindaun*. This lost paradise is envisioned as both this-worldly and cosmic. It involves human beings, the material and the unseen worlds. And its return hinges on culture heroes and ancestors.[62] *Gutpela sindaun* embraces the 'living dead' who have died but are spiritually alive, the 'living living' who have not yet tasted death, and the whole cosmos.[63]

While they await their culture heroes and earthly immortality, Melanesians influenced by this myth strive to recreate their lost paradise in the here and now.

Notes

1   Melanesia is one of the south-western sub-regions of the South Pacific, along with its Pacific regional neighbours, Micronesia in the north and Polynesia in the east. Melanesia is comprised of Fiji, New Caledonia, Papua New Guinea (PNG), Solomon Islands, Vanuatu and the Papua Province (formerly Irian Jaya) of Indonesia.

2   Garry W. Trompf, *Melanesian Religion* (Cambridge: Cambridge University Press, 1991), 71.

3   Friedrich Steinbauer, *Neo-Melanesian Dictionary* (Madang, PNG: Kristen Press, 1969), 56.

4   Steinbauer, *Neo-Melanesian Dictionary*, 172.

5   Joshua Kurung Daimoi, 'An Exploratory Missiological Study of Melanesian Ancestral Heritage from an Indigenous Evangelical Perspective' (Ph.D. diss., University of Sydney, 2004), 179.

6   Gernot Fugmann, 'Salvation in Melanesian Religions', *Point*, Vol. 6 (1984): 282.

7   Daimoi, 'An Exploratory Missiological Study of Melanesian Ancestral Heritage', 181.

8   John G. Strelan, *Search for Salvation: Studies in the History and Theology of Cargo Cults* (Adelaide: Lutheran Publishing House, 1977), 81; Maxon Mani, 'Quest for Salvation in Papua New Guinea: the Yangoruan Context', *Melanesian Journal of Theology*, Vol. 26, No. 2 (2010): 70; Doug Hanson, 'Contextual Christology for Papua New Guineans', (D.Miss diss., Western Seminary, 2012), 55; Paul G. Hiebert, R. Daniel Shaw, and Tite Tienou, *Understanding Folk Religion* (Grand Rapids, Michigan: Baker Academic, 1999), 82.

9   Daimoi, 'An Exploratory Missiological Study of Melanesian Ancestral Heritage', 181.

10 Ennio Mantovani, 'Ancestors in Melanesia: Toward a Melanesian and Christian Understanding', *Catalyst*, Vol. 20, No. 1 (1990): 26.

11 Daimoi, 'An Exploratory Missiological Study of Melanesian Ancestral Heritage', 30.

12 The notion of corporeal earthly immortality is depicted in some of the myths found among certain Melanesian cultural groups, such as the Daribi. Trompf, *Melanesian Religion*, 35. For the Manamakari or Mansren myth of the Irian Jaya people, see Peter Worsley, *The Trumpet Shall Sound: A Study of "Cargo" Cults in Melanesia* (New York: Schocken Books, 1987), 136-141.

13 Ennio Mantovani, 'Introduction to Melanesian Religions', *Point*, Vol. 6 (1984): 31.

14 Trompf, *Melanesian Religion*, 35-6; also Daimoi, 'An Exploratory Missiological Study of Melanesian Ancestral Heritage', 38-39.

15 Norman C. Habel, 'Introduction', in *Powers, Plumes and Piglets: Phenomena of Melanesian Religion*, ed. Norman C. Habel (Bedford Park: Australian Association for

the Study of Religions, reprinted 1983), 7; see also Bronislaw Malinowski, *Myth in Primitive Psychology* (London: Kegan Paul 1926), 43.

16   Steinbauer, *Neo-Melanesian Dictionary*, 208.

17   Wendy Flannery, 'Appreciating Melanesian Myths', in *Powers, Plumes and Piglets: Phenomena of Melanesian Religion*, ed. Habel, 161; also Glynn Cochrane, *Big Men and Cargo Cults* (Oxford: Clarendon, 1970), 17.

18   Italics in original. Mircea Eliade, *Myths, Dreams, and Mysteries: The Encounter between Contemporary Faiths and Archaic Realities*, transl. Philip Mairet (London: Harvill, 1960), 23.

19   Trompf, *Melanesian Religion*, 18; see also Flannery, 'Appreciating Melanesian Myths', 161.

20   Kees W. Bolle, 'Myth: An Overview', in *Encyclopaedia of Religion*, Vol. 10, ed. Lindsay Jones (New York: Macmillan, 1987), 6359.

21   Malinowski, *Myth in Primitive Psychology*, 23.

22   Trompf, *Melanesian Religion*, 71.

23   Mani, 'Towards a Theological Perspective on the Mystery of Suffering in the midst of Prosperity Theology within the Pentecostal and Evangelical Churches in Papua New Guinea, particularly Yangoru', *Melanesian Journal of Theology*, Vol. 29, No. 2 (2013): 12.

24   For the return of Saii-Urin, see Mani, 'Towards a Theological Perspective on the Mystery of Suffering', 71; and for Manamakari, see Worsley, *The Trumpet Shall Sound*, 140.

25   Daimoi, 'An Exploratory Missiological Study of Melanesian Ancestral Heritage', 182.

26   Strelan, *Search for Salvation*, 60-61.

27   Habel, 'Introduction', 7-8.

28   Flannery, 'Appreciating Melanesian Myths', 163.

29   Peter Lawrence, *Road Belong Cargo: A Study of the Cargo Movement in the Southern Madang District of New Guinea* (Melbourne: Melbourne University Press, 1964), 16.

30   Daimoi, 'An Exploratory Missiological Study of Melanesian Ancestral Heritage', 62-66.

31   Daimoi, 'An Exploratory Missiological Study of Melanesian Ancestral Heritage', 31-37.

32   Lawrence, *Road Belong Cargo*, 16; Flannery, 'Appreciating Melanesian Myths', 163-164.

33   Flannery, 'Appreciating Melanesian Myths', 163-164.

34   Flannery, 'Appreciating Melanesian Myths', 164.

35   For details on the separate creations of the two brothers Manup and Kilibob after their dispute, see Strelan, *Search for Salvation*, 60-1; see Kenelm O. L. Burridge on the separation of the two brothers' families, in *Tangu Traditions: A Study of Way of the Life, Mythology and Developing Experience of a New Guinea People* (Oxford: Clarendon,

1968), 400-402. For an ethnographic study of the Tangu people, see Kenelm O. L. Burridge, 'Tangu, Northern Madang District', in *Gods, Ghosts and Men in Melanesia: Some Religions of Australian New Guinea and the New Hebrides*, ed. Peter Lawrence and M. J. Meggitt (Melbourne: Oxford University Press, 1965), 224-249.

36 Strelan, *Search for Salvation*, 17.

37 From this point on, I will use 'culture hero' as a designation for the being often referred to as the primordial being, superhuman being, *dema*, or folk hero. I will reserve the term 'ancestor' for dead human ancestors, past and present.

38 Habel, 'Introduction', 7-8.

39 Strelan, *Search for Salvation*, 60-61.

40 For a detailed account of the Mansren myth, see Worsley, *The Trumpet Shall Sound*, 133-157.

41 The Sau myth of the Daribi people of Chimbu (Simbu) in PNG also highlights the theme of death. Trompf, *Melanesian Religion*, 35, 71.

42 Strelan, *Search for Salvation*, 17; also Friedrich Steinbauer, *Melanesian Cargo Cults: New Salvation Movements in the South Pacific*, transl. Max Wholwill (Brisbane: University of Queensland, 1979), 34-35.

43 Peter Worsley, *The Trumpet Shall Sound*, 111; cf. Patrick Gesch, 'The Cultivation of Surprise and Excess: The Encounter of Cultures in the Sepik of Papua New Guinea', in *Cargo Cults and Millenarian Movements: Transoceanic Comparisons of New Religious Movements*, ed. G. W. Trompf (New York: Moulton de Gruyter, 1990), 218-219.

44 Trompf, *Melanesian Religion*, 194.

45 Steinbauer, *Melanesian Cargo Cults*, 41.

46 Strelan, *Search for Salvation*, 60-61.

47 Habel, 'Introduction,' 8; see also Strelan, *Search for Salvation*, 59.

48 Moses Bakura, 'Towards a Melanesian Perspective on Conversion: The Interrelationship Between Communal and Individual Decision-making and its Implications for a Melanesian Communal Way of Life', *MJT*, Vol. 25, No. 1 (2009): 21.

49 Cochrane, *Big Men and Cargo Cults*, 17.

50 Daimoi, 'An Exploratory Missiological Study of Melanesian Ancestral Heritage', 39-40.

51 Ken A. McElhanon, 'Worldview', in *Evangelical Dictionary of World Missions*, ed. A. Scott Moreau (Grand Rapids, Michigan: Baker Books, 2000), 1032-1033, cited in Hanson, 'Contextualized Christology for Papua New Guineans', 36.

52 Charles H. Kraft, *Christianity in Culture: A Study in Dynamic Biblical Theologizing in Cross-Cultural Perspective* (Maryknoll, New York: Orbis Books, 1995), 53.

53 Terry C. Muck, 'Religion', in *Evangelical Dictionary of World Missions*, ed. A. Scott Moreau (Grand Rapids, Michigan: Baker Books, 2000), 818-891, cited in Hanson, 'Contextual Christology for Papua New Guineans,' 36.

54 Daimoi, 'An Exploratory Missiological Study of Melanesian Ancestral Heritage', 132.

55 Harold W. Turner, *The Roots of Science: An Investigative Journey Through the World's Religions* (Auckland: DeepSight Trust, 1998), 22.

56 Hanson, 'Contextual Christology for Papua New Guineans', 37.

57 P. Lawrence and M. J. Meggitt, 'Introduction', in *Gods, Ghosts and Men in Melanesia*, ed. Lawrence and Meggitt, 7, 9.

58 Turner, *The Roots of Science*, 19-20.

59 Turner, *The Roots of Science*, 164.

60 Lawrence, *Road Belong Cargo*, 9, 11.

61 Hanson, 'Contextual Christology for Papua New Guineans', 57.

62 Trompf, *Melanesian Religions*, 17.

63 Mani, 'Quest for Salvation in Papua New Guinea', 69-73.

The West's goddess of reason*

Daya Krishna†

What is a civilisation?

Man is distinguished from other forms of life by a very strange phenomenon. When you think of yourself, how do you think of yourself? I was just talking to a girl from Sweden this morning, and it suddenly struck me that we have different names. Imagine!

When a person tells her name, so much is hidden in it, layers upon layers of memory and hope. When you name a child, you are thinking both of the past and the future. You are giving an identity by just naming a person. I was suggesting, both as a joke and seriously, that why not change our names all the time?

Why not? When somebody asks me, 'Who are you?' I can say not just 'Daya Krishna', but give myself other names; and correspondingly, that person will think of me in different ways. Why? Because your name identifies you with a country, with a culture, with a past, with a civilisation. What is this identification?

---

* This is an edited extract from the second lecture of Professor Daya Krishna's lecture series 'Civilizations Past and Future' delivered at the Indian Institute of Advanced Study in Shimla in September 2005. This version was first published as 'Lecture 2: Understanding Civilizations—Two Case Studies, Indian and Western', Chapter 8 of Daya Krishna, *Civilizations: Nostalgia and Utopia* (New Delhi and Shimla: Sage and India Institute of Advanced Study, 2012). It is reprinted with the gracious permission of Professor Shail Mayaram and with thanks to Professor Daniel Raveh.

† Daya Krishna (1924-2007) was a leading Indian thinker, philosophy professor, and Pro Vice Chancellor at Rajasthan University. He earned his PhD from the University of Delhi. He lived in Jaipur, India.

Synkrētic

If I am William, I am something. If I am Krishna, I become something totally different. If I am a Muhammad, I become different again. Each name contains regions upon regions, provinces upon provinces of hidden meaning. Each name is different. A German's name is different, a Frenchman's name is different, an Englishman's name is different, and a South-Indian's name is again different. What is all this? I want to take you deeper into the problem of identification.

One identifies himself with a culture, and if a culture is embedded in a civilisation, then one identifies also, indirectly, with a civilisation. This civilisation has a long history, so you identify yourself with history. And history has a long, unending past; you identify with that too. But how do you understand yourself? Each human being tries to understand himself, an understanding which is in terms of going into the past.

The search for one's roots—what is this search? Why do I seek an identity in terms of the past? Why can't I be satisfied with just the present? I am here. Why do I have to go back in time to seek my identity?

Even those who talk of timelessness, about identity transcending time, always talk in terms, concepts, images, and symbols which belong to a particular tradition.

To talk of timelessness or atemporality is one thing, but the talk itself is always not merely in time, but rather it is shaped and formed by time. This time is not the time of physics, just as the space in which I live is not the space of geometry. Imagine! The space and time in which I live are not those which can be measured by geometry or physics. It is a strange thing: I live in the past, I get my identity from the past, and this past is in time, and this time gives me identity.

Let me move forward a little. What exactly is an understanding of a civilisation, and what exactly is a civilisation?

Civilisation, friends, is a strange creation of man. It is not a natural thing. It is also not something like culture, which all societies, all human beings build. It is an expression of an aspiration, of hope, of the attempt to realise an ideal, in time, through successive generations. I have said some of this before, but I would like to repeat it. This civilisation is crafted, built, imagined and stabilised, made visible, by what we would call successive creations of man. How do I understand a civilisation? By what it has created.

This creation takes place on every level. This creation is as much in the realm of politics and economy as it is in art and religion. It is also in the search for spirituality, for the transcendent; and it is, of course, in every human relationship. It is as much in the seeking for love and friendship, as in enmity and fighting. It is a strange kind of thing that we have built. After all, atom bombs and missiles are as much evidence of a civilisation as bows and arrows.

The *Mahābhārata* is full of what people call weapons of war. Everybody goes in search of weapons. Arjuna does. So does Karṇa. The epic consists of a long reflection on war, and on the justification for war. Civilisations are not merely made by peace, but they are also made by enmity, war and conflict.

Beyond this, civilisations are also built by what we may call 'a search'. What is this search? The search is for knowledge!

When you go to the past, there is a search for knowledge in various fields: in the fields of mathematics, astronomy, medicine, and so on and so forth. In every field there is a search for knowledge, and this search is a continuous endeavour. Knowledge is not fixed and static; nothing is fixed and static; everything is moving; everything is developing; everything is changing; everything is deteriorating or building up. This story of man's quest is in effect what civilisation is.

How are we to understand a long history of a quest which lasts over at least three millennia? How are we to understand it?

Friends, I would like to draw your attention to a strange situation: How can I understand my own past? I was born, and I grew up, and I am here. When I look back, how do I understand my own self? It is in a sense an impossible enterprise because, whatever I remember and whatever I identify with, I cannot say that I am just this. My days in school and college, family and friends, love, marriage, and friendship; my search for knowledge; what I have written;

what I have not done; what I have done which I would like to forget—all these things are there. But am I this?

I do not think that anyone sitting here would like to identify himself totally with anything he has done, whether good, bad, or neither. Even in a single day thousands of little things happen, thoughts cross our minds, temptations occur, and something great occurs also.

We are strange beings. We highlight only certain things. We say that 'he is this', or 'he is that'. We pick and choose. We suppress. We want to forget. I want to suggest that suppression and forgetfulness are as much a part of the seeking and the understanding of each of us as a human being, as what is remembered, what is highlighted, what is identified with. Suppression and forgetfulness are as much part of us as the picture that we want to present.

I would like to tell you a story, to introduce a case study of two civilisations. Let us see what the West identifies with, and what we—the Indian civilisation—are doing. What have we suppressed? What don't we want to remember? What don't we want to be reminded of, even if it is there? Let us find out what are the things that we simply refuse to be reminded of.

The story of civilisations is a multi-dimensional story. First, what a civilisation dreamt of and aspired to; its quest and the goals it has tried to achieve; not in one field, but in every field.

Second, how did the civilisation build itself successively, century by century, year by year, and millennium by millennium? Just imagine! When we are talking of the past, we say 'two hundred years this side', 'two hundred years that side'. Imagine! Centuries do not matter. I say '100 BC' or '100 AD' as if a hundred years do not matter at all.

Whereas in one's own life even a decade matters, even a year matters, even a day matters. On the one hand, each moment of life matters to every human being, and yet when we look at the past, there are large blanks which do not matter. Why is it so? Because we pick out the important things; we pick out the significant things; we pick out that which really makes a difference, and which is really worthwhile. The rest we want to forget; it does not matter.

The story of the West and India is interesting in two ways.

First, the West has played a trick, and we must understand that trick. The West has identified itself with Græco-Roman civilisation. Christianity was a break, a radical break in the history of the West. Hence, the West identifies itself with a pre-Christian civilisation.

Islam or the Muslims, as a counterexample, have not been able to identify with pre-Islamic civilizations. Islam has not identified itself with Persia, or Egypt; not even with the Ottoman Turks. The break in the Islamic civilisation is that it has no past before Muhammad. Islam refuses to identify with an Arab civilisation or Arab cultures which existed before Muhammad.

The Indians have no break! They have had radical breaks, but they do not treat them as breaks. We identify ourselves with the most ancient part of our civilisation, *i.e.* the Vedic civilisation. Imagine what a break it was from the Vedic time to the Upaniṣadic period.

The Upaniṣads reject, in a sense, or transcend the Veda. They call the Vedic *vidyā* '*aparā-vidyā*'.[1] They distinguish between '*parā*' and '*aparā*' and identify themselves with the '*parā*'. But what has happened to the Vedic *yajña*, the Vedic sacrifice? And where are the Vedic gods? What has happened to the Vedic pantheon? Most of the Vedic gods have disappeared. We have new gods all the time.

Not merely this, but the emergence of Jainism and Buddhism has challenged the Vedic orthodoxy at every point. And yet, India has accepted both Buddhism and Jainism as a part of its heritage. The West has merely appropriated Græco-Roman civilisation. India, on the other hand, appropriated as its past everything: Buddha and Mahāvīra as much as the ṛṣis of the Veda. Imagine! Even today people are called Bhardwaj, Bhargava, etc. Can you imagine such continuity? Even today people have these surnames, indicating Vedic 'roles' and 'positions'. What does it mean?

I started my talk referring to names. Imagine a culture or a civilisation which still has names, or surnames, belonging to the *ṛṣis* of the Vedic age. It is unbelievable! Now let us look deeper into the continuity of a civilisation and how it is preserved and kept. We talk of continuity, but what exactly continues?

Western civilisation established continuity with Græco-Roman civilisation in terms of two things.

First, knowledge. Knowledge of what? Knowledge that was certain, that was indubitable, that could be achieved by pure rational reflection, which means you did not have to open your eyes to obtain that knowledge. And yet, that knowledge was supposed to be more certain than anything you have apprehended, saw with your own eyes, felt with your senses. I am talking of mathematics. Mathematics is the strangest thing in the world. So, the West has identified itself with this great cognitive discovery that man can know a certain universal knowledge through the pure exercise of reason. The Greeks had done it, and it was from the Greek heritage that mathematics was really an exercise of reason and knowledge.

Second, Western civilisation also established continuity with Græco-Roman civilisation in terms of logic. It was mathematics and Aristotle's logic. Both these disciplines have become the paradigm examples of what Western civilisation considers itself to be rooted in. This is what the West puts in the foreground, and it forgets everything else. Imagine!

The last four thousand years of Western civilisation have been built on a vast forgetfulness, a vast act of repression. This act of repression is not merely of Græco-Roman history, of the Stoics and Epicureans, of thinking after Aristotle, but of almost the whole of Christianity. The whole thing has been sidelined by saying that this is 'theology'. No other civilisation in the past has put aside and suppressed so much of it.

I am not talking at the level of culture. Civilisation is different from culture. Civilisation is understood in terms of concepts, not images, symbols, rituals, nor even art. Civilisation is understood primarily in terms of concepts. A concept is a theoretical thing; you are building a conceptual net, and through it you are trying to understand experience and reality. This is concept; but what does it mean 'to understand'? Understanding takes place in terms of a question or a problem. Something arises in your mind, some problem wants to be solved, some question wants to be answered.

What are the questions and the problems of a civilisation? You superimpose on the human past a pattern of understanding in terms of concepts and problems. The problems and concepts have been given to you by the past. Who had set the problems in the West? Aristotle, Plato, the Pythagoreans. They had set the agenda. They had set the concepts. Imagine! There has never been a person like Aristotle, who wrote fundamental *śāstras*[2] in almost every field. Parenthetically let me just say, without elaboration or explanation at this point, that the creator of logic is not the creator of mathematics.

Therefore, any attempt to understand Western civilisation must take into account the long suppression mentioned above, as well as the relationship with a pre-Christian past which has been owned and appropriated. Any attempt to understand Western civilisation should also be in terms of what may be called 'reason', acknowledging reason's power to know everything and to determine action.

What, on the other hand, is the story of India? It is a totally different story. Has not India had a long tradition of science, astronomy, medicine, linguistics, everything? We have built temples. Temples cannot be built without knowledge of engineering, knowledge of materials, knowledge of metals, knowledge of everything. But for some reason, we ourselves do not regard this knowledge as important. Have we not contributed tremendously to the field of mathematics? It is amazing that this civilisation does not think of itself in terms of its past or knowledge of any kind.

I would like to ask my friends around this table who are interested in the Indian civilisation why it is that any product of reason, any product of intellect, any conceptual network for understanding man, society, or polity is just not there when we think of our own civilisation?

We are not interested in our very own *śāstras*! The *pramāṇa-śāstra*,[3] developed in India, is not a subject of our interest. Even grammar or language is not a subject of our interest. Some of us may talk of Pānini, but we are not interested or not interested enough in his work. Imagine! We are not interested in the millennia-long thinking which took place in this country on understanding language through language. I am sorry to say that we are simply uninterested.

Synkrētic

India's picture, as it has been built, is a picture of huge suppression. We are spiritual people; we believe only in *parā-vidyā*; we are seekers of *mokṣa* and *nirvāṇa*; we are not interested in this world. This world is unreal to us; it is *māyā*, or it is *līlā*,[4] and it does not matter. Imagine! This civilisation has been referred to in phrases like, 'The Wonder that was India'. This wonder was not merely in the realm of the spirit, but in every realm whatsoever.

You go to a temple and see the invisible behind the visible; but friends, the creation of the visible is not easy! It requires knowledge, and this knowledge has to be learnt through hard work. You cannot obtain the knowledge of mathematical relationships, or measuring, or watching the heavens without real observation. But you denigrate observation. You denigrate the senses. Can you imagine! So much observational material is reflected in Indian literature, art, everything, and yet we say that the senses do not matter.

So much thinking has taken place in India. You will be absolutely surprised. India is a land where reason and argumentation were so central to the civilisation. And yet, we identify the West with reason; we think the West is rational, that it's reason-centric, that we are not. Imagine!

In this country you had to always present a *pūrva-pakṣin's* standpoint[5] to establish anything, even in the so-called spiritual traditions of India. I want you to understand it and think about it. Let us not suppress anything. Take for example the whole development of Buddhism from Buddha onwards. Take the whole development of Jainism from Mahāvīra onwards. Take the whole development of the Upaniṣads. Take the development of the Sāṅkhya tradition. You will be absolutely amazed.

Thinker by thinker and text by text are full of arguments, and not merely of arguments but of conceptual formulations put together to understand experience. Experience was not the central thing, but it was one of the things, as it always is. Experience must be reflected upon, must be pursued. Experience is not sitting there like anything. You have to do something to have an experience. You have to imagine it; you have to close your eyes; you have to concentrate.

You have to do something! And yet doing has been denigrated in this country.

I'm telling you, there has never been a civilisation like the Indian! And yet, we know very little, too little about it. I am saying this with full responsibility and humility. We do not know our own civilisation. We have built a false picture of it. I believe that this false picture has been built as a response, a reaction and a defence-mechanism to the West.

If the West has formulated a picture according to which 'we are rational', 'we are logical', 'we believe in mathematics', 'we believe in measurement', 'we believe in objectivity', 'our heart is in logic and mathematics', emphasising observation, experiment and a continuous formulation and reformulation, we have formulated just the opposed picture.

We find the truth once and for all; we just repeat, we do not innovate; reason is not important to us; observation is not important to us; experiment is not important to us; senses are not important to us; mind is not important; *buddhi*[6] is not important; only *prajñā*[7] is important, or so some may think.

We do not believe in the distinctions between good and bad, truth and falsity, the beautiful and the not beautiful. Imagine the picture that we have built of ourselves. I suggest that this picture, taken by some as self-evident, is a build-up of the eighteenth century onwards. In the nineteenth century it was built both by the West and by us. These so-called contrasts between India and the West are presented by S. Radhakrishnan in his book *Eastern Religions and Western Thought*.[8] Imagine! We have no thought at all!

What a condemnation of our civilisation, what a suppression; India is full of thought! If anybody says that India is not full of thought, there is something wrong with him. And if someone says that the West has no religions, he does not know the West. I am absolutely surprised that a man of the stature of Radhakrishnan contrasts eastern religions and Western thought. He should have contrasted Western thought with Indian thought. There is power in Indian thought, and it has the capacity of confronting Western thought. It should!

The picture that we have built is a picture of a vast suppression, as if India did not have an intellect; as if it did not have reason; as if it did not have senses and observation. This is absolutely unbelievable. And contrasted with the West—the West's suppression is as vast a suppression. The West has no religiosity? Imagine! The Greeks used to worship gods like us. They had gods and goddesses in plenty. Forget about mathematics and logic!

Large parts of Græco-Roman civilisation, including at the intellectual level, have nothing to do with mathematics and logic. It was practical reason, not theoretical reason which dominated. It was the concern with the emotions and passions, and their control, which occupied both the Stoics and the Epicureans. After the coming of Christianity, reason was 'at a discount'. It was the era of faith; millennia, thousands of years of faith; and yet we suppress it from our consciousness. I want to suggest that the understanding of civilisations, like the understanding of the 'personal past' of a human being, is full of suppression. It is all about what we want to highlight and what we do not want to highlight.

The history and historiography of Western civilisation, as it is told, conceal large aspects of this very civilisation. Take as another example the fact that churches were built, marvellous churches, as wonderful as our temples and sometimes even more wonderful. But the West itself suppresses it, and only talks of the external architecture, and not the internal experience that occurs when you go into a church.

What I am trying to suggest, unpleasant or unacceptable as it may sound, is that the understanding of civilisations is a strange enterprise. Man has built so much, and yet, when we look back at the past, we do not see it as it really is. We pick and choose, and identify ourselves only with certain things, thus rejecting, forgetting, or suppressing all the rest.

I would like to reinforce my previous suggestion and argue that the West has consolidated its own picture by rejecting, almost totally, at the intellectual level, the whole history of its past. It has identified itself so much and so deeply with the story of merely the last four hundred years and with some parts of Greece, that it is not able to give it up.

Moreover, in the present day the West sees the necessity of repudiating even these last four hundred years. The West is in a moment of crisis, where it finds that the 'safe' and 'beautiful' house it has built in terms of conceptual structures is no longer adequate. Therefore, the question the West must now deal with is what to do with it? How to go forward when every concept and each methodology has been questioned, when all the past formulations of the problems are no more relevant and valid? The Indians must address the same problem.

The Indian dilemma is different form the Western dilemma. The Western dilemma is how to repudiate, how to cope with the questioning of its own concepts, its own old methodology; how to cope with the questioning of reason itself in its traditional formulation. Both mathematics and logic, as I argued, are facing this dilemma.

I jokingly told a friend that there is a scandal in the temple of the Goddess of Reason in the West. One simply cannot believe in mathematics and logic in the same way one did for the last more than two thousand years. What do we do with it? After all, these are the foundations: mathematics in relation to what we may call 'the objective world', and logic in relation to thought itself. Both are in ruins, both are shattered. What do we do?

Let us go back to the history of Indian civilisation, taking inspiration from it in order to figure out what to do in the present for the future. The West must do the same but let us focus on India.

Notes

1 *vidyā* – knowledge; *aparāvidyā* – lesser, fragmented, worldly knowledge; *parā* – ultimate; *aparā* – not ultimate, lesser.

2 *śāstras* – scientific or critical texts.

3 *pramāṇa-śāstra* – philosophical, knowledge-centered texts.

4 *māyā* and *līla* – 'cosmic illusion' and 'master-game'; terms used to derogate the phenomenal, daily, worldly aspect of the human life, thus indicating a clear preference for the metaphysical or the trans-worldly experience.

5 a *pūrva-pakṣin*'s standpoint – a counter-perspective; the perspective of 'the other' or, more accurately, others in the plural.

6 *buddhi* – intellect.

7 *prajñā* – insight, enlightenment, the noetic dimension of spiritual experience.

8 See Sarvepalli Radhakrishnan, *Eastern Religions and Western Thought* (Oxford: Oxford University Press, 1940).

On Asian and Western minds*

Emerita Quito†

Philosophy began in the East—*Ex oriente lux*.[1] It was in Asia that the first thinkers asked about the nature and origin of the cosmos, that the first seers experienced the Supreme Being in their own way.

Historical research reveals that Plato departed from Athens after the defeat of the Athenians in the Peloponnesian wars. In his travels, he encountered an Indian in Africa who served as the conduit of Indian philosophy.[2] Plato was exposed to the philosophy of the East in this encounter. It is not surprising, then, that his Dialogues are now divided into two: those he wrote before he left Athens, and those he wrote after his long trip.

Aristotle and the other Greeks could not accept Plato's theories which contained a notion that I term un-Greek, namely that there could exist a World of Ideas that men have not experienced in any way.

Since Aristotle was a philosopher whose feet were literally planted on the ground of experience, the Platonic notion was never accepted by the Greeks.

---

* This is an edited extract from the introduction and conclusion to Emerita Quito's *The Merging Philosophy of East & West* (Manila: De La Salle University Press, 1991). It is reprinted with the gracious permission of Dr Quito's estate.

† Emerita Quito (1929-2017) was a professor emerita, chair of the philosophy department and dean at De La Salle University. She held a PhD in philosophy from the University of Fribourg. She lived in Manila, the Philippines.

Synkrētic

The pedagogical clash between Plato, the teacher, and Aristotle, the pupil, caused a branching out of the philosophical trunk. The Aristotelian branch dominated the Platonic by the force of sheer logic, whereas the Platonic, which is truly ancient and Eastern, suffered a repudiation.

Philosophy, however, has come a long way since its origin in the East. The West, building new systems on top of the old, has enriched and strengthened its own weak points. While philosophy originated in Asia, the West has substantially improved on it to such an extent that some of its philosophies are decidedly better formulated than—though not necessarily superior to—the East's in scope and magnitude, style and substance, and latitude or perspective.

I believe in giving Asia its due, and will try to express Asian thought in simple, lucid, and readable terms, intelligible to anyone making the acquaintance of Asian philosophy for the first time.

In order to understand Asian philosophy, it is imperative to put away all complexes, whether of superiority or inferiority. There are, however, gross differences between East and West which should be accepted as axiomatic from the very start.

First, the Western mind thinks in a linear manner. Western man invariably thinks in terms of time, as beginning and end, and his concept of eternity is but an extension of the end to an invisible no-end, and of the beginning to an unknown no-beginning.

The Asian, on the other hand, thinks of time in a cyclical manner. For him, the beginning and end of events or of individuals are but links in a chain of beginning-ends where the end of one immediately gives rise to another beginning in a perpetual manner. Nothing really ends; nothing really begins absolutely. Once in existence, always in existence, and a non-existent will never become, but will remain forever in the bosom of nothingness.[3]

Thus, the Western mind thinks naturally of creation at the beginning of the world of things and annihilation at the end of the same. The Asian mind summarily dismisses absolute creation and absolute annihilation. The fact that things exist *now* is an indication that they have *always* existed. They were never lifted from nothing into something by way of creation, and they will never cease to be; they will always exist in a different mode.

Second, there is no dichotomy between a way of life and a way of thinking in Asia. Religion and philosophy are one. No gap exists between philosophy and life, contemplation and action, theory and practice. And this is perhaps the reason philosophical theory has not soared as high as it did and still does in the West for, commensurate with theory, the Asian must accomplish in practice, which is not easy. The West has but to theorise and speculate; no application to life is necessary. Such are the Platonic, Hegelian, Kantian, Fichtean theories to which the Western philosophers render lip service.

Thirdly, the Asian mind resorts to intuition if logic is no longer able to solve a life problem. One should therefore not be surprised at its propensity for mysticism, its appeals to super-consciousness, or its countenancing the existence of a third eye or sixth sense.

By using the seven disciplines of Western philosophy—*psychology, ethics, theodicy, epistemology, metaphysics, cosmology,* and *logic*—to compare Asian and Western philosophy, we may easily discern further similarities and differences.

In PSYCHOLOGY, the study of human nature, Asian and Western thinkers have different perceptions of man.

In the West, man is an individual, special and unique, whose individuality is based on personal characteristics emanating from a soul that is his and his alone. In Asia, man is looked upon as a speck in the universe of things; he does not possess the importance accorded him in the West. His existence is merely a continuation of another existence in a long and continuous chain.

The etymology of "psychology" (*psyche-* meaning "soul", and *-logos* meaning "word") is suggestive of the Western preoccupation with the duality of man. Body and soul are the two components of the human person, from which arises the difficulty of tying these two components into a single unity. Throughout the history of Western philosophy, this has always posed a problem.

Plato did not attempt to conjoin them. He said that the soul of man inhabited the World of Ideas 'up above the heavens', while his body inhabited the sensible world below. So that, when the soul descended into the body in the *Phaedrus*, it forgot what it once knew.[4] Plato saw the body as a sort of prison, which he held responsible for consigning to oblivion ideas the soul once knew. He never taught an indissoluble union of body and soul.

Aristotle did conjoin man's body and soul in his doctrine of hylomorphism (*hyle-* meaning "matter", and *-morphe* meaning "form").[5] He said that every being was made up of matter and form.

A table has matter and form. Matter can be of two kinds: primary and secondary. Primary matter is the ingredient in all beings. It cannot be created nor annihilated since it is an underlying substrate in all things. Secondary matter is what is perceived as coloured, textured, shaped, its bulk and weight. Secondary matter can undergo accidental changes if the table is re-shaped, shortened, re-painted, etc. The table can also burn, in which case its substance seems to be annihilated, and a new one, ashes, created in its place.

Aristotle's doctrine states that primary matter remains unchanged, whatever formal changes occur. In this case, the primary matter of the table was retained in the ashes, since primary matter is the common substrate of all things. Only the secondary matter and the form were involved in the change from table to ashes.

Hylomorphism similarly applies to the human being. The human person is made up of matter (the body) and form (the soul). For Aristotle, the body is just as important a component of man as the soul. If, for Plato, the body is like a prison or a glass case that dims the brilliance of a burning candle—in either case a liability—for Aristotle the body is necessary, if only for acquiring knowledge.

Aristotle believed that man's soul was a *tabula rasa* at birth, and that the only way to fill up this blank tablet was to allow the outside world to penetrate it through the bodily senses. 'There is nothing in the mind without having been in the senses' is an important doctrine of Aristotle's.[6] Hence, the body is necessary as a contact point between the soul and the material world.

When man dies, does the soul die as well as the body? The answer given in Western philosophy is that it does not. Two proofs are given. One is that the soul is simple, *i.e.* it has no parts. If death means the disintegration of parts, the soul cannot die because it has no parts. The other proof is that the soul is spiritual, *i.e.* it is non-material. This argument is based on the principle of *agere sequitur esse*—'action follows essence.'[7] As is the tree, so are its fruits. Man has spiritual activities like thinking, therefore man must have a spiritual component responsible for them. The body is not spiritual, hence the soul is the source of all spiritual activities. A spiritual being is by definition immortal.[8] Therefore, man's soul is immortal; it will survive the body's death.

In the East, there is no difficulty in proving immortality. To begin with, Eastern philosophers do not put any emphasis on the duality of man's nature. Man is one self. This self is the *atman* that is the seat of consciousness. The *atman* is man's deepest selfhood where man is truly man. Even in sleep, consciousness is never turned off. If so, then this consciousness must exist beyond death, because it depends not on the body but on the *atman*.

The concept of freedom is another point of divergence between East and West. In the West, freedom is such a valuable commodity that all of man's values centre on this concept. The categories of guilt, responsibility, retribution, and the noble and ignoble depend on freedom. No ethics is possible without freedom. The Westerner prides himself on enjoying freedom to the point that he has built his philosophies around it.

In the East, freedom does not merit any attention. The reason could lie in the lack of freedom surrounding man's birth. Man is born 'without having been consulted' as the existentialists say.[9] He has no choice of parents, place and date of birth, bodily feature, mental power, physical capacity, etc. His goals, ambitions, desires, and propensities are already laid out by the circumstances of his birth. Why, then, fuss over freedom?

Ideogenesis, the theory of how we form ideas, is another point of difference. In the West, there is only one way to arrive at ideas. An external sense like touch perceives a tree. The internal sense extracts the tree's substance, such as its bulk, weight, and mass. Then, the intellect eliminates its colour, size, and shape to arrive at the essence of a tree. Finally, the passive intellect defines the tree's essence as 'a plant about 10 feet tall, rooted to the ground and having twigs and leaves.' This essence is non-material because its colour, size, and shape have been dropped. For the West, there is no other path to knowledge.

Eastern thinkers accept other ways of ideation, such as intuition, inspiration, seeing in a mystical way. Words like *rishi* which means "seeing", and *vidya* meaning "to see", abound in the writings of Indian thinkers. In Chinese philosophy, the "heart" is given emphasis. One thinks with the heart and not with the mind. When one forms an idea without passing through the usual medium of the senses, this process is called inspiration. When one "sees" what other eyes do not normally see, this is called mystical vision.

In the East, man is *atman*, seat of consciousness. This consciousness has access to a universal or cosmic consciousness, and the only hindrance is man's individuality which is rooted in his body. However, the body is not a hindrance as it is for Plato. In Eastern writings, the body is subservient to the *atman*, which can overpower it.

In line with this conception of man, the Asian brand of ETHICS has a basis different from that of personal responsibility.

Asian ethics is based on one's caste. To every station in life there corresponds a certain behaviour according to which a person must live. In Asia, therefore, ethics is based on the group and not on the individual. There are no moral laws for the individual.

The moral law in the West, on the other hand, is aimed at the individual as expressed in "Thou shalt..." and "Thou shalt not..." Individual conscience plays an important role. The natural moral law expressed in the dictum 'Do good and avoid evil' applies to everyone without regard to status, age, or colour.[10]

In Asia, no such law is impressed on the mind of man. Right and wrong depend on one's status or caste. The brahmin[11] follows *noblesse oblige* as is demanded of royalty. The brahmin who does not act like a brahmin is doing evil; likewise for the other castes.

In the West, the eternal law is a universal mandate that commands everything. A specific law governs plants, animals, minerals, heavenly bodies, and so on. The eternal law is responsible for universal order. For Christian thinkers, the eternal law is the divine mind that sees to it that a semblance of order is maintained in the universe.

The Asian equivalent of the eternal law is *Rta*.[12] Like its Western counterpart, the *Rta* is an all-encompassing law covering all beings. However, it is not the mind of a divine being governing all beings since this idea is unacceptable in the East.

The ethics of the West considers freedom to be a *sine qua non* of culpability or responsibility. Without freedom a person cannot be blameworthy. Hence, freedom is heavily debated. Morality is an empty concept without freedom.

Asian ethics lacks the concept of freedom. This may be because man has no choice regarding the "soul" he will inherit in the cycle of rebirth. Without this choice, how can moral blame be imputed to him? Hence, responsibility in the East is based on a man's caste, into which he is born according to the inexorable law of *karma*.

This may be the reason that, in the East, there is resignation to one's fate and forbearance in suffering. Instead of griping over something that can't be changed, the Easterner tries to live in harmony and quiet resignation. There is wisdom in this attitude that is often misunderstood in the West.

Since freedom is highly valued in the West, the individual takes it upon himself to assert, alter, or demolish it with impunity, which he considers his inalienable right. Concomitant with it is responsibility, which the Westerner assumes along with freedom. In the East, people do not even attempt to alter their destiny, which they believe is set and unalterable.

Easterners do not emphasise their rights but only their duties, for the simple reason that rights are based on freedom, which is not given due importance in the East. Westerners, on the other hand, insist on their rights more than their duties because rights are positively deduced from freedom, while duties are indirectly deduced from rights.

In view of the above considerations, it is not difficult to see why Asian philosophy developed the way it did. Man is reborn because he is but one link in a chain. If he has "sins" to pay for, he would, by applying the law of *karma*, compensate for them by prolonging his stay on earth, which for the Indians is hell itself.

In both East and West, almost all disciplines in philosophy are intimately linked with THEODICY, the study of the Supreme Being. For instance, without the concept of the deity in the West being a personal God, ethics would have to conceive of a personal judge to mete out rewards and punishments.

In the East, the Supreme Being is impersonal, so that the idea of a personal judge is uncalled for. Who or what then determines guilt or culpability? It is *Rta*, the inexorable law and unforgiving wheel of justice 'which grinds exceedingly slow but exceedingly fine.'[13] There is no court of appeals possible in the East. This explains why there are higher moral standards there than in the West. Perhaps this is an inaccurate way of expressing this belief. Asians simply know that there are no alibis for doing evil, even if done accidentally or unintentionally.

In the West, one can bargain or plead mitigated guilt due to circumstances beyond one's control. The same does not happen in the East.

Retribution also differs in East and West because of their divergent concepts of the Supreme Beings. With a personal judge, one's guilt can be easily determined and condemnation or rewards swiftly meted out. That's why, in the West, men go to heaven, hell, or the limbo called purgatory to be cleansed of the remaining dross of their guilt. In the East, the remaining guilt will automatically mean *samsara* or rebirth. Only the pure and cleansed will go to *nirvana* and be exempted from rebirth.

In EPISTEMOLOGY or the science of knowledge, thinking in the East never fails to emphasise the spiritual and non-material manner of knowing. Whereas some Western thinkers over-emphasise the sense or material aspect of knowledge to the exclusion of the spiritual, in the East the material aspect is always coupled with the spiritual.

But it would be an oversimplification to presume that the West is materialistic, the East spiritualistic. The human being, both spirit and matter, cannot be sliced in half and neatly categorised into two rubrics. The human being is one. East and West agree on this much.

One wonders how the first Asian philosophers conceived of a pantheistic Supreme Being. Long before the dawn of civilisation, some Indian *gurus* who taught ancient wisdom to their selected pupils found unorthodox ways to communicate the idea of a Supreme Being as seen in the Upanishads. Upon being asked by a student what Brahman[14] is, all the teacher could utter was silence. When the teacher finally spoke, he said, 'There is no word to contain Brahman. Brahman is all and thou art that'.[15] In this one statement the teacher was able to convey that Brahman is more than anyone can think, and that any word would fail to express Brahman.

By speculating that Brahman is everything, one does not have to confront the idea of creation. Brahman is really second to none—either at the beginning or at the end, neither a producer nor produced, but both or neither. At first blush, this concept may seem ridiculous. How can one be neither a producer nor produced and yet be both or neither? This idea goes against the cardinal rules of logic. And yet, did not Nicolas of Cusa, himself a cardinal of the Church, say that the Supreme Being is a *coincidentia oppositorum*, a coincidence of opposites?[16]

The Supreme Being therefore cannot be classified. He (or it) transcends all classifications. Did not Jean-Paul Sartre try to prove God's non-existence by calling the Supreme Being an *en-soi-pour-soi*—that is, a contradictory being, because *en-soi* contradicts *pour-soi*?[17] Sartre concluded that, not only did God not exist, but it was impossible for him to exist.

And yet, this contradiction seems to be the mark of a Supreme Being, which is the very argument laid down in the Upanishads. The Supreme Being can be all or none, or both or neither, even a coincidence of opposites. That is one way of saying that the Supreme Being is not arrived at by any process of human logic.

While the West fumbled in its use of the principle of causation, 'Anything that comes into existence has a cause,'[18] engendering all of its conceptual errors regarding the Supreme Being, the East wisely taught that cause and effect could be one and the same. By saying that Brahman was second to none, neither producer nor produced, these philosophers swept away all human categories of time, space, contraries, and contradictories.

In METAPHYSICS or the study of being, Western thinkers put a great weight on the stamp of individuality since the individual has but one life. For the thinkers of the East, the individual is likened to a drop of water which merges with the ocean of being, evermore to be distinguished as a drop of water once the individual enters *nirvana*.

Eastern metaphysics does not bother with the minutiae and hairline distinctions which Western metaphysicians devote a lot of time to.[19] While the West made a quasi-science out of metaphysics, the East dwelt on the religious aspects of all philosophy, such that, in Asia, philosophy is religion and religion is philosophy.

In COSMOLOGY or the study of the cosmos, the East considers the world to form part of the entire universe, in which rules or laws govern both the earth and human beings. In the West, the laws governing the earth are not the same as those that govern human beings, because the latter are considered free whereas the earth is not.

The Chinese speak of this earth in a respectful manner, owing to their being a this-worldly people. Their concept of the earth—along with that of heaven, *tao*, and the ruler—is based on their abiding faith in its permanence. Indeed, people come and go, but the earth remains forever. Since they are of the East, the Chinese do not meddle with the laws of the earth, but submit to them unconditionally.

In the West, the earth must accommodate man's desires, otherwise what would being "master of the universe" be for? If night must be made day, let one light a million bulbs. If one must harvest three times a year, let the researchers look for ways and means to achieve it, even at the expense of nature.

Science is of supreme importance to the West because it values technological advancement, itself the fruit of the scientific method. The East has no philosophy of science and does not put any value on it.

In LOGIC, the study of reasoning, both East and West subscribe to a sort of logic. The West is influenced to a great extent by Aristotelian logic, and Indian philosophy by *Nyāya* logic.[20]

The Chinese have a special kind of logic known as the logic of the "white horse".[21] There was once a king who ordered that under no circumstances should any horse be allowed into the premises. But a white horse was allowed in under the excuse that the white horse was not any horse for three reasons:

1. "Horse" has no colour, form, or shape, while "white horse" has colour, form, and shape.

2. If I asked for any horse, I could be given a black, brown, or white horse. But if I asked for a *white* horse, I could not be given any other horse than a white one.

3. "Any horse" is only an idea in the mind, while "white horse" superimposes the colour white on "any horse". There is thus a difference between "any horse" and "white horse".

No matter how crude, *Nyāya* logic was still a kind of logic that antedated Aristotelian logic by several centuries. It is therefore not true that the East is merely intuitive and not rational. What the East insists upon is that logic and intuition have their own domains that need not overlap. But the West claims that 'everything can be explained by logic', that 'everything must make sense' by applying it.

The logic of the East is based on nature, which by all standards is the most logical because it is the most regular. Logic is natural and unforgiving. If one overindulges in food and drink, one gets sick; if one commits felonies, one suffers retribution; if one follows nature, one is in harmony.

Logic in the East is evidently not scientific. It has nothing to do with reasoning. Terms are not divided systematically into clearcut classifications. Logic in the West, meanwhile, is scientific.

Philosophy is ultimately human before it is Eastern or Western. It is the human being and not the Chinese, Indian, or Greek who philosophises. If a philosophical idea is truly universal, it will transcend boundaries.

Synkrētic

But other human factors affect philosophy. Before the European invasions, philosophy was at its peak in China, India, and the Middle East. After these invasions, philosophy declined in these areas. An invasion does something to the psyche of a people. The philosophical thought of a nation influences its mores and values. It constitutes the spirit of a people.

To understand Asia, therefore, one must first understand its philosophy.

Notes

Except where indicated, these are not the author's notes. They are provided by Synkrētic to clarify references and other details of interest.

1 *Ex oriente lux*, 'out of the East, light'. It refers to the belief, popular among some 19th century European writers, 'that greater wisdom and deeper spirituality can be found in Eastern religions than in the materialistic West'. See John Bowker, *Concise Oxford Dictionary of World Religions* (Oxford: Oxford University Press, 2003), online version.

2 There are divergent hypotheses and legends surrounding Plato's travels to Kyrene, Italy, and Egypt in quest for knowledge. One source suggests that 'Plato wanted to meet Indians as well' in his travels. Whether or not he met Indian philosophers, they likely influenced Plato's doctrines indirectly, including his theory of the immortality of the soul. See Felix Jacoby, *Die Fragmente der Griechischen Historiker*, Part Four, ed. G. Schepens (Leiden: Brill, 1998), 262.

3 *Author's note – Bhagavad Gita II*, 16.

4 Quito may be referring to part 247c in which 'those that are called immortal, when they reach the top, pass outside and take their place on the outer surface of the heaven…and they behold the things outside of the heaven…[that] was never worthily sung by any earthly poet, nor will it ever be.' Plato, *Phaedrus*, Plato in Twelve Volumes, Volume 9, translated by Harold N. Fowler (Cambridge, MA: Harvard University Press, 1925), 247.

5 *Hylomorphism* is not Aristotle's own term but a portmanteau scholars created for it. He lays the foundations of this theory in his *Physics* and *Metaphysics*. This doctrine influenced medieval Christian philosophers, including Thomas Aquinas who studied it in his *On Being and Essence* (1256). Long after its decline in the West, the school of Thomism, and through it Aristotle's ideas, have left a strong mark on many Filipino philosophers including Emerita Quito.

6 'Nothing is in the intellect that was not first in the senses', or *Nihil est in intellectu quod non sit prius in sensu*, is Thomas Aquinas' version of an axiom developed by Aristotle's peripatetic school. See Aquinas, *De Veritate*, Q2, A3, a19.

7 *Agere sequitur ad esse in actu*, 'Doing follows upon being in actuality'. A scholastic maxim coined by St. Thomas Aquinas. It appears in his *Summa Contra Gentiles* (1259-1265) and is echoed in his *Summa Theologica* (posth. 1485). See Dietrich Bonhoeffer, *Act and Being*, Volume 2 (Minneapolis: Fortress Press, 1996), 103.

8 Quito supports this claim by inserting the following definition in brackets: 'Because the word "mortal" comes from the Latin *mors* meaning death, and adding "im-" negates death, immortal means "not capable of dying".'

9 Quito later attributed the idea that we are born without being 'consulted' to Martin Heidegger's *Being and Time* (1927). Her exact wording echoes Søren Kierkegaard's *Fear and Trembling* (1843): 'Who am I? How did I come into the world? *Why was I not consulted?*' See Quito, *Critique of Historical Theory* (Manila: De La Salle University

Press, 2002), 95; Kierkegaard, cited in Martin Cohen, *Philosophical Tales* (Malden, MA: Blackwell Publishing, 2008), 181.

10 The injunction 'Do good and avoid evil' is based on 'Good is to be done and pursued, and evil is to be avoided' found in Aquinas' *Summa Theologica*, part I-II, 94, 2. See Germain G. Grisez, 'First Principle of Practical Reason: A Commentary on the Summa Theologiae, 1-2, Question 94, Article 2, in *Natural Law Forum*, paper 107 (1965): 168.

11 The *brahmin* are a class (*varna*) in Hinduism. They were typically priests, kings, philosophers, ascetics, teachers, including those called *guru*. There are similarities between Hinduism's caste system and Plato's *Republic*, which some see as evidence that Indian philosophy directly influenced Ancient Greek doctrines. See John Bussanich, *Ancient Ethics*, eds. Jörg Hardy and George Rudebusch (Göttingen: Vandenhoeck & Ruprecht, 2014), 44-45; A.N. Marlow, 'Hinduism and Buddhism in Greek Philosophy', in *Philosophy East and West*, Vol. 4, No. 1 (April 1954): 42.

12 Often compared to the Chinese *Tao*, the Sanskrit concept *Rta*, which means 'true, proper, right, and honest' in its everyday sense, occurs over 120 times in the *Rigveda* and 89 times in other texts. The term contains ideas about cosmic order, a moral law governing the universe, and ritualistic sacrifice to the gods. See G.N. Chakravarthy, *The Concept of Cosmic Harmony in the Rg Veda* (Prasaranga, University of Mysore, 1966), 37; Swami Parmeshwaranand, *Encyclopaedic Dictionary of Vedic Terms*, Volume 1 (New Delhi: Sarup & Sons, 2006), 529, 534.

13 Though the idea can be traced to Plutarch in the first century, this modern form is Henry Wadsworth Longfellow's translation of Friedrich von Logau's poem *Retribution* (1654): 'Though the mills of God grind slowly, yet they grind exceedingly small; Though with patience he stands waiting, with exactness grinds he all.' See Margaret Miner and Hugh Rawson, *Oxford Dictionary of American Quotations* (Oxford: Oxford University Press, 2006), 289.

14 *Brahman* is Hinduism's highest metaphysical concept. In the Upanishads and Vedas, it is described as the principle of ultimate reality, the absolute, the universal, the cosmic principle, the single unity behind all things, God, etc.

15 The passage of the Upanishads to which Quito is alluding is unclear. The original text does not provide a source.

16 The 15th century German bishop Nicolas of Cusa has been called the first modern philosopher. His concept of a coincidence of opposites influenced later Western scholars and the analytic psychologist Carl Jung. See H.S. Webb, '*Coincidentia Oppositorum*', in D.A. Leeming, K. Madden and S. Marlan (eds.) *Encyclopedia of Psychology and Religion*, Springer, Boston, MA (2010), available at: <https://doi.org/10.1007/978-0-387-71802-6_118>.

17 'Each human reality is at the same time a direct project to metamorphose its own For-Itself [*pour-soi*] into an In-Itself-For-Itself [*en-soi-pour-soi*]...which religions call God. Thus the passion of man is the reverse of that of Christ, for man loses himself as man in order that God may be born.' Jean-Paul Sartre, *Being and Nothingness: An Essay on Phenomenological Ontology*, transl. Hazel E. Barnes (New York: Philosophical Library, 1956), 615.

18   'Anything that comes into existence has a cause' is the first premise of the cosmological argument for the existence of God. It was argued by the 11ᵗʰ century Persian
philosopher Abu Hamid Al-Ghazali. See Bruce Reichenbach, 'Cosmological Argument', *The Stanford Encyclopedia of Philosophy* (Winter 2021 Edition), Edward N. Zalta
(ed.), <https://plato.stanford.edu/archives/win2021/entries/cosmological-argu-
ment/>.

19   Quito notes in passing that 'Western metaphysics is so complex in its myriad topics
that it would be baseless to compare Eastern and Western metaphysics.' She lists
these topics as including debates over *act and potency, substance and accident, matter and
form, real and possible being; univocity, equivocity and analogy of being, unity, truth and goodness
of being etc.*

20   Meaning 'method of reasoning' in Sanskrit, *Nyāya* is one of the six orthodox
schools of Indian philosophy. Its foundational text is Askapāda Gautama's *Nyāya
Sūtras*, which developed its distinctive epistemology and logic.

21   Although it predates him, the third century BC Chinese logician Gongsun Longzi's
'On the White Horse' is the earliest known philosophical discussion of this problem. See Zhenbin Sun, 'Cracking the white horse puzzle', in *Journal of East-West
Thought*, Vol. 3, Issue 3 (2013): 97-106; and A.C. Graham, *Disputers of the Tao: Philosophical Argument in Ancient China* (Ann Arbor, Michigan: Open Court, 1989), 87-89.

The mystery of the god Io

Byron Rangiwai*

In 1913, Percy Smith, the founder of *The Journal of the Polynesian Society*, published findings on Māori religion that shocked experts in the colonial capital of London. This truth 'hitherto unknown to Europeans', which he translated from his source H.T. Whatahoro's testimony, who himself learned it from a Māori priest fifty years earlier, was indeed stunning.

In *The Lore of the Whare-wānanga*, Whatahoro and Smith claimed that Māori tribes, long thought to be polytheistic, had once worshipped a Supreme God. They suggested that this creator of heaven and earth was believed to rule over the world, the minor gods and men, and that his name was Io.[1]

There were three potential issues with this claim.

The first was that this monotheistic deity mapped neatly onto the image of the Judæo-Christian God whose name had begun spreading throughout Māori tribes exposed to missionary influences.

The second was that Whatahoro, who collected the source material from two Māori priests, was a baptised Christian when he interviewed them. Even at the time, his reliability was questioned.[2]

---

* Byron Rangiwai is a Senior Lecturer at Unitec Institute of Technology. He holds PhDs in Indigenous Studies from Auckland University of Technology and the University of Otago. He lives in Auckland, Aotearoa New Zealand.

And the third was that few people had ever heard of Io. As the Māori scholar Te Rangi Hīroa noted, 'the discovery of a supreme god named Io in New Zealand was a surprise to Maori and Pakeha alike.'[3]

These facts have fed an enduring controversy over the authenticity of the Māori god Io. This is a complicated and extensive debate.[†] Skeptics believe that Io was either an accidental or intentional colonial construct used to present Māori culture as semicivilised to European audiences, because, it was thought, worshipping a Supreme God placed it on a higher rung of an imagined hierarchy of races. Māori believers, meanwhile, accept Io as their god, whether they identify him with the Christian faith, Māori tradition, or both.

In his book *The Invention of God in Indigenous Societies*, James L. Cox explores the literature on Io in great detail, from the perspectives of both Māori and Pākehā scholars.

I will not enter here into a debate about Io's authenticity because, from a Māori theological perspective, hard definitions on spiritual matters are nonsensical.

For Māori, time is not linear but cyclical and is best understood metaphorically as walking backwards into the future.[4] As Roma Mere Roberts writes, this well-known aphorism 'highlights the importance of seeking to understand the present and make informed decisions about the future through reference to the past'.[5] By looking back to the past, Māori gain insights about how to act in the present and navigate the future.

When Māori were introduced to the Bible, we made connections between ourselves and the stories and traditions of the ancient Isrælites.[6] Our Māori prophets, who resisted colonisation and missionary Christianity by creating syncretistic religious movements, interpreted their situation through the lens of the Bible.

---

† H.T. Whatahoro, 'Io of the hidden face', in *Synkrētic* №1 (Feb 2022): 189-204.

Māori used the past—the biblical past in this case—to make sense of their present and future.

Whether Io is an 'authentic' Māori god is therefore a debate for scholars only concerned with linear constructions of time. In his search for the 'High God' in indigenous cultures including Māori, for instance, James Cox concludes that

> the debate over Io… is of principal concern to those who, either for ideological reasons…or from Christian theological motives, find it necessary to 'invent' a God with attributes similar to the Christian deity…for veiled and at time surreptitious purposes, which makes an alleged Māori belief in a Supreme Creator incidental to the predisposed underlying motives of those promoting the idea.[7]

From the purely empirical standpoint, Io's authenticity has been heavily critiqued. However, Māori understandings very often fall outside the conventions of Western academia.[8]

For his part, the Reverend Māori Marsden, a priest or *tohunga* trained in the tradition of Io and an Anglican priest critical of Western academic approaches, maintained that only 'Maori from within the culture' can adequately 'describe the main features of the consciousness in the experience of the Maori'.[9] For Marsden, an authentic approach to understanding the spiritual affairs of Māori—including the mysteries of Io—was closer to 'poetic imagery' than to 'the empirical approach of the social anthropologist'.[10]

If we take the Māori theological approach of *Atuatanga* as our departure point, which accepts the divine as normal and valid, we will see the limits of the purely empirical debate on the existence and authenticity of Io.

The word *Atua* refers to an ancestor with continuing influence or a god, demon, supernatural being, deity, ghost, strange being or object of superstitious regard. The term *Atuatanga* is then created by adding the suffix *-tanga*, which designates the quality of the base noun. *Atuatanga* pertains to Māori theology and spirituality, whether one is referring to ancestor deities with continuing influence, *ngā Atua*, or the Christian God called *Te Atua*. I define *Atuatanga* quite simply as all things *Atua*.

The concept of God in any given society at any given time reflects that society. Whether he be real, invented, or the result of religious syncretism, Io is as real as any object of perception to his believers. Moreover, concepts of God shift, change and evolve over time in all societies, adding another layer of richness to the debate over Io.

The Māori worldview is open and holistic. Our genealogy or *whakapapa* helps Māori to understand ourselves and the world around us. *Whakapapa*, which means "to layer", is the basis for understanding our spiritual and physical place in the cosmos. It provides us with the foundation upon which we stand as Māori.

Māori life is understood in spiritual terms. Birth, life, and death are viewed as physical facets of spiritual life. Māori concepts such as *mana* (spiritual power), *tapu* (restriction), *noa* (free from restriction), *mauri* (life force), and *wairua* (soul) are part of everyday life for Māori.

Somewhat inaccurately referred to as the gods, *ngā Atua* reside and are active in the physical world. They are more accurately described as ancestor deities with continuing influence over particular domains. For example, Tangaroa is the *Atua* of the sea and Tāne is the *Atua* of the forest.[11] *Iwi* (tribes), *hapū* (clans), and *whānau* (families) also had specific *Atua*, as well as *kaitiaki* (custodians) and *taniwha* (monsters, guardians) that protected them and, conversely, punished people for breaching codes of behaviour. These entities could also be turned against one's enemies.[12]

Māori history and theology begins with creation narratives that speak of emergence, growth, and separation. These narratives vary somewhat from *iwi* to *iwi*, but the dominant theme, as with other creation stories, is that of moving from darkness to light, from *Te Pō* to *Te Ao Mārama*.

Of the many different Māori creation narratives, there are three main ones in the literature: those concerned with Io, the separation of Ranginui and Papatūānuku, and the creation of the first human being by *Atua*.

The notion of Io as a supreme *Atua* is a debatable one. Many scholars have argued that Io was a post-Christian invention and that 'such a tradition is inauthentic as it was intentionally created in response to foreign ideas'.[13] Others have claimed that the Io narrative already existed in Māori society but that it was revived and adapted by some *tohunga* to resist Christianity's advances, focusing first on those ideas from Māori culture that most closely resembled those in Christianity.

Christianity was absorbed by Māori into the prevailing belief system, producing a uniquely Māori type of Christianity, which for some also includes the incorporation of the previous *Atua*. Some argue that, if Io was taught by *tohunga* and accepted by certain Māori communities at the time of contact with Europeans, then the tradition is authentic, since all traditions naturally evolve over time.[14]

In the present day, Io is still worshipped among Ngāpuhi *iwi* in the far north of Aotearoa New Zealand and by a number of other tribes. In his works, Reverend Māori Marsden argued that Io was eternal and located in *Te Korekore*, which he described as a realm suspended between

non-being and being: that is, the realm of potential being. This is the realm of primal, elemental energy or latent being. It is here that the seed-stuff of the universe and all created things gestate. It is the womb from which all things proceed.[15]

Beyond its interest to scholars and believers, the Io creation story is brimming with theological, cosmological, and philosophical interest.

Io began creation through a 'process of genealogical recitation or naming'.[16] The creation process moved through a series of 'principal epochs': first the void (*Te Korekore*), then the abyss (*Te Kōwhao*), and finally night (*Te Pō*). Io then made the 'state of being' come into existence as a 'seed' in the abyss of non-being, which grew and expanded like a plant. Inside the seed, Io had placed a *mauri*, the life-force which caused its gestation through various stages of growth. This is what made the seed grow from a taproot (*Te Pū*) to a vine (*Te Aka*). It then moved into a new stage of seeking (*Te Rapunga*) that ended in that of elemental and pure energy (*Te Hihiri*).

Io then fashioned the realms of the subconscious (*Te Mahara*), which expanded into those of cognition and knowledge (*Te Whē*). He then exhaled the breath of life (*Te Hauora*) into the universe, creating the corporeal world that paved the way for the earth, sky, and spirit world (*Te Ao Wairua*).

The primordial parents, Papatūānuku and Ranginui, clasped together in an unending embrace, had several offspring who lived in the dark realm between them. Their firstborn was called Tāne.[17] Io irritated the primal parents' children with the permanent darkness around them to stimulate their search for the light.[18] Resenting that the world was pitch black, Tāne pushed his parents Ranginui and Papatūānuku apart. This final act created the world of life and light as we know it (*Te Ao Mārama*).[19]

Although Io officially delegated these tasks to the primal father Ranginui and his son Tāne, he continued to manage the creation process through his spirit messengers.[20]

It is a singular trait of modern Māori religion that the gods (*ngā Atua*) and God (*Te Atua*), who for some is Io, are placed side by side and not in conflict.[21] On the question of how this could be so, we should recall Marsden's point that only cultural insiders could understand the intricacies of a Māori worldview.[22] This holds true for the notion of Io.

Māori views on the identity and authenticity of Io are still in development. In some tribal traditions, cosmological *whakapapa* begins with Io, while in others it begins with *Te Kore*, the pre-creation void mentioned earlier. Those who follow the Io tradition believe that he wove together the very fabric of the universe. For the *tohunga* Te Mātorohanga and Nēpia Pōhūhū, whose testimony informed the first published account of Io in Whatahoro's *Lore of the Whare-wānanga*, he was not a derivative of the Christian God introduced by missionaries, as critics claim, but an authentically Māori one.[23]

For those Māori who subscribe to a belief in Io, he is the genuine starting point of Māori cosmology. He is its 'supreme god',[24] the 'original creator of potentiality',[25] the starting point of *whakapapa*.[26] Io is described as the 'great god of all',[27] the Creator of the universe, the 'Soul of Things'.[28] He is the source of all things in the Māori world,[29] even the creator of the traditional primal parents Papatūā-nuku and Ranginui.[30] Like the prime mover of Aristotle's *Metaphysics*,[31] he is the 'uncaused'[32] first cause of creation.[33]

For believers, Io outranks all other *atua* as supreme *Atua*,[34] the Great Spirit,[35] a 'unique figure' among Māori gods.[36] He is simply the Supreme Being,[37] the 'ultimate God'.[38] This makes Io, contro-versially for other Māori traditions, the creator of the minor gods. Thus, the Māori theologian Wayne Te Kaawa writes that Io is the 'first or original cause of creation and is the source of Atua [the Māori gods]'.[39] Another scholar goes so far as to view these Māori gods as agents of Io's will.[40] This, in turn, makes Io the creator of human beings.[41]

Followers of Io who are also Christians have connected him to Jesus, seeing him as the voice of Io manifested in the word.[42] To understand this point, we ought to recall the late historian Dame Judith Binney's observation on the Māori reception of Christian be-liefs. It was 'rarely a case of Māori abandoning their long-held beliefs,' she writes, but of the old being 'meshed and intertwined with the new.' Māori followers 'indigenised' Christianity.[43]

Scholars who have critiqued Io as a pale imitation of Jehovah may thus have it backwards. For believers, the Bible did not furnish materials for fashioning Io so much as confirmation of *Io*'s fashion-ing of the world. The Māori indigenisation of Christianity did not create but adjusted new myths to the old. It did this by identifying Io with the 'Word made flesh' of John 1:14, that is with Jesus.[44] Thus, while Io skeptics see him as a colonial hoax injected into Māori culture from without, his believers see him as anticipating the Christian gospel by millennia. In Io's light, Jesus is Māorised.

Some Māori thinkers remain unconvinced.

For some, Io is a product of Māori culture. Taina Pohatu sees it as a concept for the primacy source from which *mauri*, the universal life force, emanates.[45] He suggests that the recitation of Io's many names can invoke *mauri*, which 'occurs where the names of Io are mentioned'.[46]

But others like Ritāne Wallace question the authority of the Io tradition.[47] Though skeptical, he sees the Io tradition as paradoxically both an assimilation of Christian monotheism and a syncretic means of resisting against the influence of Pākehā, white New-Zealanders.[48] Certainly, Māori have a strong history of such practices.

In this vein, Rawiri Taonui sees Io as a creature of the Māori tendency to amalgamate Christian belief systems with indigenous traditions. Io, he writes, is

a more sophisticated construct complete with genealogies and narratives. Io was said to be the Supreme Being of Māori who created the heavens and earth, the first man and from him the first woman. Whiro, usually a navigator in Polynesian traditions, was transposed as the devil. There was a heaven and hell, and angels.[49]

Other writers not only reject Io as a corruption of Māori tradition by Christianity, but as a 'distortion' of Christianity itself.[50]

Yet, there is some evidence that the Io tradition existed in some tribal areas before colonial contact. In his research, the celebrated Māori historian and Catholic priest Pā Henare Tate traced the belief in Io to seven tribes and districts in Aotearoa New Zealand.[51] Relying on both Māori and Pākehā sources, Father Tate cautiously concluded on the note that the Io tradition was sufficiently well established and geographically dispersed 'that we may dare to accept *Io* as an authentic Māori term to speak of the One whom Christians have also called *Atua*,' that is God.[52]

The many views about Io are all valid aspects of Māori spirituality. This apparent logical contradiction is explained by the concept of *wairua*, a word for spirit which refers to the way in which Māori understand concepts in spiritual ways. Without this spirit, scholars looking in and using empirical research methods to investigate Māori culture may come to understand everything except what is essential to it. The mystery of Io cannot be grasped without *wairua*. While there is an abundance of evidence to show that Io was an invention as the critics claim,[53] these facts alone do nothing to explain the spiritual experiences of Māori believers in Io.

Whatever the outcome of the academic debate, Io is real to those who believe. Even as some Māori see him as a colonial protrusion in our culture, yet others, just as authentically Māori, recite *karakia* prayers to their Supreme God. This is disagreeable to those who critique Percy Smith and H.T. Whatahoro for allegedly re-engineering the Māori pantheon. But uncritically rejecting Io as a fake god risks repeating the mistake Smith and Whatahoro are accused of making, that of playing the part of arbiters of the sacred truths of a living culture.

Io is believed, what is believed is real, therefore Io is real—to his believers. Whether this syllogism is acceptable to Western philosophy is beside the point. What it does prove is that Māori tradition skilfully absorbed colonial Western culture, philosophy, and religion into its categories and did so on its own terms. Māori thinkers thus breathed new life into values, ideas, and maybe even gods that lay dying in Europe.

Notes

1 See Percy Smith, 'Introduction', in H.T. Whatahoro, *The Lore of the Whare-wananga: Or, teachings of the Maori College on religion, cosmogony, and history, written down by H. T. Whatahoro from the teachings of Te Matorohanga and Nepia Pohuhu, priests of the Whare-wananga of the East coast, New Zealand*, Part I. 'Things Celestial', transl. S. Percy Smith (New Plymouth: N.Z., 1913), i.

2 James L. Cox, *The Invention of God in Indigenous Societies* (Utrecht: Acumen Publishing, 2014), 57.

3 Peter Buck, *The Coming of the Maori* (Wellington: Whitcombe & Tombs, 1950), 526.

4 Nepia Mahuika, 'Kōrero Tuku Iho: Reconfiguring Oral History and Oral Tradition' (unpublished doctoral thesis, University of Waikato, 2010); Byron Rangiwai, 'Back to the Future: Using Prophecy to Support Māori Student Success in Tertiary Education', *Te Kaharoa: The eJournal on Indigenous Pacific Issues*, Vol. 17, No. 1 (2021); Byron Rangiwai, 'Walking Backwards into the Future: Prophecy as an Approach for Embedding Indigenous Values in Tertiary Education', *Te Kaharoa: The eJournal on Indigenous Pacific Issues*, Vol. 17, No. 1 (2021).

5 Roma Mere Roberts, 'Walking Backwards into the Future: Māori Views on Genetically Modified Organisms', *Perspectives on Indigenous Knowledge*, *WINHEC Journal*, Vol. 17, No. 1 (2005): 8.

6 Byron Rangiwai, 'A Kaupapa Māori Study of the Positive Impacts of Syncretism on the Development of Christian Faith among Māori from My Faith-World Perspective' (Unpublished doctoral thesis, University of Otago, 2019).

7 Cox, *The Invention of God*, 65–66.

8 Byron Rangiwai, '"Stories are Knowledge, and Knowledge is Literature": Viewing and Re-Viewing Sites/Cites of Mātauranga Māori as an Alternative to Traditional Western Literature Reviews', *Te Kaharoa: The eJournal on Indigenous Pacific Issues*, Vol. 11, No. 1 (2018): 489–92.

9 Maori Marsden, 'God, Man and Universe: A Maori World View', in *Te Ao Hurirhui: The World Moves On. Aspects of Maoritanga*, ed. Michael King (Wellington: Hicks Smith and Sons, 1975), 218.

10 Marsden, 'God, Man and Universe', 219.

11 John C. Moorfield, *Te Aka—Māori–English, English–Māori Dictionary* (Auckland: Pearson, 2011).

12 David R. Simmons, *Iconography of New Zealand Maori Religion* (Leiden: E. J. Brill, 1986).

13 Michael P. J. Reilly, 'Te Tīmatanga Mai O Te Ao: The Beginning of the World', in *Te Kōparapara: An Introduction to the Māori World*, ed. Michael Reilly, Suzanne Duncan, Gianna Leoni, Lachy Paterson, Lyn Carter, Matui Rātima and Poia Rewi (Auckland: Auckland University Press, 2018), 13.

14 Reilly, 'Te Tīmatanga Mai O Te Ao', 13.

15   Maori Marsden, *The Woven Universe: Selected Writings of Rev. Māori Marsden* (Ōtaki: Estate of Rev. Māori Marsden, 2003), 20.

16   Reilly, 'Te Tīmatanga Mai O Te Ao', 13.

17   Ani Mikaere, *Colonising Myths—Māori Realities: He Rukuruku Whakaaro* (Wellington: Huia, 2011); Marsden, *The Woven Universe*; Michael P. J. Reilly, 'Te Tīmatanga Mai O Ngā Atua', in *Ki Te Whaiao: An Introduction to Māori Culture and Society*, ed. Tania M. Ka'ai, John. C. Moorfield, Michael P. J. Reilly and Sharon Mosley (Auckland: Pearson, 2004); Reilly, 'Te Tīmatanga Mai O Te Ao'.

18   Alexander W. Reed. *Reed Book of Māori Mythology* (Auckland: Reed, 2004); Reilly, 'Te Tīmatanga Mai O Te Ao'.

19   Marsden, *The Woven Universe*; Reilly, 'Te Tīmatanga Mai O Te Ao'.

20   Reed, *Reed Book of Māori Mythology*; Reilly, 'Te Tīmatanga Mai O Te Ao'.

21   Rangiwai, 'A Kaupapa Māori Study', 219.

22   Marsden, 'God, Man and Universe'.

23   Bronwyn Elsmore, *Mana from Heaven: A Century of Maori Prophets in New Zealand* (Auckland: Reed, 1999); Percy Smith, 'Percy Smith "Te Kauae-runga - Ngā kōrero a Te Mātorohanga rāua ko Nepia Pohuhu"', transl. Percy Smith, *Memoirs of the Polynesian Society*, Vol. 3 (New Plymouth: Printed by Thomas Avery, 1913).

24   T.P. Rollo, 'Mā Te Wai Ka Piki Ake Te Hauora', *New Zealand Journal of Music Therapy*, Vol. 11 (2013): 54.

25   Rebecca Wirihana, Cherryl Smith and Takirirangi Smith, 'Māori Indigenous Healing Practices in Aotearoa (New Zealand)', in *The Routledge International Handbook of Race, Culture and Mental Health*, ed. Roy Moodley and Eunjung Lee (Abingdon, Oxfordshire: Routledge, 2020), 530.

26   Kuni Jenkins and Helen M. Harte, *Traditional Maori Parenting: An Historical Review of Literature of Traditional Maori Child Rearing Practices in Pre-European Times* (Auckland: Te Kahio Mana Ririki, 2011).

27   Te Haupapa-o-Tane, 'Io, The Supreme God, and Other Gods of the Maori', *The Journal of the Polynesian Society*, Vol. 29, No. 3 (1920): 141.

28   Hare Hongi, 'The Gods of Maori Worship. Sons of Light', *The Journal of the Polynesian Society*, Vol. 29, No. 1 (1920): 27.

29   Jonathan Te Rire, 'Taxonomy – Māori Whakapapa versus Western Science', *International Journal of Arts & Science*, Vol. 5, No. 3 (2012): 59–73; Jordan Waiti and S. Awatere, 'Kaihekengaru: Māori Surfers and a Sense of Place', *Journal of Coastal Research*, Special Issue No. 87 (2019): 35–43.

30   Manuka Henare, 'Te Tangata, Te Taonga, Te Hau: Maori Concepts of Property', Paper presented to the Conference on Property and the Constitution, Wellington for the Laws and Institutions in a Bicultural Society Research Project, Waikato University, 18 July 1998; Ella Henry and Hone Pene, 'Kaupapa Mari: Locating Indigenous Ontology, Epistemology and Methodology in the Academy', *Organization*, Vol. 8, No. 2 (2001): 234–42.

31   See Aristotle, 'Lambda 7', *The Metaphysics* (London: Penguin, 2004), 372.

32 Whaanga, 'Maori Values can Reinvigorate a New Zealand Philosophy', 67.

33 Piripi Whaanga, 'Maori Values can Reinvigorate a New Zealand Philosophy' (unpublished master's thesis, Victoria University of Wellington, 2012).

34 Lisa Pohatu, 'Iron Maori: A Kaupapa Māori Driven Hauora Initiative' (unpublished master's thesis, University of Otago, 2015).

35 Donny R. Tuakiritetangata and Alicia Ibarra-Lemay, 'Tūhonotanga—A Māori Perspective of Healing and Well-being through Ongoing and Regained Connection of Self, Culture, Kin, Land and Sky', *Genealogy*, Vol. 5, No. 2 (2021): 1–12.

36 Wayne M. R. Te Kaawa, 'Re-Visioning Christology through a Māori Lens' (unpublished doctoral thesis, University of Otago, 2020), 40.

37 Hirini G. Reedy, 'Te Tohu-a-Tuu: A Study of the Warrior Arts of the Maori' (unpublished master's thesis, Massey University, 1996), 26.

38 Ruth Lemon, 'The Impact of New Media on Māori Culture and Belief Systems', *Working Papers in Culture, Discourse and Communication*, Vol. 1, No. 1 (2001): 4.

39 Te Kaawa, 'Re-Visioning Christology through a Māori Lens', 40.

40 Jonathan Te Rire, 'The Dissipation of Indigeneity through Religion' (unpublished master's thesis, University of Otago, 2009), 32.

41 Wiremu NiaNia, Allister Tere Bush and David Epston, '"I Will Not Leave My Baby Behind": A Cook Island Māori Family's Experience of New Zealand Māori Traditional Healing', *Australian and New Zealand Journal of Family Therapy*, Vol. 34, No. 1 (2013): 13.

42 Marsden, *The Woven Universe*.

43 Judith Binney, 'The Coming of the Pākehā 1820–1840', in *Tangata Whenua: An Illustrated History*, ed. A. Anderson, J. Binney and A. Harris (Wellington: Bridget Williams Books, 2014), 201.

44 Tony Ballantyne, *Webs of Empire: Locating New Zealand's Colonial Past* (Wellington: Bridget Williams Books, 2012), 158.

45 Taina W. Pohatu, 'Mauri—Rethinking Human Wellbeing', *MAI Review*, No. 3 (2011): 1.

46 Carl Mika, 'The Utterance, the Body and the Law: Seeking an Approach to Concretizing the Sacredness of Maori Language', *Sites: A Journal of Social Anthropology and Cultural Studies*, Vol. 4, No. 2 (2007): 184.

47 R. Wallace, 'Kotahi Anō Te Tupuna O Te Tangata Māori, Ko Ranginui E Tū Nei, Ko Papatūānuku E Takato Nei: Colonisation through Christianity' (unpublished master's thesis, University of Waikato, 2021).

48 Wallace, 'Kotahi Anō Te Tupuna O Te Tangata Māori'.

49 Rawiri Taonui, 'Nga Tatai-Whakapapa: Dynamics in Māori Oral Tradition' (unpublished doctoral thesis, University of Auckland, 2005). 37.

50 See, for example, Eruena R. Prendergast-Tarena, 'He Atua, He Tipua, He Takata Rānei: The Dynamics of Changes in South Island Māori Oral Traditions' (unpublished master's thesis, University of Canterbury, 2008), 28.

51 According to Pa Tate, the Io tradition is found in Ngāti Kahungunu, Waikato, Ngāi Tahu, Te Tairāwhiti, Te Rarawa, Ngāpuhi and Ngāti Whātua. See Henare A. Tate, 'Towards Some Foundations of a Systematic Māori Theology: He Tirohanga Anganui Ki Ūtahi Kaupapa Hōhonu Mō Te Whakapono Māori' (unpublished doctoral thesis, University of Divinity, 2010).

52 Tate, 'Towards Some Foundations', 279.

53 Cox, *The Invention of God*, 65–66.

Logic as rectification of thought*

Hu Shih[†]

That philosophy is conditioned by its method, and that the development of philosophy is dependent upon the development of the logical method, are facts which find abundant illustrations in the history of philosophy both of the West and of the East.

Modern philosophy in Continental Europe and in England began with a *Discourse on Method* and a *Novum Organum*. But the history of modern philosophy in China furnishes a still more instructive illustration.

When the philosophers of the Sung dynasty (960-1277 AD), especially Cheng Hao (1032-1085) and his brother Cheng Yi (1033-1108), sought to revive the Confucian philosophy, they discovered a little book entitled *Ta Hsueh*, or *The Great Learning*, which had for over a thousand years remained one of the forty odd books in the collection known as the *Li Ki*. This little book, of about 1,750 words and unknown authorship, was then singled out from the *Li Ki* and later exalted to the enviable position of one of the "Four Books" of Confucianism.

---

*   This is an edited extract of Hu Shih's PhD thesis, published as *The Development of the Logical Method in Ancient China* (Shanghai: The Oriental Book Company, 1922). This work is in the public domain.

†   Hu Shih (1891-1962) was Professor of Philosophy at National Peking University. He held a BA from Cornell University and PhD in philosophy from Columbia University. He lived in Shanghai, Beijing, New York City, Taipei.

Synkrētic

The reason for this interesting incident lies in the fact that these philosophers were looking for a *Discourse on Method,* and found in this little book the only work of the Confucian school which furnished what they considered a workable logical method. The main thesis in this book is summed up in the following passage:

> When things are thoroughly investigated, knowledge will be extended to the utmost. When knowledge is extended to the utmost, our ideas will be made true. When our ideas are made true, our minds will be rectified. When our minds are rectified, our individual character will be improved. When our individual character is improved, our family will be well ordered. When the families are well ordered, the state will be well governed. When the states are well governed, the whole world will be at peace.

The most important part of this statement consists of the three opening sentences. The school of Sung, represented chiefly by the Cheng brothers and Chu Hsi (1129-1200), maintained that everything has a reason (理) and that "to investigate into things" means to find out the reason in the particular things. As Chu Hsi writes: 'The saying (in the *Ta Hsueh*) that the extension of knowledge depends on the investigation of things, means that in order to extend our knowledge we must study everything and find out exhaustively its reason. For in every human soul there is knowledge, and in every thing there is a reason. It is only because we have not sufficiently investigated into the reason of things that our knowledge is so incomplete. Therefore, in the scheme of *The Great Learning* (which was taken by the Sung philosophers to mean 'learning for adults') the student is asked first to study all the things under heaven, beginning with the known principles (reason) and seeking to reach the utmost. After sufficient labour has been devoted to it, the day will come when all things will suddenly become clear and intelligible. When that time has arrived, then we shall have penetrated into the interior and the exterior, the apparent and the hidden principles of all things, and understood the whole nature and function of our minds.'[1]

This method of beginning with accumulative learning and leading to the final stage of sudden enlightenment continued to be the logical method of Neo-Confucianism until the Ming dynasty (1368-1644) when Wang Yang-ming (1472-1529) revolted against Said Wang Yang-ming: 'In former years, I said to my friend Chien, "If to be a sage or a virtuous man one must investigate everything under heaven, how can at present any man possess such tremendous power?" Pointing to the bamboos in front of the pavilion, I asked him to investigate them. Day and night, Chien entered into an investigation of the reasons in the bamboo. Having exhausted his mind and thought on it, he fell sick at the end of three days. At that time, I thought it was because his energy and strength were not equal to the task. So, I myself undertook to carry on the investigation. Day and night I failed to understand the reason in the bamboo. I was so tired that I fell sick after seven days. In consequence, we both confessed with a sigh that, without the great power and ability required to carry on the investigation of things, we were disqualified to become sages or virtuous men.'[2]

Accordingly, Wang Yang-ming rejected the method of the Sung school and founded a new school on what he considered to be the original text of the *Ta Hsueh*. The new school holds that 'the objects under heaven need not be investigated and the task of "investigating things" can only be carried out in and with reference to the individual's character and mind.'[3]

Apart from the mind, there is neither reason nor thing. 'The ruler of the body is the mind. That which proceeds from the mind is the idea. The nature (本體) of the idea is knowledge. That on which the idea rests is the thing. For instance, when the idea rests on serving one's parents, then serving one's parents is the thing.'[4] Therefore, Wang Yang-ming holds that the word *kueh* (格) in the phrase *kueh wuh* (格物) does not mean "to investigate into" as the Sung philosophers had maintained. It means "to rectify" as in Mencius' saying, 'The great man rectifies (格) the mind of his prince.' The doctrine of *kueh wuh*, therefore, does not mean "to investigate into things" but "to remove from the mind that which is not right and to restore its original nature of rightness."[5] It is, in short, to bring forth the 'intuitive knowledge' (良知) of the mind.

'Knowledge is the nature of the mind. The mind is naturally capable of knowing,' Wang Yang-ming writes. 'Conquer the selfish passions and reinstate reason, and the intuitive knowledge of the mind will be freed from its impediments and will function to its full capacity. That is what is meant by the extension of knowledge to the utmost. When knowledge is extended to the utmost, the ideas will be rectified.'[6]

To sum up, the whole history of modern Chinese philosophy from the eleventh century to the present day has centered on the interpretation of a little book of 1,750 words and unknown authorship. Indeed, the whole controversy between the Sung school and the Ming school of Neo-Confucianism may be said to be a controversy over the question whether the two words *kueh wuh* should be interpreted as "to investigate into things" or as "to rectify the mind in order to have intuitive knowledge."

As I now look back on the history of Chinese philosophy of the last 900 years, I cannot but feel profoundly impressed by the conditioning influence of the logical method on the development of philosophy. The most important fact in this long period of controversy is that the philosophers, in their search for a method, have found a little treatise which gives an outline of a method, or what appears to be a method, without a concrete statement of its detailed operations. This enables the philosophers to read into it whatever procedure they were able to conceive of.

It is clear that the interpretation which the Cheng brothers and Chu Hsi gave to the phrase *kueh wuh* comes very near to the inductive method: It begins with seeking the reason in things and aims at the final enlightenment through synthesis. But it is an inductive method without the requisite details of procedure.

The story told above, of Wang Yang-ming's attempt to investigate the principles of the bamboo, is an excellent instance of the barrenness of an inductive method without the necessary inductive procedure. This barrenness and futility have forced Wang Yang-ming to resort to the theory of intuitive knowledge, which exalts the mind as co-extensive with cosmic reason, thus avoiding the futile efforts to seek the reason in all things under heaven.

But both the Sung and the Ming philosophers agreed on one point. Both Chu Hsi and Wang Yang-ming agreed that the word *wuh* (things) meant "affairs" (*sze*).[7] This humanistic interpretation of one word has determined the whole nature and scope of modern Chinese philosophy. It has limited philosophy to the realm of human "affairs" and relations. Wang maintained that the "investigation of things" can only be carried out in and with reference to the individual's character and mind.

Even the Sung school, which sought to know the reason in everything, did so only in so far as such investigation tends to 'make our ideas true (sincere) and firm' and thereby to 'rectify our minds'.[8] Not equipped with a scientific method for the investigation of natural objects, they, too, confined themselves to the problems of moral and political philosophy. Thus, neither the one nor the other of the two great epochs of modern Chinese philosophy has made any contribution to the development of the sciences. There may have been many other causes which account for the absence of scientific learning in China, but it is surely no exaggeration to say that the nature of the method of philosophy has been one of the most important causes.

This account of the development of methodology in modern Chinese philosophy, which may seem unnecessarily lengthy, is intended to be my excuse for writing the present essay on the development of the logical method in ancient China. For I believe the great revival of philosophical speculation in the eleventh, twelfth, and sixteenth centuries was, most unfortunately, greatly hampered by the fact that the work which has served as the *Novum Organum* of practically all the schools of modern Chinese philosophy was probably written by some Confucian of the fourth or third century BC who, in setting forth the doctrine of extending one's knowledge to the utmost through the investigation of things, was probably unconsciously influenced by the scientific tendencies of that age.[9]

But because the scientific influence was at most unconsciously felt, because the scientific methods for the investigation of things which were developed by the non-Confucian schools of the era were never explicitly stated, and because the whole spirit of the *Ta Hsueh*, as well as of the other standard Confucian works, was purely rationalistic and moralistic—the development of philosophy and science in modern[10] China has greatly suffered for lack of an adequate logical method.

Now that China has come into contact with the other thought-systems of the world, it has seemed to some that the lack of methodology in modern Chinese philosophy can now be supplied by introducing into China the philosophical and scientific methods which have developed in the Western world from the time of Aristotle to this day. This would be sufficient if China were content to regard the problem of methodology as merely a problem of "mental discipline" in the schools or even as one of acquiring a working method for the laboratories. But as I see it, the problem is not really so simple. The problem as I conceive it is only one phase of a still larger and more fundamental problem which New China must face.

This larger problem is: How can we Chinese feel at ease in this new world which at first sight appears to be so much at variance with what we have long regarded as our own civilisation?

For it is perfectly natural and justifiable that a nation with a glorious past and with a distinctive civilisation of its own making should never feel quite at home in a new civilisation, if that new civilisation is looked upon as imported from alien lands and forced upon it by external necessities of national existence. And it would surely be a great loss to mankind at large if the acceptance of this new civilisation should take the form of abrupt displacement instead of organic assimilation, thereby causing the disappearance of the old civilisation. The real problem, therefore, may be restated thus: How can we best assimilate modern civilisation in such a manner as to make it congenial and congruous and continuous with the civilisation of our own making?

This larger problem presents itself in every phase of the great conflict between the old civilisation and the new. In art, in literature, in politics, and in social life in general, the underlying problem is fundamentally the same. The solution of this great problem, as far as I can see, will depend solely on the foresight and the sense of historical continuity of the intellectual leaders of New China, and on the tact and skill with which they can successfully connect the best in modern civilisation with the best in our own civilisation.

For our present purpose, the more specific problem is: Where can we find a congenial stock with which we may organically link the thought-systems of modern Europe and America, so that we may further build up our own science and philosophy on the new foundation of an internal assimilation of the old and the new? It is, therefore, no mere task of introducing a few school textbooks on logic.

My own surmise goes somewhat like this. Confucianism has long outlived its vitality. The new schools of Sung and Ming rejuvenated the long-dead Confucianism by reading into it two logical methods which never belonged to it. These two methods are: the theory of investigating into the reason in everything for the purpose of extending one's knowledge to the utmost, which is the method of the Sung school; and the theory of intuitive knowledge, which is the method of the school of Wang Yang-ming.

While fully recognising the merits of the philosophy of Wang Yang-ming, I cannot but think that his logical theory is wholly incompatible with the spirit and procedure of science. The Sung philosophers were right in their interpretation of the doctrine of "investigating into things." But their logical method was rendered fruitless by: (1) the lack of an experimental procedure; (2) its failure to recognise the active and directing role played by the mind in the investigating of things; and most unfortunately of all, (3) its construing of "things" to mean "affairs."

Aside from these two schools, Confucianism is long dead. I am firmly of the opinion that the future of Chinese philosophy depends upon its emancipation from the moralistic and rationalistic fetters of Confucianism. This emancipation cannot be accomplished by any wholesale importation of Western philosophies alone. It can be achieved only by putting Confucianism back in its proper place; that is, by restoring it to its historical background. Confucianism was once only one of the many rival systems flourishing in ancient China. The dethronement of Confucianism, therefore, will be assured when it is regarded not as the solitary source of spiritual, moral, and philosophical authority, but merely as one star in a great galaxy of philosophical luminaries.

In other words, the future of Chinese philosophy would seem to depend much on the revival of those great philosophical schools which once flourished side by side with the school of Confucius in ancient China. That this need is dimly and semiconsciously perceived by our thinking people may be seen in the fact that, while the reactionary movement to constitutionally establish Confucianism either as the national religion or as the national system of moral education is vigorously opposed by all the more thoughtful leaders both in and out of parliament, there is hardly a single periodical of any intellectual influence which has not printed in the last several years articles on the philosophical systems of the non-Confucian schools.

For my own part, I believe that the revival of the non-Confucian schools is absolutely necessary because it is in these schools that we may hope to find the congenial soil in which to transplant the best products of Western philosophy and science. This is especially true with regard to the problem of methodology.

The emphasis on experience as against dogmatism and rationalism, the highly developed scientific method in all its phases of operation, and the historical or evolutionary view of truth and morality, these—which I consider to be the most important contributions of modern philosophy in the Western world—can all find their remote but highly developed precursors in those great non-Confucian schools of the fifth, fourth, and third centuries BC.

It would therefore seem to be the duty of New China to study these long-neglected native systems in the light and with the aid of modern Western philosophy. When the philosophies of ancient China are reinterpreted in terms of modern philosophy, and when modern philosophy is interpreted in terms of the native systems of China, then, and not until then, can Chinese philosophers and students of philosophy truly feel at ease with the new methods and instrumentalities of speculation and research.

I do not wish my advocacy for the revival of the philosophical schools of ancient China to be understood as prompted by a desire to claim for China the honour of *priority* in the discovery of those methods and theories which have hitherto been regarded as exclusively Western in origin. I am the last man to take pride in priority as such.

Mere priority in invention or discovery without subsequent efforts to improve and perfect the original crudities can only be a matter for regret, certainly not for vainglory. When I look at a mariner's compass and think of the marvellous discoveries which the Europeans have made therewith, I cannot but feel a sense of shame to recall the superstitious uses which I myself have seen made of this great invention of ancient Chinese genius.

My interest in the rediscovery of the logical theories and methods of ancient China, as I have repeatedly said above, is primarily pedagogical. I have the strongest desire to make my own people see that these methods of the West are not totally alien to the Chinese mind and that, on the contrary, they are the instruments by means of which and in the light of which much of the lost treasures of Chinese philosophy can be recovered.

More important still, I hope that by this comparative study the Chinese student of philosophy may be enabled to criticise these precursory theories and methods in the light of the more modern and more complete developments, and to understand why the ancient Chinese antecedents have failed to achieve the great results which their modern counterparts have achieved. The reader may come to grasp, for instance, why the theories of natural and social evolution in ancient China have failed to accomplish the revolutionary effect which the Darwinian theory has produced on modern thought.

Furthermore, I hope that such a comparative study may save China from many of the blunders attendant upon an uncritical importation of European philosophy, blunders such as wastefulness in teaching the old-fashioned textbooks of formal logic in Chinese schools, or the acceptance of Herbert Spencer's political philosophy together with the Darwinian theory of evolution.

Synkrētic

Such, then, is my excuse in making the present study of the development of logical method in ancient China. May this study, which is the first of its kind in any language not excepting the Chinese, serve to introduce to the Western world the great schools of thought in ancient China!

Notes

1 Chu Hsi's commentary on the fifth section of the *Ta Hsueh*. *Cf.* Sun Chi Fung's *History of Rational Philosophy* (1667), Vol. 2, p. 10 of the 1879 edition.

2 Wang Yang-ming, *Records of Discourses*, translated by F. G. Henke in *The Philosophy of Wang Yang-ming*, 177-178, which is a translation of the first volume of his selected works, first published by Sze Pong-yao in 1636 and republished by Fang Hsuoh-fu in 1906. I have here and in the following quotations revised Henke's translations.

3 *Loc. cit.* transl. Henke, 178.

4 *Recorded Instructions for Practice*, 9. In Henke, 59.

5 *Loc. cit.*

6 *Recorded Instructions for Practice*, 9. In Henke, 59.

7 Chu Hsi, in his commentary on the opening chapter of the *Ta Hsueh*, said: "'Things' is equivalent to 'affairs'. Wang Yang-ming said 'Things are affairs.'" (See his *Inquiry Regarding the Great Learning*, 45, transl. Henke, 213).

8 See Huang Chung-hsi, *History of the Philosophical Schools of the Sung and Yuen Dynasties* (written in the seventeenth century, revised by Chuan Chu Wang (1704-1755), first published in 1838, and republished in 1879), Vol. 10, pp. 18 and 46.

9 If this assertion needs any proof, note the unconscious influence of a scientific age on such Confucians as Mencius, as is seen, for example, in the following quotations: 'Having thoroughly employed the powers of their eyes, the sages have left behind them the try-square, the compasses, the level and the tape-measure, which may be infinitely used for making squares and circles and for leveling and straightening. Having thoroughly employed the powers of their ears, they have left behind them the six tonal regulators for the infinite use in standardising the five notes. Having thoroughly employed their mental powers, they have left behind them their benevolent policies in government in order that benevolence may extend to the whole empire" (Mencius, IV, Pt. I, 1). 'High as the heavens are, distant as the stars seem if we only seek their cause (故), the equinoxes of a thousand years can be calculated while sitting.' (Bk. IV, Pt. II, 26; the equinoxes, of course, are those in a lunar calendar and fall on different dates in different years). Many similar passages could be cited.

10 "Modern China", so far as philosophy and literature are concerned, dates back to the Tang dynasty (AD 618-906).

RESPONSES
What is Filipino philosophy?

On snow and the Filipino mind*

Leonardo N. Mercado†

Being is the core of Western philosophy. We see this centrality, for instance, in scholastic philosophy and in existentialism.

Since language mirrors thought, philosophies also reflect the languages on which they are based. When Aristotle wrote his *Categories*,[1] he was actually reflecting the Greek parts of speech. In general, the structure of sentences in Western languages can be simplified to having a subject and a predicate linked by the verb 'to be'.

Language is the house of philosophy. If Being is most important in Western philosophies, should it also be the concern of Filipino philosophy? An analogy may clarify the question.

Because temperate countries experience plenty of snow, people there have made it a major part of their culture. Their agricultural practices and way of life have been accommodated to the eventuality of winter. They have words to depict the various states of snow and weather: their homes are designed to cope with snow; they have winter sports and other things connected with a snow culture. In

---

*   This is an edited extract of Leonardo N. Mercado, Chapter 5, 'The Counterpart of Being', in *The Filipino Mind Philippine Philosophical Studies II* (Washington, D.C.: The Council for Research in Values and Philosophy, 1994), 85, 87, 89, 90. It is reproduced with the gracious permission of the Council for Research in Values and Philosophy.

†   Rev. Fr. Leonardo N. Mercado, SVD (1935-2020) was a Catholic missionary and a leading thinker on Filipino philosophy. He earned a PhD in philosophy from the University of Santo Tomas. He lived in Quezon City, the Philippines.

countries with four seasons, languages are tense-oriented. English, for instance, has a dozen tenses.[2]

On the other hand, Filipinos do not have snow. So, why should they be concerned with snow? Filipinos naturally are more concerned with other meaningful aspects of the weather that affect their lives. Because Filipinos have no snow, they have no original word for it. But they have quite a vocabulary for things like rice in all its states, that is from the seed to its planting, harvesting, and cooking stage. Because the two seasons in the Philippines are basically *tag-init* (hot season) and *tag-ulan* (rainy season), tenses in Philippine languages are not stressed.[3] We shall return to this point later.

Language therefore mirrors the concerns of life, and consequently mirrors a people's worldview or philosophy. Hence, Filipino philosophers primarily concerned with Being are like Filipinos concerned with snow!

The epistemological consequence is that English and other Western languages tend to judge things as *either/or*. A Filipino tends to think *both/and*, which mentality suits his concern for harmony. He shares this logic with his Asian neighbours.[4]

The *either/or* mentality leads to universal and cultural imperialism because of its zeal to reduce truth to essences. Truth for its own sake, even at the sacrifice of persons, is the goal of *either/or* thinking. We can therefore understand why Church history in the West has been marked by wars and persecutions for the sake of orthodoxy.

On the other hand, the *both/and* mentality leads to respecting pluralism. For the Filipino, truth must not be sacrificed out of respect for other persons, but harmony is a higher value than truth. Truth is not just conformity between the mind and the object.

Comparative Asian philosophy is important because it provides insights into Filipino philosophy. In the metaphor of family resemblance, not all the members of the family look the same because the totality of traits are, so to speak, not in every individual. Thus, Chinese and Indian philosophies are different, but they have a family resemblance.

Taoism, which stresses the harmony of the yin and yang principles, is actually a philosophy of Becoming. The Chinese language,
like the Philippine languages, also does not have the verb 'to be'.
Yet, Chinese philosophy can go deep in its speculations.

While Filipino philosophy has some features common to yin-
yang philosophy, there are also differences.[5]

From the foregoing evidence, we can therefore conclude that the
counterpart of Being in Filipino philosophy is Becoming.

We said above that Being is the core of Western philosophy,
partly because of the structure of the Western languages. In the
history of Western philosophy, 'in most, though not in all, philosophical systems Being was given prominence while Becoming was
placed in an inferior and subordinate role.'[6] That is why, beginning
with Plato, ideas came to be the most important concern: idea was
translated to Being. In the history of Western thought, ideas were
considered as eternal. Thus, scholastic philosophy was concerned
with eternal truths.

If Becoming is a major concern of Filipino philosophy, does this
mean a neglect of Being? Before we can answer the question, first a
short digression.

The idea of the holy has two dimensions: the transcendent and
the immanent. Western thought is concerned with the holy as transcendent, but Filipinos prefer to view the holy as immanent.[7] Since
the model preferred depends upon the culture, those who uphold
one should not impose theirs on others.

Likewise, the law has two sides: right and duty. Western thought
gives more importance to right because it values the individual
more.

On the other hand, the Filipino preference for the immanent
over the transcendent, duty over right, also has its counterpart in the
preference for Becoming over Being.

Notes

1 *Synkrētic* – Aristotle, *The Categories*, transl. E. M. Edghill (Whitefish, Montana: Kessinger Publishing, 2004).

2 Leonardo N. Mercado, *Elements of Filipino Philosophy* (Tacloban City: Divine Word University Publications, 1974), 108.

3 Mercado, *Elements of Filipino Philosophy*, 107-110.

4 Felix Wilfred, 'Dialogue Gasping for Breath? Towards New Frontiers in Interreligious Dialogue', *FABC Papers*, No. 49 (1987), 43-46.

5 See Leonardo N. Mercado, Chapter 6, 'Evil', in *The Filipino Mind Philippine Philosophical Studies II* (Washington, D.C.: The Council for Research in Values and Philosophy, 1994), 93-105.

6 Milac Capek, 'Change', *The Encyclopedia of Philosophy*, 1967, II, 76.

7 Leonardo N. Mercado, 'Religious Models and Filipino Thought', *Solidarity*, No. 128 (October-December 1990): 21-23; see also Leonardo N. Mercado, *Inculturation and Filipino Theology* (Manila: Divine Word Publications, 1992), 43-73.

North Sampalokese
is better than Plato's Greek*

Roque J. Ferriols†

No one can create a Filipino or any other philosophy except by accident.

Zhuang Zhou did not try to develop a Chinese philosophy. He simply awoke to the Way within him and around him, tried to awaken even more, knew that what he lived could not be put into words—when all that can be said has been said, the most important thing cannot be said—yet felt compelled to say all that he could say. Hundreds of years later, what he said still lives and is called Chinese philosophy. He is surprised. It is the Way that matters to him, not the label.

What more German than Hegel or Nietzsche? Yet neither are in agonies to be Germanic. They are too fascinated by the striving to see [the truth], by the visions that occasionally break [over] them, to engage in dramatics about identity. At the beginning of *Discours de la méthode*, Descartes says half-proudly, half-apologetically, that he is writing it in French.[1] For the rest of the work, he simply philosoph-

* This is an edited extract of Roque J. Ferriols, S.J., 'A Memoir of Six Years', in *Philippine Studies*, Vol. 22, No. 3-4 (1974): 338-345. It is reproduced with the gracious permission of the publisher, Ateneo de Manila University.

† Roque J. Ferriols, S.J. (1924-2021) was a Jesuit priest and Ateneo de Manila professor who pioneered the teaching of philosophy in Filipino. He earned his PhD from Fordham University. He lived in Quezon City, the Philippines.

ises. No symptoms of an anguished thrust to Frenchness. He is too French for that.

When I try to philosophise in Filipino, it is with the intent to live and to help awaken other people into living. Each language is a way of being alive that is irreducible. No, Filipino is not my favourite language. But it is a good language.

[I have been asked,] 'How do you translate philosophical terms?' That is really no problem. Most English philosophical terms are really Latin words (*subjectivum, objectivum, intuitio, praedicatum*) somewhat mispronounced and misspelled (subjective, objective, intuition, predicate). Or Greek words similarly distorted (metaphysics). The Germans sometimes use Latin and Greek (*subjektiv, Metaphysik*) or create their own terms (*Mitzumachung*) or do both at the same time (*Objekt, Gegenstand*). We followed the German model.

But this question was not usually asked as a request for suggestions on how to proceed or for information on how we proceeded. Usually, it was asked rhetorically, as a way of saying: 'You cannot do this.' Sometimes so bitterly as to mean: 'You cannot do this to me.' Often the question was a cover for a presupposition that what English and Spanish are allowed to do cannot be allowed to Tagalog or any Filipino language. So, intuition is 'derived from' the Latin. Coffee and alcohol are 'derived from' the Arabic. But *sumbalilong*[2] is a 'corruption of' the Spanish, *istrok*[3] is 'corrupted from' the English.

Another form this question took was: 'How do you say "being" in Filipino?' with a facial aha-this-shows-you-cannot-do-philosophy-in-Filipino expression. There are many ways of answering that question. One is: 'as inadequately as in English.' The English word 'being' does not really express the central deed of metaphysics. Another answer is: 'What philosopher have you in mind?' 'Being' in Bertrand Russell[4] is a different word from 'being' in Heidegger.[5]

'Are you still doing it?' The questioner is usually an English-speaking academic, fifty to sixty years old. He is taken up with obvious facial preparations to assume a grief-stricken pose the moment he hears the, he hopes, inevitable 'No'. Chagrin as he hears 'Yes'.

The asker feels threatened by this continuing effort to philosophise in Filipino.

The question proceeds from the hidden conviction of the asker that nothing profound has happened in any Filipino language, that translations of foreign terms are not mere ornaments or helps but the very life blood of Filipino thought. Can there be any depth, he asks, in a Filipino centre? The Lord save him from his own superciliousness. He himself cannot.

A little over half a hundred years ago—according to reliable hearsay—I saw first light on floor twelve of the Philippine General Hospital. Later, I saw more and more light in Sampalok.

Trying to make friends in the playground, I talked to my peers in something I thought was Tagalog and was laughed at.

In North Sampalok, nobody felt superior to you if you spoke with a different accent or mixed Ilocanisms[6] with your Tagalog. Not three kilometres away, the little sons and daughters of the Tagalese[7] were enforcing elitist norms. Slowly, I came to know that my language was not Tagalog but North Sampalokese.

Twenty-five years after I had left home, I was in Wao, Lanao del Sur. A man a little older than me called me by my name. After a few minutes of talking, I too could call him by his name. He was an old neighbour. 'How did you know I was here?' 'I recognised you on the altar when you were saying Mass.'[8] He had a farm in one of the *barrios*.[9] He could not live in our old neighbourhood after it had become too dense. We talked in North Sampalokese.

In six years, one comes to know that, for human thinking, North Sampalokese is better than Plato's Greek.

Notes

These notes are provided by Synkrētic to clarify references and other details of interest.

1   'And if I write in French, which is the language of my country, in preference to Latin, which is that of my preceptors, it is because I expect that those who make use of their unprejudiced natural Reason will be better judges of my opinions than those who give heed to the writings of the ancients only,' he writes. See René Descartes, 'A Discourse on Method', in *French and English Philosophers: Descartes, Voltaire, Rousseau, Hobbes: The Five Foot Shelf of Classics*, Vol. XXXIV, Charles W. Eliot, ed. (New York: Cosimo Classics, 2009), 62.

2   *Sumbalilo(ng)* is the Tagalog word for 'sombrero' and is derived from this masculine Spanish noun. See Pedro Serrano Laktaw, *Diccionario Tagálog-Hispano* (Manila: Santos y Bernal, Islas Filipinas, 1914), 1210.

3   *Istrok* is the Tagalog word for 'stroke' and is derived from this same English noun.

4   'The world of being is unchangeable, rigid, exact, delightful to the mathematician, the logician, the builder of metaphysical systems, and all who love perfection more than life.' Bertrand Russell, *The Problems of Philosophy* (Oxford: Oxford University Press, 2001), 57.

5   'Philosophy is en route to the Being of being, that is, to being with respect to Being. [...] The Being of being rests in Beingness. But this—the *ousia* [Beingness]—Plato calls *idea* and Aristotle the *energeia* [actuality].' Martin Heidegger, *What is Philosophy?*, transl. Jean T. Wilde and William Kluback (Lanham, Maryland: Rowman & Littlefield, 1956), 55.

6   An *Ilocanism* is a word from the Ilocano language used in Tagalog, much as *tête-à-tête* is a Frenchism in English.

7   An adjectival noun here relating to the Tagalog people, and more generally to the Filipino people in archaic usage.

8   His neighbour is referring to the fact that Father Ferriols, a Jesuit priest, had celebrated a Catholic religious service.

9   *Barrios*, a Spanish word that is itself an Arabism, are urban or municipal districts, often on the outskirts of a town.

Filipino logic*

Florentino T. Timbreza[†]

In the 1960s and 1970s, no Filipino teacher of philosophy would ever have believed there to be such a thing as Filipino philosophy. At the time, Western thought was the only acceptable one.

But if philosophy begins in wonder as Plato and Aristotle claimed, then there is a Filipino philosophy, insofar as Filipinos also marvel at the mystery of existence. 'All human beings by nature desire to know,' as Aristotle famously observed.[1] The Greeks do not have a monopoly on the desire to know.

If philosophy arises out of human experience, as the existentialist and phenomenologist teach, then there is a Filipino philosophy inasmuch as there is a distinctly Filipino experience.

And if philosophy is found in every culture, as the sociologist and anthropologist have discovered, then there is a Filipino philosophy, since the Filipinos have a culture as rich as that of any people.

If, finally, thought and language are intertwined, with the latter embodying the former, as linguists and philosophers of language suggest, then Filipino philosophy exists because there is also a

---

*   This is an edited extract from Florentino T. Timbreza's *Filipino Philosophy Today* (Mandaluyong City: National Book Store, 2008), xi-xxv, 187-191. It is reprinted with the gracious permission of Dr Florentino T. Timbreza.

†   Florentino T. Timbreza is a University Fellow and former Full Professor at De La Salle University-Manila. He wrote the first philosophy PhD in the Filipino language at the University of Santo Tomas. He is based in Manila, the Philippines.

Filipino language—and in fact over 80 varieties of it, each of which reflects a different facet of human reality.

Our ability to philosophise, therefore, does not depend on our being Chinese, Greek, Indian, German, French, or Filipino. We do not need to become Westerners, nor speak English or French, to be awed by the mystery of life. It is enough to be born human with an indigenous experience, inherent culture, and a native language.

Filipinos, too, have their own philosophical worldview, a picture of reality which provides a plausible explanation of human life. Filipino thought is more of a philosophy of life than a philosophy of being, just as it was for the Greeks. It's still too young to have a metaphysics of its own, although Fr. Ferriols' concepts of *meron* (being), *wala* (nonbeing), and *pagmemeron* (becoming) have taken initial steps in this direction.[2]

Filipinos have not devised a system of definition. Instead, they tend to use metaphors, analogies, and similes. It is the scholar's arduous task to assemble these fragments of a philosophy of life into a coherent whole.

Some sinologists suggest that Confucius himself referred to his *Lunyu*, also known as *The Analects of Confucius*, as being based on a collection of wise sayings by the Chinese people's ancestors.[3] There is no reason that we cannot do the same thing with the corpus of Filipino myths, parables, legends, proverbs, and sayings we inherited from our own forebears.

Who else could articulate a Filipino philosophy if not the Filipinos themselves? It would be the high point of irony to leave this task to foreigners.

If the Western syllogism is taken as the norm, then Filipino logic is identical with it in its theoretical form. Yet, the latter is *distinct* and *unique* on account of six core differences. Unlike its abstract, impersonal, universal, and scientific Western cousin, Filipino logic is more metaphorical, concrete, personal, moralistic, rhetorical, and theological.

This can make Filipino reasoning seem faulty from the stance of Western logic. Fallacies of false premises or false cause are often committed. People are prone to jumping to conclusions, indulging in pure speculative arguments, taking items out of context, and assuming premises without proof.

However, Filipino logic should be understood in the context of the people's mental framework. Western thought is logical and empirical. Every statement is supported by facts. Every conclusion should logically follow from its premises. Every pronouncement must be backed by proof. Every utterance must be verifiable and observable. Filipino thinking, on the other hand, is nonlogical and nonempirical. It is more intuitive than sequential, more functional than empirical, more practical than inferential.

The Filipino does not need to prove his statements. He does not need to define his terms; he does not need to justify his thought. He directly intuits the truth of statements. He seems to immediately apprehend knowledge of a practical kind about the nature of life, human nature, the world, etc. We see this, for instance, in the penetrating wisdom of the popular proverb, *Ang taong nagigipit, kahit sa patalim ay kakapit*, which means: 'A man who is in danger will cling even to a knife.' While it may formally prove nothing, its truth is obvious to anyone who has experienced all-consuming fear, loss, or despair.

Because we, Filipinos, have developed an indigenous philosophy and logic, it's important that we philosophise with it, and not with that of other races. Thinking with another's thoughts is like eating pre-chewed food. When we think through another's thoughts, we become subconsciously subservient to their owner. This is one of the reasons many Filipinos still have a colonial mentality.

Until when shall we remain prisoners of other people's thoughts? Why should we not articulate our own? If not now, when?

Reflecting on our culture and language can help us discern our philosophy of life, our values, and our Filipino identity.

Notes

These notes are provided by Synkrëtic to clarify references and other details of interest.

1 This the first sentence of Aristotle's *Metaphysics*, here based on W.D. Ross' translation: 'All men by nature desire to know.' See Aristotle, *The Works of Aristotle*, transl. W.D. Ross (Oxford: Clarendon Press, 1954), 980.

2 See, for example, Nemesio S. Que and Augustin Martin G. Rodriguez, eds., *Pagdiriwang Sa Meron: A Festival of Thought Celebrating Fr. Roque J. Ferriols, S.J.* (Quezon City: Ateneo de Manila University, 1997).

3 See, relatedly, Daniel E. Bell's suggestion that 'a strain of Chinese wisdom [was] preserved in the "Confucian" Classics'. Bell, *Confucian Political Ethics* (Princeton: Princeton University Press, 2010), 89.

Philosophy must transcend man*

Claro R. Ceniza†

Some students regard philosophy as the most irrelevant of subjects. This is probably so because the ideas we teach them are foreign ideas which are alien to our Filipino experience.

One prevalent theory for this general feeling of the irrelevance of philosophy to our practical lives is that, in the over two thousand years that men have philosophised, philosophers have not agreed on any definitive answers to the philosophical questions. There appear to be as many answers to the questions as there are philosophers who have proposed answers to them. Hence, to many a common man, philosophy seems to be an exercise in futility. I do not agree with this thesis.

Many of the original problems of philosophy have in fact already been answered—or the way to their answers has in fact already been given. Note that the ancients asked themselves, 'What is the world made of?', and gave various answers to this question.

*   This is an edited excerpt from Claro R. Ceniza, 'Self-Identity and the Filipino Philosophy', in *Sophia*, Vol. XII, No. 1, May-August 1982, Trimestral Journal of the Department of Philosophy, De La Salle University, Manila, the Philippines, pp. 22-25. It is based on a lecture delivered at a De La Salle University Philosophy Week Celebration between 15-19 March 1982. It is reproduced with the gracious permission of the Claro Rafols Ceniza Estate.

†   Claro R. Ceniza (1927-2001) was a Full Professor at De La Salle University and a leading metaphysician, logician and philosopher of science. Dr Ceniza earned a PhD from Syracuse University. He lived in Manila, the Philippines.

'Water', said Thales.[1] 'The Boundless', said Anaximander.[2] 'Fire', according to Heraclitus.[3] 'The atoms and the void', answered Leucippus and Democritus.[4] And yet today, almost all—if not all—physics textbooks are in agreement as to the ultimate, or at least the penultimate, constituents of matter.

But it may be remarked that it was physics, not philosophy, which answered that question. In reply, we can only say that, formerly, physics was a branch of philosophy. It was then called natural philosophy. It just happens that when a philosophical problem is answered—or nearly answered—it ceases to be a philosophical problem. The discipline is taken over by a new-born science.

Who now thinks that the sun, the stars, and the planets are carried in their heavenly courses by intelligences? Science tells us it is gravity—or some curvature in the Space-Time continuum—that is responsible for the motions of the heavenly bodies. People once thought that diseases were caused by demons and angry spirits. Today, practically everyone believes that they are caused by germs or other physical malfunctioning. It used to be thought that earthquakes were caused by giant animals moving under the earth. Now we know they are caused by movements of the earth's crust. Storms and lightning, as well as wars and pestilences, used to be blamed on the gods. Today, we are wont to explain them in terms of natural causes. The question of the origin of man has been answered to the satisfaction of most scientists and philosophers as due to the mechanism of evolution theorised by Darwin,[5] Mendel,[6] and others.

Even the beginning of the universe is no longer regarded as unanswerable in principle and the consensus among scientists and philosophers appears to be that the world did not begin according to the literal account given by the first chapters of Genesis.[7] Much of the human psyche and man's consequent behaviour have been explained and mapped by psychology, and a great deal of our social behaviour has been clarified by sociology.

The problem of the nature of Space and Time and their relation to the physical world have been greatly enlightened by the General Theory of Relativity, which, incidentally, I believe decisively—that is, as decisively as is possible at this point, at any rate—answers the question of whether the world is mind-dependent or possesses a reality outside of the perceiving mind; whether causal laws are happenstances, as Hume claimed,[8] or proceed from a category of the mind, as Kant believed,[9] or are due to the geometrical structure of Space-Time as Relativity itself suggests,[10] and are, therefore, objective.

Philosophy is relevant and not a waste of time provided we take care to make it relevant to the student's personal concerns. There has to be a balance between objective lessons and student response. We must allow the students some leeway for discussions, even if we disagree with the opinions they express. We must, if possible, situate the lessons and examples in terms of the students' personal experiences—especially their experiences as Filipinos.

Nevertheless, a national philosophy must not be the ultimate goal of Filipino philosophising. We must graduate from nationalism to a more global approach. The next great step is humanism: to think from the viewpoint of humanity. We should no longer think merely as Filipinos, as Frenchmen, Germans, or Americans. But, although this is important, this also cannot be the sole purpose of philosophy.

For philosophy must also transcend the exclusive concentration on man. Philosophy must still step forward and, I think, throw its light on being itself. Being is Plato's Form of the Good which, like the sun,[11] enlightens all things and gives us understanding of all around us.

This, I think, is the course that Filipino philosophy ought to take.

Notes

These notes are provided by Synkrētic to clarify references, and other details of interest.

1 Aristotle writes that, on the question of the nature or principle from which all others spring, 'Thales, the founder of this kind of philosophy, says that it is water (that is why he declares that the earth rests on water).' Aristotle, *The Works of Aristotle*, transl. W.D. Ross (Oxford: Clarendon Press, 1954), 983b6.

2 Anaximander speculated that the origin of the world 'has its source in the boundless (*apeiron*), literally, "without limits".' Robin Waterfield, ed., *The First Philosophers: The Presocratics and Sophists* (Oxford: Oxford University, Press), 5.

3 Heraclitus theorised that, through no act of man or the gods, '*all things* become *fire* at one time or another [...] it ever was and is and will be: ever-living *fire*, kindling in measures and being extinguished in measures.' Cited in Aryeh Finkelberg, *Heraclitus and Thales' Conceptual Scheme: A Historical Study* (Leiden: Koninklijke Brill, 2017), 65.

4 Leucippus was the first philosopher to speculate on the existence of atoms. His theory also presupposed a void in the universe, which later inspired Newton. Leucippus' student Democritus developed his materialistic model of the universe. See Bernard Pullman, *The Atom in the History of Human Thought* (Oxford: Oxford University Press, 1995), 31-32.

5 Charles Darwin, *On the Origin of Species: By Means of Natural Selection*, eds. Mary Carolyn Waldrep, Thomas Crawford (Mineola, New York: Dover, 2006).

6 Gregor Mendel, *Experiments in Plant Hybridisation* (New York: Cosimo, 2008).

7 Genesis 1:1-2:3.

8 For an introduction to David Hume's theory of causation, see C.M. Lorkowski, 'David Hume: Causation', *Internet Encyclopedia of Philosophy*, available at: < https://iep.utm.edu/hume-cau/>.

9 For a comparison between Kantian and Humean theories of causality, see Graciela De Pierris and Michael Friedman, 'Kant and Hume on Causality', in *The Stanford Encyclopedia of Philosophy*, Winter 2018 Edition, Edward N. Zalta (ed.), available at: <https://plato.stanford.edu/archives/win2018/entries/kant-hume-causality/>.

10 See, among others, James J. Callahan, *The Geometry of Spacetime: An Introduction to Special and General Relativity* (New York: Springer, 2013).

11 Ceniza is alluding to the famous analogy of the sun in *The Republic*, which Plato uses to explain the Good. See Plato, *Plato in Twelve Volumes*, Vols. 5 & 6, transl. Paul Shorey (London, William Heinemann Ltd., 1969), 507b–509c.

The Philippines' greatest female philosopher*

Anne Quito†

At 12:40am on 17 September 2017, Emerita Quito,[1] one of the Philippines' greatest philosophers, finally got her wish.[2] The 88-year-old former De La Salle University dean and author of more than 20 books died of respiratory failure in Manila. She was a trail-blazing scholar, a prolific writer, and a sought-after lecturer. She was also my grand aunt.

Once at the apex of Asian philosophy circles, Quito passed away in near obscurity, quietly whiling away her last years watching reruns of her favourite French game show, *Des chiffres et des lettres*. 'I have one prayer to God when I wake up every morning: Take me. I'm ready,' she said when I last visited her in June 2016. 'I don't only feel old,' she told me without a hint of nostalgia, 'I feel ancient.'

Quito dedicated her life to the realm of ideas. Educated at the Université de Fribourg in Switzerland and the Sorbonne in Paris, she garnered the *Chevalier dans l'Ordre des Palmes Académiques*, France's highest academic decoration in 1984. She was honoured as the Philippines' most outstanding educator a year later. She mastered six languages (including Urdu) and was a superb writer who chewed, challenged and interpreted Western philosophy for

---

* This edited extract of a piece first published in *Quartz* on 18 September 2017 is reprinted with permission.

† Anne Quito is a staff journalist at *Quartz*. She holds a Master's degree in Visual Culture from Georgetown University and a Master of Fine Arts in Design Criticism from the School of Visual Arts. She is based in New York City, USA.

the Asian context with great insight and precision. Her 1969 dissertation, *The Notion of Participatory Freedom in the Philosophy of Louis Lavelle*, was the first work by a Filipino that the Université de Fribourg published.

Philosophy isn't very popular in the Philippines. Culture usually means pop culture there—Beyoncé will trump Barthes any day. Philosophy is even linguistically associated with foolishness in the national language. 'On the popular or grassroots level, the term *"pilosopo"* (Filipino word for "philosopher") is a pejorative name for anyone who argues lengthily, whether rightly or wrongly,' as Quito wrote in a 1983 essay analysing the Filipinos' cultural aversion to rigorous thinking.[3]

Perhaps that is why one of the Philippines' most decorated intellectuals—and mould-breaking female professionals—never gained a larger following outside the classroom. Or maybe it was because she was an uncompromising personality who refused to preen for the celebrity-obsessed media.

Quito rarely broke out of her serious, no-nonsense demeanour while on campus. She wore an ascetic's uniform for years—straight black skirt and simple, short-sleeved blouse—recalling the nun's habit she wore as Sister Mary Paul when she briefly joined the Catholic convent of Assumption Sisters in Paris.

Quito's students remember her as a brilliant but stern scholar who had no tolerance for laziness. 'We were afraid of her. But we wanted to like her. So we tried. All we needed to do was read around 2,000 books,' says her former student, Milette Zamora. 'She never really gave us the answers, she made us get them on our own,' she recalls.

'She has no patience for bullshit,' adds Laureen Velasco, another of Quito's students. 'She would have made a very bad politician.'

Her former secretary Gabi Bongales recalls how popular her classes were despite her reputation. '[Students knew that] if Dr Quito gave them a failing grade, they deserved it, so no one complained.'

Those who breached Quito's stern veneer saw her generous and nurturing side. 'I was struck by her sincere professional interest in my work in creative writing and my feminist advocacy to expose and eradicate insidious practices of sexism,' recalls fellow De La Salle University professor Marjorie Evasco-Pernia.

Among my fondest memories of Lola Emy, as we called her, is of sitting on her chequered living room floor for French language lessons with my cousins. Fresh from a trip from Paris, she rewarded each child who managed to twist their tongue to utter a perfect *bonjour* or *croissant*. The prize that day was a retractable ballpoint pen printed with the words *je ne suis pas un stylo*. It was an existential joke, my dad later explained. I cherished the gag gift from my usually impassive grand aunt.

After she retired at age 59, Lola Emy continued to travel and give occasional lectures abroad. She collected paintings and lived on the royalties of her books. The last time we were together, I watched her divide her money among her nephews and nieces, gleefully distributing banknotes like cards from a deck. Never married and with no children, she was determined to give it all away before she died.

Unsentimental till the end, she refused a wake and asked to be cremated right away.

Late in her career, she was consumed by the task of defining philosophy for the masses. 'I grasped at Asian philosophy as a solution, like a drowning man would clutch a floating log in turbulent waters,' she wrote in her 1991 book *The Merging Philosophy of East & West*. 'I believe in giving Asia its due, and will try to express Asian thought in simple, lucid and readable terms, intelligible to anyone.'[4]

Notes

1 Dr Emerita Quito's academic biography can be accessed on the De La Salle University website, available at: <https://www.dlsu.edu.ph/university-fellows/dr-emerita-quitoi/>.

2 For the full text, see Anne Quito, 'The Philippines' greatest female philosopher has died', *Quartz*, 18 September 2017, available at: <https://qz.com/725370/emerita-quito-the-greatest-forgotten-filipino-philosopher-has-died/>.

3 Emerita Quito, *The State of Philosophy in the Philippines* (Manila: De La Salle University Press, 1983), 9.

4 Quito, *The Merging Philosophy of East & West* (Manila: De La Salle University Press, 1991), 3.

Abulad's postmodern reading of Kant

*Daryl Mendoza**

Arguably the premier Kantian scholar in the Philippines, Romualdo Abulad was highly regarded for his readings of Kant and particularly the *Critique of Pure Reason*.[1] Abulad's philosophical project of postmodernism should be viewed in this light.

Despite postmodernism being a watchword in Western intellectual circles from around the mid-1970s, it was not as well known in the Philippines until relatively recently. In 2000, Abulad inaugurated its reception with his programmatic essay, 'What is Postmodernism?'[2]

Prior to this, essays in the Philippines did not account for postmodernism's structure and genesis. Abulad's peculiar reading of postmodernism was influential in Filipino philosophical circles because he explained both. While many works on postmodernism set out from poststructuralism, Abulad began with an unusual source: Immanuel Kant. A 1998 essay already foreshadowed his philosophical trajectory:

Thus, it cannot be said that my interest in Postmodern Philosophy contradicts my ceaseless interest in Kantianism. On the contrary, there is a way to prove that the true direction of Kant's thinking ineluctably leads to insights which belong even to our own time. I shall, therefore, endeavor to integrate the two things which nowadays never cease to occupy me: Kant and Postmodernism.[3]

---

*   Daryl Mendoza is Assistant Professor at the University of San Carlos. His research interests include Baudrillard, Marxism and post-modernism. He is based in Cebu City, the Philippines.

Abulad's reading of Kant that I explicated takes the form of binaries. These should not be read as hypostasised concepts, but as strategic devices that guide without calcifying his thought.

The overarching strategic binary in Abulad's philosophy is that between the *via negativa* and *via positiva*, the negative and positive ways respectively. This device informs his reading of Kant and, crucially, his appropriation of it for understanding postmodernism.

Abulad's binary emphasises two important divisions in the *Critique*.

It first divides the *Critique* between its Transcendental Doctrine of Elements on the one hand, and the Transcendental Doctrine of Method on the other. It next demarcates the former along the lines of what can and cannot be known. In the *Critique*, the boundary between Kant's 'country of truth' and 'stormy ocean' falls at the end of the Transcendental Logic Analytic, before the Transcendental Logic Dialectic.[4] Abulad considers the first general division of the *Critique of Pure Reason* as the *via negativa*, and as a necessary condition for the *via positiva* of the second general division. Similarly, he treated Kant's thesis on the knowable as his *via positiva*, and his thesis on what is unknowable as his *via negativa*.

Building on these divisions, Abulad's reading of Kant established two important premises in his thought.

The first premise was the importance of making a critique as radical as Kant's to wipe the slate clean and of building a new consciousness on this foundation. The second concerned the necessity of evaluating the faculty of reason to establish the limits of knowledge, which should inform action. Abulad would later apply these premises, drawn from his reading of Kant, to postmodernism.[5]

Paolo Bolaños observed that Abulad's essays tended to take readers with him on 'a journey back to the history of philosophy of his own peculiar telling, that is, his own philosophical *Denkbild*, often a fusion of horizons between the East and the West, but always Abulad's own constellation of concepts borrowed from the history of thought.'[6]

This 'peculiar telling' was the foam from which his theory of postmodernism arose. One also finds therein Abulad's two peculiar premises based on his binary of the *via negativa* and *via positiva*. Thus, Abulad replicated the structure of his reading of Kant in his reading of what he called postmodernism. That is, Abulad's account of postmodernism is also structured along the lines of the *via negativa* and *via positiva*.

Abulad's postmodernism sprouted from the rubble in the aftermath of Kant's devastating critique. In 2011, going beyond describing the German professor as its pioneer,[7] Abulad finally presented Kant as the father of postmodernism, just as Descartes was the father of modern philosophy.[8]

Abulad's contributions to Filipino philosophy can be assessed using the conditions he set out in his own writings on this topic. It must be a conscious, original, authentically Filipino attempt at academic philosophy. 'Filipino philosophy is Filipino,' as he put it tersely.[9]

By his own criteria, Abulad's work on continental philosophy, his idiosyncratic reading of Kant's postmodernism, and his life-long commitment to his country mark him out as a distinguished Filipino philosopher. Born in the province of Quezon, Philippines, Romualdo E. Abulad was a teacher's teacher who taught at numerous universities over five decades and who never left his home country for opportunities abroad, even when these were offered to him.

Abulad was a teacher and mentor who saw in philosophy not only a profession or vocation, but a way of life. But if he has taught us anything, it is that even the example of his own philosophical method and conclusions should be purged completely and without reserve.

Notes

1   See Daryl Mendoza, 'Reading Abulad's Reading of Kant: Postmodernism and the Possibility of a Filipino Philosophy', in *Phavisminda Journal*, Special Issue, Vol. 18 (2019): 121.

2   Romualdo Abulad, 'What is Postmodernism?,' *Karunungan*, Vol. 17 (2000): 34-54.

3   Romualdo Abulad, 'Kant and Postmodernism', *Phavisminda Journal*, Vol. 2 (May 1998): 32.

4   See B295/A236-B324/A268, in Immanuel Kant, *Critique of Pure Reason*, transl. Marcus Weigelt (London: Penguin, 2008), 251.

5   See Mendoza, 'Reading Abulad's Reading of Kant', 125.

6   Paolo Bolaños, 'Introduction to the Special Tribute Section: Abulad, Philosophy, and Intellectual Generosity', *Kritike: An Online Journal of Philosophy*, Vol. 13, No. 2 (December 2019): 7.

7   Romualdo Abulad, 'Contemporary Filipino Philosophy', in *Karunungan*, Vol. 5 (1988): 1-13; and Romualdo Abulad, 'Immanuel Kant as a Pioneer of Postmodernity', in *The Thomasian Philosopher*, Vol. 26 (2005): 120-128.

8   See Romualdo Abulad, 'Immanuel Kant as the Father of Postmodernity', *Zeferino Gonzales Quadricentennial Lecture Series*, UST Martyr's Hall, 19 February 2011. Unpublished; also quoted in Mendoza, 'Reading Abulad's Reading of Kant'.

9   See Romualdo Abulad, 'Options For a Filipino Philosophy', in *Karunungan*, Vol. 1 (1984): 17-30; Romualdo Abulad, 'Kant and Postmodernism'; Mendoza, 'Reading Abulad's Reading of Kant', 137-138.

How to outgrow Kant*

Rolando M. Gripaldo†

The early Filipino philosophers were Enlightenment thinkers in that they were influenced by the European Enlightenment.

The Enlightenment movement of the 18th century in Central Europe travelled to Spain in the first half of the 19th century and reached the Philippines in the second half of that century. José Rizal, who bought all the works of Voltaire, was an Enlightenment thinker.[1] He subscribed to the ideas of the Enlightenment: the dominance of *reason* with its capacity to emancipate mankind from its woes; the primacy of education as a tool for enlightenment; the inevitability of progress brought about by science and technology; the deistic belief that God created the universe with the laws of nature and left it perfectly working by itself, never to interfere with it again; the confidence that man can solve all his problems because these are humanly, not divinely, created; and the like.

It is a fact that there are Filipino philosophers. However, there are only a few of them. Most Filipinos engaged in philosophy are just *teachers* or *scholars* of philosophy. They have not yet graduated to become genuine philosophers. They master a philosopher—say,

*   This is an edited extract of Rolando M. Gripaldo, 'The Making of a Filipino Philosopher', *Philosophia: International Journal of Philosophy*, Vol. 37, No. 1 (2008): 23-36. It is reproduced with the gracious permission of *Philosophia*.

†   Rolando M. Gripaldo (1947-2017) was a Full Professor of philosophy at De La Salle University and the editor of the journal *Philosophia*. He held a PhD from the University of the Philippines. He lived in Manila, the Philippines.

Immanuel Kant, St. Thomas Aquinas, Friedrich Nietzsche, or Plato—or they specialise in a branch of philosophy such as ethics, æsthetics, philosophy of religion, or metaphysics. They try to learn a little of the other branches of philosophy to be able to relate those ideas to the ideas in their respective specialisations. In other cases, they simply do not read some schools or traditions of philosophy, which they consider either as not genuine philosophy or as too technical for their understanding to fathom, as in the philosophy of mathematics. But hardly if ever do they reflect or philosophise on their own.

To master a philosopher's philosophy or to master a field of specialisation within a discipline is good, but Filipinos need to grow either outside or within that philosopher or that specialisation. One ought not to be a Kantian forever, if by "Kantian" we mean we simply mouth Kant's ideas in our lectures and writings, that is to say, we do not innovate. We simply imitate Kant—we mimic his ideas and even probably also his mannerisms. We can quote or para-phrase from his three *Critiques*[2] cover to cover, know the ins and outs of his life, and so on. We become an intellectual through him.

Many of the Filipinos are like this Kantian. They become Nietz-schean or Heideggerian or Rortyan through and through. They forget about their own independence of mind. They forget that they can innovate or tread a new path. Ralph Waldo Emerson teaches that one should be an independent intellectual because to imitate is suicide.[3] If all that one wants in life is just to become a Kantian, or to mimic Kant, then in effect he or she is an *intellectual suicide*. Ber-trand Russell and G.E. Moore were *young Hegelians*,[4] but eventually they rejected Hegel and formulated their own individual philo-sophies. Plotinus studied Plato, but he did not end up just becoming a Platonist; he made a novel approach to Plato and became a neo-Platonist. It is said that Plato's immediate successor in the Academy was a Platonist,[5] but, unlike Aristotle, he was easily forgotten or taken for granted in history.

In contemporary times, we can cite Alfred North Whitehead, who became a neo-Heraclitean by affirming the reality of the Her-aclitean flux while employing the results of modern physics,[6] and

Claro R. Ceniza, who became a neo-Parmenidean when he tried to reconcile the views of Parmenides on *the One* and those of Heraclitus on *the Many*.[7]

Pythagoras—and many of the ancient Greeks—restudied the question that Thales earlier raised: 'What is the universe made of?' or 'What is the ultimate reality?', and independently offered a solution.

In short, we have at least three ways to become a genuine philosopher. We can: (1) innovate (from Kantian to neo-Kantian); (2) reject an old philosophical thought and create a new path to philosophising; and (3) review old philosophical questions and offer a new insight.

The Filipinos need also to recognise that any cultural setting is rooted in history. Culture over time is history. If they look back in their history, their philosophical beginnings and their developmental trajectory are influenced by a Western orientation. If we examine what is going on in philosophy in the Philippines today, it is basically Western in outlook with some occasional pockets of what is known as the Oriental outlook.

What is needed are philosophical innovations that are distinctively the product of profound philosophical minds, something that will separate one's thoughts from the thoughts of others before him or her. And, I think, this is one of the great challenges of a would-be Filipino philosopher.

Notes

The text of note 5 is Dr Gripaldo's. All other notes are provided by Synkrētic to clarify references and other details of interest.

1 José Rizal (1861-1896) is widely considered to be the Philippines' pre-eminent national hero. An influential novelist, political activist and revolutionary, he read Voltaire during his medical studies in Madrid. See Raul J. Bonoan, 'The Enlightenment, Deism, and Rizal', in *Philippine Studies*, Vol. 40, No. 1 (First Quarter 1992): 53-67.

2 The *Critique of Pure Reason* (1781), *Critique of Practical Reason* (1788), and *Critique of the Power of Judgment* (1790). Immanuel Kant, *Three Critiques: Three-Volume Set*, transl. Werner S. Pluhar (Indianapolis: Hackett Publishing, 2002).

3 'There is a time in every man's education when he arrives at the conviction that envy is ignorance, that imitation is suicide…' Ralph Waldo Emerson, *Self-Reliance* (Morrisville, North Carolina: Logos Books, 2019), 9.

4 Morton White, *The Age of Analysis* (New York: Mentor Books, 1955), 13, 17.

5 Speusippus adhered to the philosophy of Plato. Though he rejected the world of Forms, he did not make a significant innovation in Plato's philosophy. See Diogenes Laërtius, *Lives of the Eminent Philosophers*, transl. Robert Drew Hicks, Volume 1, Book 4, Loeb Classical Library (Cambridge: Harvard University Press, 1925), 374-379.

6 Alfred North Whitehead, *Process and Reality: An Essay in Cosmology*, eds. David Ray Griffin and Donald W. Sherburne (New York: The Free Press, 1929).

7 Claro R. Ceniza, *Thought, necessity and existence: Metaphysics and epistemology for lay philosophers: Written in the spirit of Parmenides of Elea* (Manila: De La Salle University Press, 2001).

Filipino philosophy?*

Noel S. Pariñas[†]

Inspired by Martin Heidegger's *What is Philosophy?*, the question 'what is Filipino philosophy?' entails the logical presumption that there is a Filipino philosophy. But is there really?

Undeniably, philosophy is fundamentally Greek. The Greek mathematician Pythagoras coined the term *philosophia* from the words *philos* or *philia* and *sophos* or *sophia*. Their nominal meanings are associated with "love, passion, or friend" and "wisdom" respectively. But it is not only by way of etymology that philosophy is said to be Greek, for the Western tradition claims that philosophy itself started in Greece. The father of philosophy, Socrates, was Greek and the first philosophers were Greeks.

The term 'Greek philosophy' is therefore a tautology.[1] It is tautological because philosophy is Greek by its very nature. For this reason, even 'Western philosophy' is practically redundant. As a necessary consequence, 'philosophy' implies that it is precisely Greek and Western. So, to speak of 'Western philosophy' or 'Greek philosophy' is to fall into the logic of redundancy. I will make use of wine as an analogy. By definition, 'wine' results from the fermentation of grapes. 'Grape wine', then, is a tautology.

---

* An earlier version of this paper was first published as N. Pariñas, 'Filipino Philosophy?', in *Academia Letters*, Article 442, available at: <https://doi.org/10.20935/AL442>. This edited extract contains substantial changes.

† Noel S. Pariñas is a Senior Education Program Specialist at the National Educators Academy of the Philippines. He holds a PhD from Benguet State University and JD from Baguio University. He lives in Baguio City, the Philippines.

The word 'logic' was coined by a Greek thinker, Parmenides, from the Greek word *logos*, which may mean reason or discourse.[2] If philosophy is 'love of wisdom' and we search for wisdom using logic, then logic is the tool of every philosophical inquiry. Even the tool of philosophy is Greek. How is it possible to argue that there is non-Greek logic if logic originated in Greece and was systematically developed by a Greek thinker, Aristotle, who is regarded as the father of logic?[3]

This is the reason why Chinese philosophy, Indian philosophy, and all other Eastern philosophies are not acknowledged as legitimate philosophies—because they are non-Greek, that is non-Western. In short, to classify them as philosophies is an error. To classify certain products as 'strawberry wine', 'rice wine', etc., is similarly an error since 'wine' is the product of fermented grapes.

For these reasons, there can be no Filipino philosophy, properly speaking. How could there be a Filipino philosophy when, as Alfred North Whitehead famously concluded in *Process and Reality*, the 'safest general characterization of philosophical tradition is that it consists of a series of footnotes to Plato?'[4]

Still, some thinkers claim and insist that Filipino philosophy exists on the grounds that a philosophy is Filipino if the author's language, citizenship, or categories are Filipino.

The first argument is problematic. Merely translating Plato's texts from Greek to Filipino neither makes his philosophy Filipino, nor alters the identity of philosophy itself.

Secondly, the philosopher's citizenship is not a sufficient condition either. I would not consider Plato's philosophy Filipino even if, hypothetically, he became a naturalised Filipino citizen.

Lastly, it is even harder to establish a Filipino philosophy on the basis of the categories used. Which categories could be agreed to be authentically Filipino? Their claimed cultural purity would in most cases be highly dubious.

Despite the impossibility of there being a Filipino philosophy, there can still be Filipino philosophers. Although philosophy is Greek, we can distinguish a German from a French, American, or

Filipino philosopher. Each uses their own vernacular to philosophise in originally Greek categories, so to speak.

A philosopher is not identified by their citizenship but by their nationality.[5] Paulo Freire[6] is a Brazilian philosopher because his nationality is Brazilian, even if he changed citizenship. Yet, we cannot say that Paulo Freire's philosophy is a, let alone the, Brazilian philosophy.

In like manner, we cannot generalise about German philosophy on the basis of Martin Heidegger's works. Nor do Jacques Derrida's books give us a privileged insight into something called French philosophy. Nationality, therefore, is prefixed to a philosopher's name not for the purposes of induction or generalisation, but of identification.

As Fr. Ranhilio Aquino argued, the idea of a purely Filipino philosophy is no less absurd than that of a British physics, a German mathematics, or a Greek geometry. If it 'is in the nature of science in fact to be no respecter of national boundaries,' as he asked, 'should that be less true of philosophy?'[7]

Who, then, is a Filipino philosopher?

One is said to be a Filipino philosopher if, despite the cultural Greekness of philosophy's methods, one is rooted to the Filipino historical experience. But because the discipline of philosophy is a system of references, rules, and standards imposed by the West, one is only crowned with the title of philosopher for playing its game.

Whenever we talk about Filipino philosophy, we are using the West's standards as a yardstick to measure and judge non-Western systems of thought.

Notes

1 Martin Heidegger, *What is Philosophy?* (Washington: Rowman & Littlefield Publishers, Inc, 1956), 109.

2 *Synkrētic* – See Robert Sherrick Brumbaugh, *The philosophers of Greece* (New York: SUNY Press, 1981), 50.

3 *Synkrētic* – For an introduction to Aristotle's logic, a collection of works known as the *Organon*, see Robin Smith, 'Aristotle's Logic', *The Stanford Encyclopedia of Philosophy* (Fall 2020 Edition), Edward N. Zalta (ed.), available at: <https://plato.stanford.edu/archives/fall2020/entries/aristotle-logic/>.

4 Alfred North Whitehead, *Process and Reality* (New York: Macmillan Company, 1969), 39.

5 'The philosopher must be a citizen of no country'. Michael Walzer quoting Ludwig Wittgenstein, 'Philosophy and Democracy', in *Political Theory*, Vol. 9, No. 3 (August 1981): 379.

6 *Synkrētic* – Paulo Freire was an influential philosopher of education who founded the critical pedagogy movement. See *Pedagogy of the Oppressed* (London: Penguin, 1985).

7 Fr. Ranhilio C. Aquino, 'Filipino Philosophy?', in *The Manila Times*, 19 June 2019, available at: <https://bit.ly/3pu9VB7>.

STORIES

How koalas lost their tails*

David Unaipon†

I

Aboriginal folklore

Perhaps someday Australian writers will use Aboriginal myths and weave literature from them, the same as other writers have done with the Roman, Greek, Norse, and Arthurian legends. If there is anything in the scientific theory that our Aboriginals are descendants of the Dravidians (a very ancient Indian race)[1] then Aboriginal folklore may be among the oldest in the world.

The Aboriginals are great storytellers. The *mooncumbulli* (the wise old man) telling the story puts in every detail. He acts and dramatises every incident with gesture, with changed intonations he leads his hearers from point to point in the story. A little simple legend told to the tribe under primitive conditions would take all the evening to relate. The Aboriginals have a myth connected with nearly all the constellations and bright stars in the heavens.

---

* These lightly edited pieces are drawn from David Unaipon's original typescript in the State Library of New South Wales, 'Volume 2: Typescript of *Legendary Tales of the Australian Aborigines* by David Unaipon, 1924-1925'. This work is under copyright and is reproduced with the permission of the Mitchell Library, State Library of New South Wales, and courtesy of the copyright-holder, Ms Judy Kropinyieri. For the full published work, see David Unaipon, *Legendary Tales of the Australian Aborigines*, eds. Stephen Muecke and Adam Shoemaker (Carlton: Miegunyah, 2006).

† David Unaipon (1872-1967) was a leading Ngarrindjeri thinker, inventor, preacher, and a pioneering Aboriginal writer in English. He was educated at the Point McLeay Mission School. He lived in South Australia, Australia.

Nearly all the tribes scattered about Australia have traditions of their flight from a land in the nor'-west, beyond the sea, into Australia. That land may probably be the ancient continent of Lemuria.[2] The traditions also relate that the Aboriginals were driven into Australia by a plague of fierce ants, or by a prehistoric race as fierce and as innumerable as ants. Like the Isrælites, the Aboriginals seem to have had a Moses, a lawgiver, a leader, who guided them in their Exodus from Lemuria. His name is Ngurunderi.[3]

This mythological being, who now lives in the heavens, gave the Aboriginals their tribal laws and customs, Aboriginal myths, legends, and stories were told to laughing and open-eyed children centuries before our present-day European culture began. These stories stand today as a link between the dawn of the world and our latest civilisation.

II

Belief of the Aborigine in a Great Spirit

The belief in a Supreme Being and in religious instruction, as well as religious ceremonies and worship, are not the experiences of the Jew and Muslim alone. Neither did it belong to one particular age or place, but it is universal and belongs to every age. This wonderful experience of a longing for something beautiful and noble, something spiritually Divine, lives within the bosom of the nations of the past as it does today.

Wonderful is the soul of man. A capacity for the Great Spirit of the Eternal God. Go back into those ancient civilisations and review the wonders. Those sensational discoveries in the valley of the Nile or in the jungles of Indochina, or let your mind be carried away to far-off Peru or Yucatan, or think of the grandeur that once was Rome's, the glories that once belonged to Greece. Amongst these ruins are monuments and fragments of magnificent temples erected to their gods. These are evidence that man is a worshipping creature irrespective of colour, language, or clime. The only difference is that a nation's conception of the Great Spirit alters its form of worship.

Synkrētic

The Jews have their synagogue, where they find delight and satisfaction in the offering of sacrifice and the singing of psalms to God Jehovah. The Muslims have their mosque, where they love to bow in reverent attitude praying to Allah, their God, and to Muhammad the prophet. The Christian churches of today, churches of various denominations, have people worshipping, some within humble buildings, some worshipping in beautiful churches and cathedrals with towers and spires, artistic windows, decorated ceilings and walls, sculptured pulpits, altars, and fonts, with the genius of a Raphael and Michelangelo—as it was in the past, so it is today. People in every clime still bowing and worshipping their gods, material gods hewn and fashioned in rock and clay and wood. God's animals, birds, and reptiles, these they believe possess the spirit of the Deity.

Not so with the Aboriginals of Australia. We build no place of worship, neither do we erect altars for the offering of sacrifice, but, notwithstanding this lack of religious ceremonies, we believe in a Great Spirit and the Son of the Great Spirit. There arose among the Aborigines a great teacher, Ngurunderi; he was an elect of the Great Spirit. And he spoke to our forefathers thus:

'Children, there is a Great Spirit above whose dwelling-place is Wyerriwarr. It is His will that you should know Him as Hyarrinumb; I am the Whole Spirit and ye are part of the whole, I am your Provider and Protector. It has been my pleasure to give you the privilege to sojourn awhile in the flesh state to fulfil my great plan. Remember (*porun*) children (*wukone illawin*) your life is like unto a day, and during this short period on earth you are to educate yourself by your conduct to yourself as a part of Myself and your conduct to others, with the knowledge that they are part of Myself. Live as children of your Great Father. *Nol kal undutch me wee*, control your appetites and desires. Remember, never allow yourself to become slaves to your appetite or desire, never allow your mind to suffer pain or fear, lest you become selfish, and selfishness causes misery to yourself, your wife and children and relations, and those with whom you come into contact. Selfishness is not of the Great Spirit. Cultivate everything good, moderation in food and pleasure, be generous to others, develop a healthy state of mind and body. Body and mind ought to be governed by good and pure morals with kindness for others, remembering that they are a part of that Great Spirit from whence you came.'

This knowledge develops the soul, which is a part of the Whole Spirit, to a state fit to become a companion to the Great Spirit. To this end, the little boys and girls are placed in the hands of the elders with their wives to be educated. The children's first education is the control of their appetites. During this training, they travel from one hunting-ground to another for years.

The children endeavour day by day to control their appetites. They do this by their moderation in taking food and their conduct to those who may be weaker in body or mind, and their moral behaviour to either sex. The children also submit themselves to the test of whether they are able to control pain. The first test may be the knocking out of their front teeth by a blow from a stone axe, and the cutting of their bodies with flint knives and the sprinkling of ashes into the wound (ashes burned from a particular shrub or tree) which intensifies the pain, yet also has a healing effect.

They lie upon live fire coal or stones heated red-hot for a moment. Youths submit themselves to having their beards plucked like you would a dead fowl or turkey, or to sitting in a bull-ants' bed. All kinds of cruel methods are adopted to test and train the children to experience what pain is like and how to control it.

There are stages of inflicting great pain every day, and the mind and body develop accordingly. The last training is that of the control of fear. Night after night, men are selected to make up some terrible story of great and ugly monsters. Monsters like the mythological Bunyip and the Muldarpi, a demon that disguises itself in all kinds of forms like a kangaroo, wombat, or waterfowl to trap the hunter, or a butterfly with beautiful colouring such as children like to capture. And at night, during a thunderstorm they relate ghost stories, and the children sit and listen. After the story, the elder will lead them to their camp selected during the day.

'Children you are to sleep in the burying ground of your forefathers.' They spend the night in the cemetery, and at sunrise present themselves to the elder, showing no sign of a disturbed night. By this act, they prove to the elder the control of fear.

Then, on a particular day, all members of the tribe meet upon a sacred spot set aside for the purpose, and an elder, in the presence of the congregation, will declare that the boys and girls are men and women. And all men of the congregation stand, and the female portion will sit with head bowed, the men alone with faces turned and with spear and nulla[4] pointing to the setting sun shout, '*Kay kay!*' meaning:

'Well done children, you have already fought the battle of life and have conquered. Manhood and womanhood is complete in you. The Great Spirit is pleased. He is now awaiting your presence in Wyerriwarr, the Home of the Spirits.'

III

The voice of the Great Spirit

It is interesting to learn how all races of men have wrestled with the problem of good and evil. The Australian Aboriginals have a greater and deeper sense of morality and religion than is generally known. From a very early age, the mothers and the old men of the tribe instruct the children by means of tales and stories. This is one of the many stories that is handed down from generation to generation by my people.

In the beginning, the Great Spirit used to speak directly every day to his people. The tribe could not see the Great Spirit, but they could hear his voice, and they used to assemble early every morning to hear him. Gradually, however, the tribe grew weary of listening to the Great Spirit and they said one to the other: 'Oh, I am tired of this listening to a voice. I cannot see whom it belongs to. So, let us go and enjoy ourselves by making our own corroborrees.'[5]

The Great Spirit was grieved when he heard all this, so he sent his servant Ngurunderi to call all the tribes together again once more. 'The Great Spirit will not speak again to you, but he wishes to give you a sign,' said Ngurunderi. So, all the tribes came to the meeting. When everyone was seated on the ground, Ngurunderi asked them all to be very silent.

Suddenly a terrific rending noise was heard. Now, Ngurunderi had so placed all the tribes that the meeting was being held around a large gumtree. The tribes looked and saw this huge tree being slowly split open by some invisible force. Also, down out of the sky came an enormous *thalung* (tongue), which disappeared into the middle of the gumtree, and then the tree closed up again.

Ngurunderi said to the tribes: 'You may go away now to your hunting and corroborrees.'

Away went the tribes to enjoy themselves. After a long time, some of them began to grow weary of pleasure, and longed to hear again the Great Spirit. So, some of them asked Ngurunderi if he would call upon the Great Spirit to speak to them again.

Ngurunderi answered: 'No, the Great Spirit will never speak to you again.'

The tribes went to the sacred burial grounds to ask the dead to help them, but, of course, the dead did not answer. Then they asked the great Nebalee (the same as the English Nebulæ), who lives in the Milky Way, if he would help them, but there was still no answer, and the tribes at last cried aloud. They began to fear that they would never get in touch with the Great Spirit again.

The tribes finally appealed to Wyyunggurree, the wise old blackfellow who lives in the South Cross. He told them to gather about the big gumtree again. When all were there, Wyyunggurree asked: 'Did you not see the *thalung* go into this tree?' 'Yes,' answered the tribes.

'Well,' said Wyyunggurree, 'take that as a sign that the *thalung* of the Great Spirit is in all things.'

Thus it is today that the Aboriginals know that the Great Spirit is in all things and speaks through every form of Nature. *Thalung* speaks through the voice of the wind; he rides on the storm; he speaks out from the thunder. *Thalung* is everywhere, and manifests through the colour of the bush, the birds, the flowers, the fish, the streams. In fact, in everything that the Aboriginal sees, hears, tastes, smells, and feels there is *Thalung*.

IV

Nhung e umpie

Human nature is the same in the Australian Aboriginal as it is in the white, brown, or yellow man irrespective of nationality, language, and religion.

We may presume that it makes no difference if we go back to distant ages, to earlier periods the evidence of which our ancestors have placed on record. We find there, in the remains of ancient civilisation of the great Nineveh, Greece, Rome, and Egypt, great walls and fortune as a defence against the enemy who attempted to invade their cities. Writing and carving clearly demonstrate this point; it was an eye for an eye and a tooth for a tooth.

Now, amidst the rising and falling of King and Emperor, there arose mighty men who caught a higher inspiration and were filled with knowledge and wisdom. They endeavoured to raise their people to lofty ideals and to instil into the hearts and minds of their respective races a spirit of brotherhood and good will. Now, it is not necessary for me to mention those noble and inspired characters of every age.

The Buddha, Muhammad, and Christ, these men have established religions and teachings to knit the bond of the race in love and sympathy. The question arises: Have these religions and teachings fulfilled all conditions for the benefit of the human race? Now, each nation may accept and follow the teachings of a Buddha, a Muhammad, and Christ. Each was a great man in his time and their influences are felt, and they are with us, today.

Now, there arose among my people a man who claimed to be (as others did) also sent by God with a message and teaching and we speak of him as Ngurunderi. He was a sacred man who—like all Prophets, Teachers, and Philosophers—found that he was confronted by a great social problem of his race. How was he to overcome the vile nature of the human race? Spears, nulla-nullas, boomerangs, pointing sticks, and bone witchcraft could not allay this cankerous disease.

Now, as if inspired, Ngurunderi instituted the custom of *nhung e umpie*.[6] Now, *Nhung e umpie* is a portion of the navel cord at birth from mother and child. Now, the gut or intestine is treated in a way that preserves it, for it is kept for a considerable time, then placed within a roll of Emu feathers, and then wound round with fibre from the bark of the tree or mallee.[7] This makes it safe and transferable from one hunting ground to another, and when it is sent on a long mission as a bond of friendship.

Now, it is only the privilege of a certain female member of the tribe to be selected to give the gut. She must be the daughter of a mother who also was selected for a navel gut. These mothers must come from a direct line of noble womanhood, being of good and pure moral character. She submits the gut to a *mooncumbulli*, that is to the Philosopher of the tribe, and it remains in his possession until he sees fit or thinks it proper to present it to a tribe.

But supposing there were a break in the line of these women, then the woman who is the next of kin on the mother's side would take up this great and important position. This is a coveted position among the women, with each girl, when they are educated to become good, striving for this position. No one knows that, from some one of them, a selection will be made.

I would like to call your attention to the Christian faith. In Luke 1:42, one of the Gospels, you will find these words: 'Blessed art thou among women, and blessed is the fruit of thy womb.' In Luke 1:46-48, 'Mary said, My soul doth magnify the Lord, and my spirit hath rejoiced in God my Saviour. For he hath regarded the low estate of his handmaiden: for, behold, from henceforth all generations shall call me blessed.'

Now, the gut or part of the intestine linking mother and child has a great significance to us. We look upon it as coming from that part of a woman within which dwell all good wishes of pity and sympathy.

There are two parts embodied in this one gut. First, that of the well-trained moral of perfect womanhood, which is recognised with a great deal of reverence. Secondly, there is that portion of the children's innocence and purity which offers itself for a great development of life. Through challenges, it shows itself capable of developing to prove it rightfully inherited its mother's qualities. Thirdly, the navel cord is symbolic of a string that binds the peculiarities of mother to child. As a mother and child are linked to each other before birth, so the *nhung e umpie* must be linked as mother and child.

The navel cord is a physical reality so *nhung e umpie* should be so: true love, true fellowship, true pity. Let this symbol so bind you. Now, we look upon the navel cord with reverence, just as the Christian reveres the house of God, its fount, Altar and Sacrament. It is an all-powerful custom that can bind any two tribes in a bond of good fellowship and brotherhood. Distance makes no difference to whether it is conveyed and submitted to a tribe. It is accepted with honour. It is a law in itself.

V

How Teddy lost his tail

Once upon a time, long long ago, before the animal, bird, reptile, and insect life came to Australia, they occupied the many islands that existed in the ocean Karramia, a place of the beginning of day, where all is peace and rest. The Kangaroo tribe lived upon one island, the Eagle-Hawk tribe upon another, the Iguana tribe upon another.

Now, upon one beautiful island with high and lofty mountain peaks, reaching into the sky and with deep valleys clothed with great, giant gumtrees, there lived the Teddy Bear[8] with his tribe. The Teddy Bears were a wise and intelligent tribe. The elders would take the young Teddy Bears up into the mountains and instruct them in the knowledge of astronomy. One night, as they were gazing into the sky, their attention was drawn to a streak of light away in the south.

'That is strange,' said the elder of the tribe, staring at the light in the south. Then he looked to the north and saw another light shining against the northern sky. Night after night, the elders of the Bear tribe would climb to the mountain top to hold consultation as to the source of this mysterious light that appeared at intervals during the night. The elder of the tribe, a venerable old bear, eventually felt convinced that he had arrived at a solution of the mystery, and he said:

'Children, tomorrow, just as day breaks, let every man bear, woman bear, and child bear gather and carry to yonder mountain a bundle of sticks. This must be done for seven sun risings.'

So, every bear able to work began the tedious labour of carrying sticks to the mountain top. On the evening of the seventh rising sun, everything was in readiness. The great Philosopher Bear gave instructions that all the bears should attend and watch, and they all congregated on the mountain where the sticks were stacked. Then the Philosopher with another elder of the tribe sat upon the mountain to watch the result. At sunset everyone was awaiting instructions.

Presently the small voice pierced the air: 'Fire the wood heap.'

They began rubbing the sticks together until they kindled a spark and the wood heap was set ablaze. It made a huge bonfire, and the flames leapt up lighting the darkness for miles around and across the sea.

The Elder Bear, who was sitting gazing intently through the darkness, saw answering flashes around the horizon, north, south, east, and west.

'The problem is solved,' said the Philosopher Bear. 'We shall discuss it further tomorrow.'

Next morning, all the bears rose early and sat around in orderly groups on ledges of rocks, on boughs of trees, and in every available place, awaiting the arrival of the Philosopher Bear. Then they started to chatter among themselves, and their voices gradually grew louder. One of their number seeing the Philosopher approaching, shouted: 'Order!' The Elder took his place among them and began to address them. There was an instant silence, as they strained their ears to hear what he was about to say.

'Children,' he said, 'there are other lands like ours all around us, which are occupied by strange and queer people I am not able to describe, as I have never seen them; but I do say that there are other forms of life. Prepare your canoes, north, south, east and west, and scour the oceans and bring me information.'

The male bears dragged their canoes into the water and set out on their voyage of discovery. They paddled for a long time until they eventually landed in beautiful new countries, and they went about among the new tribes, noticing their customs and the kind of people they were, and when they had learned all they could of them they returned to the Elder. Each explorer told his story, one describing the kangaroo, one the emu, and another the iguana, the platypus, the eagle-hawk, the lyrebird, and so forth. And very wonderful the descriptions sounded to the people who had never seen any land but their own.

After a week, the Elder gave instructions to build many, many canoes, saying: 'We will paddle our way to the great new country.'

All the male bears set to work making canoes, some making as many as a dozen. At last, they were completed and they paddled across the sea till they reached Australia. The landing-place was at Shoalhaven. After they had lived in Australia for some time, wandering away into the Blue Mountains, and up and down the Paramatta, Hawkesbury, Hunter, and the great Murray Rivers, they thought it would be nice to ask the kangaroos, the emus, the eagle-hawks, the iguanas, and all the animal, bird, reptile and insect tribes to come down and share this wonderful country. So, once more, they set out in their canoes and brought them back with them, distributing to them various parts of Australia.

When they returned to their home at Shoalhaven, they met with stormy weather and paddled through the angry surf, their canoes being so tossed about that every bear fell out of the canoes and had to swim ashore. The hungry sharks followed them and bit their tails off, and that accident completely subdued the adventurous spirit of the Teddy Bears.

Notes

These notes are provided by Synkrētic to clarify references and other details of interest.

1 The popular 19th century Dravidian Theory according to which Aboriginal Australians descended from this Indian tribe has been debunked. However, recent genetic and linguistic research supports the claim that Dravidian people migrated to Australia 4,000 years ago. Kumud Merani, 'The Story Untold - The links between Australian Aboriginal and Indian tribes, *SBS Hindi*, 10 July 2019, available at: <https://www.sbs.com.au/language/english/audio/the-story-untold-the-links-between-australian-aboriginal-and-indian-tribes>.

2 *Lemuria*, a hypothetical lost continent in the Indian Ocean, was popularised by theosophical and occult writers.

3 *Ngurunderi* (Unaipon writes *Narrundari*, also written *Ngarrinderi*) likely refers to one of the Ngarrindjeri people's Dreaming heroes who carried out great feats, including creating the River Murray by chasing a cod out of a stream.

4 A *nulla* (from *nulla-nulla*, also *waddy*, and *boondi*) is an Aboriginal Australian hardwood club or hunting stick.

5 *Corroborree* (from the Dharug language *garaabara*) refers to varied meetings involving Australian Aboriginal people.

6 *Nhung e umpie* is spelled *ngia-ngiampe* in modern texts.

7 *mallee* is a term, widely used in southern Australia, to describe shrubs or trees growing from an underground lignotuber. This growth habit is observed in *Eucalyptus* trees as a defence against fire.

8 *Teddy Bear* is Unaipon's term for the koala (*Phascolarctos cinereus*), which did once have an external tail, now lost.

The brief, insignificant history of Peter Abraham Stanhope*

Mary Rokonadravu†

I

At 11:42pm on 1 November 2016, Peter Abraham Stanhope sat at his family's old mahogany dining table and slit his wrists. He had folded three clean bath towels on which to place his hands so as to not make a mess. He watched the news first; switched on to Fiji One Television crackling against the sudden rain, part of the storm approaching from the east. The islands of Wakaya and Makogai were already cloaked in rain well before nightfall. He showered first, of course. Ate his dinner of fried pork sausages, three sausages to be exact. Some cassava,[1] fried to a crisp. Just the way he liked it. He folded his laundry—one cotton shirt, one pair of cotton trousers, one pair of well-worn polyester underwear he had bought from Gulabdas & Son two years before.

The fragrance of citrus—lime and oranges from the soap powder—permeated the living room as he meticulously laid out his clean, folded clothes. He opened a can of skipjack tuna chunks and fed Sona, his old cat—the cat's name meaning "arsehole", the result

* This story was shortlisted for the 2017 Commonwealth Short Story Prize. It was first published by *adda*, the online literary magazine of the Commonwealth Foundation, on 2 January 2018.

† Mary Rokonadravu is a Fijian writer and communications manager in the Pacific office of the World Wildlife Fund (WWF). She holds an MA in Pacific Studies from the University of the South Pacific. She lives in Suva, Fiji.

of a lost bet with old Maciu Smith, Mac, his old diabetic workmate, now house-bound in Vulcan's Lane with both legs amputated from the knees down and addicted to Korean soap dramas on Sky Television. He had visited Mac during the day; said he was going to Suva on the morning ferry, if Mac could see to Sona who ate tuna chunks and appreciated the odd belly rub.

'Fuck you!' Mac had roared into the quiet afternoon. 'Yeah, I gonna send one of the kids to feed Sona. If you stay longer, I'll make them take me up the fucken steps and I gonna stay until you get back. And answer your phone when I call you!' They had both worked at PAFCO, the Pacific Fishing Company, driving forklift loads of frozen skipjack, albacore, and bigeye between the Korean fishing boats and the cannery. That was in a better time, when the Japanese still ran the cannery, before the Government took over. At least, that was the general opinion in town.

He remembered to sweep up his toenail clippings from earlier in the day, fold them into an old *Fiji Times* page, and put them into the rubbish bin. He knew the Wesleyan Chapel deacon, the *Vakatawa*, would find him on Sunday morning. He wanted the house, and himself, clean.

His daughter, Caroline, married to a snivelling American who sold computers, lived in Maine. Peter had the fall postcards and winter Christmas cards pinned on the kitchen walls. His son, Jona, was dead. The men who killed him were now on trial. He had watched them in the news for two weeks. Then rung his nephew Samuela in Suva. He received the diver's knife from Bob's Hook, Line and Sinker a week later. It did not need sharpening. He read his Bible before he put his wrist on the towels and cut. His hands lay limp on the table, as if momentarily resting from a dinner of baked chicken and potatoes, as if someone at table were telling an interesting story, about an elopement maybe, or sharing a sermon from a Sunday past, and the hushed table was all ears. Were it a painting, the title *Abraham's Dinner* would be apt.

His people have been in the town for one hundred and fifty years.

Let us begin with that. The town.

Synkrētic

Levuka sits on a black rock, the Pacific at her toes. A tiny row of clapboard stores on its main thoroughfare. With no declaration to creativity, the name Beach Street stuck to the macadam road that once was igneous pebbles salted by the sea. A few stores are of old coral and limestone patched with concrete. There is a Catholic cathedral of modest proportion. A Wesleyan chapel of even more modest proportion. A Masonic temple, oldest in the South Pacific, razed to the ground by good, I-am-born-again-and-the-rest-of-you-will-burn-in-Hell Christian folk. A tuna cannery a rabbi from Baltimore comes to cleanse to kosher twice a year. A little powerhouse hums electricity into the cannery, into homes perched like limpets onto steep, craggy volcanic slopes, into streetlights guiding night-shift workers back home or cigarette-puffing boys jogging to the bakeries for rising dough and morning buns and loaves.

There is no drone of a first fly. They must be at the fish cannery at the southern end of town, drunk at the mixing of fish meal for pet food and fertiliser. The whole town cowers under this regular stench. It slips into the wood walls laying termites intoxicated; sinks into oiled mahogany floors, into the snake beans outside the Steinmetz's kitchen on Church Street; into hand-washed PAFCO, FEA,[2] and PWD[3] overalls on clotheslines along the 199 steps of Mission Hill. The only sound is a mud wasp smoothening the walls of its mud house behind the old German-made woodstove.

He lives alone. Stopped going to church thirty years ago. If no one finds him within a few days, he will bloat in the tropical heat. Then there will be liquid on the mahogany chair and on the mahogany floor.

He knew the church would not permit him a Christian burial—how awful that he took his own life! Burn in Hell! So he wrote letters. One to Mac telling him to have prayers in the living room—he had cleaned the room, gotten on his knees and polished the wood floor. Washed and ironed the curtains. Fluffed out the cushions. Put his wife's best crochet piece on the coffee table. On all the palm-stands and side tables, little pieces of crochet-edged linen with embroidered daisies. He wrote another letter to Caroline. When you come to your senses and leave that American, home will be waiting for you. Do not believe any superstition. My spirit will not be here. I am going to your brother.

The last three things he did that night, before sitting to watch the news, before moving to the mahogany dining table, was to wash and season the cast iron skillet, put a fresh roll of toilet paper on the holder, and call his son's mobile number. His son was gone, as was the phone, but he called it every night. He had called it for the last three years. He had never been able to sleep without calling. He knew he called more for himself than for Jona. But in a very deep, hidden place, he wished Jona to know, if he were watching at all, that his father was still here. Still calling. He hesitated at the telephone. He knew it was the last call. He wanted it to be right. He dialled the number very slowly. His eyes fixed on the lights of Levuka, at the foot of the hill from him, this little bastard of a town that had kept his family for two hundred years, as a voice came over the line: *The number you are trying to call is not available. Please hold while your call is diverted.*

He held the line until it clicked. Then he stood to walk to the mahogany table in the next room.

II

He could have been a Genghis Khan. A unifier of clans. Lord of the flat earth. He could have been born in a valley of foaling horses. In a springtime melt of ice setting loose chill waters from the mountains of the goddesses. He belonged in a country of pilgrimages; prayer flags drenched in mist; yaks hot with the intent of service hunched against winter storms. Loving and losing a woman. With an army of bareback-riding archers laying waste to entire nations—this could have been his story. Like the Genghis of history, he too was born with a blood clot fisted in his palm. But he arrived centuries late; in a latitude placing him on an island. By the time it came to him, there had been thousands of fuckings between strange and varied people in strange and varied places across tides of race, religion, work, humour, and time—should the most faithful of genealogists in his family tree piece the details together, as they did over the years, only names and years surfaced like flotsam. Floating. Meaningless. Unattached to ship, person, or place. His many bloods cursed him to nothingness on all sides. The only truth in the life of his family, passed on between generations, across continents and islands, was fish.

His were a herring people once. Then cod. Then his great-great-grandfather came down south following whales. He was a caulker, a handler of oakum to seal barrels. Without him, blubber, salted pork, whale oil, and flour would be impossible to carry through the Pacific. But in Levuka, he jumped ship. There was a young American on shore, sharp and fast with the chisel and mallet, quick to put out boats. David Whippy was from Nantucket, Massachusetts, loved by the chief. Whippy had several wives. A pineapple plantation next to his thatched kingdom. Several pigs tamed from the hills. Bought and sold *bêche-de-mer*, the smoked sea cucumber prized in China. It was rumoured David Whippy had homes and estates all over the islands. That he made a lot from boats but made the most from *bêche-de-mer*. Peter's great-great-grandfather, William Jacob Stanhope, did not need convincing. He swam ashore in the dark and the American hid him in the smokehouse when the crew came ashore to look for the deserter.

In a few short years, William J. Stanhope made a small fortune from sandalwood found in Bua on the island of Vanua Levu. Used his money to set up a calico shop. Imported bales of calico and silks from Port Jackson, Melbourne, San Francisco, and Macau. In his gratitude to David Whippy, he promised never to impinge on business the American conducted. So Stanhope built a fortune on calico, silk, needles, china, scissors, violins, pianofortes, threads, soup tureens, serving platters, saucepans, birdcages, Indian teas, and earthen pots for wild orchids Fijians brought from the cold and misty highlands. The Stanhope fortune was built on little things. Little reminders of what settlers had left behind to come to the heat and desolation of the tropics. Every planter's wife, missionary's wife, trader's wife looked forward to going to Levuka to enter the Stanhope Store, which sat between Morris & Hedstrom and Hennings.

William Jacob Stanhope married a brown woman, Elenoa; Eleanor to the English tongue. In the old Stanhope family home at the summit of Mission Hill, beside the Methodist mission and above the Williams', the Vollmer, and the Powell homes, Elenoa sits unsmiling in every single family portrait. She was not unhappy, though. Elenoa of Navosa ruled the Stanhope home with an iron fist. The story goes that when Fiji's first English governor of the colony, Sir Arthur Gordon, walked into the store and thought her a native worker, she unflinchingly served him a severely burnt side of beef at the Stanhope Sunday table, ignoring her husband's cutting stare. And that she continually served the governor this dish until he apologised. They became good friends afterward, it is said. The entire botanical collection the early British colonisers brought in from Mauritius, Ceylon, and India was shared with the Stanhope matriarch.

And when the *Leonidas*, the first boat to arrive in Fiji with indentured labourers from India, arrived on 14 May 1879, the brown Mrs Stanhope managed to recruit two young Indian coolies, a strapping young man and his wife. It is said in the islands that the Stanhope home was the first to serve the most exquisite curries, had its own herb and spice gardens, and at the time of Diwali, the festival of lights the Indian coolies celebrated, Mrs Stanhope sat alongside her Indian cook, as brown as her own brown skin, and made balls of the most perfect ladoos. Testament to the Stanhope fortune is that the Stanhope children did not attend school at the Levuka Public School, or with a hired governess, both boys were sent to boarding schools in Port Jackson, Australia.

It is said that when the younger of the boys, Silas, told his parents of his intention to marry the lovely Fijian girl, Tarusila of Nairai, who had been taught by missionaries and now taught at the mission school in Delana, his mother sipped her cup of Ceylon tea and calmly told him to lift the girl's skirt and check the colour of her buttocks. Mr Stanhope spoke to his wife that night, reminding her of her own colour, but she shushed him with a wave of her left hand and put out the night lamp, robbing him of his reading.

'Don't talk to me like that, William,' she said in the dark, 'and don't forget if you never meet me, you might be marry the black girl from Lovoni who don' talk English like me. An' who gonna cook your pineapple pie like the one I make, eh? Your died grandfather from London?'

This is the tragedy of any family fortune, that if not managed well and held collectively, it disintegrates into portions until all that is shared is name only, a few candlesticks, a few empty shells from World War Two, remains of what American soldiers left behind when they and the Royal New Zealand Air Force used Fiji as a base. It happened to the Stanhopes.

'It matter who you gonna married,' Elenoa had said a hundred years before. William had written her words in one of his journals and showed it to her as a hymn. 'It matter who you gonna married. If you marry the bitch, she gonna cut your balls and sell it on the wharf after eating all the money.'

The only Stanhope line to manage to save a little money, save the family home, and keep one of the cotton estates, did so because the man who carried the name, Alexander Stanhope, married a Madrasi woman, Vellamma, planter of tamarinds and maker of pickles, the saviour of lands and homes. She was Peter Abraham Stanhope's mother and, had she been alive to watch her son's slow demise, she would have rubbed a bongo chilli on his asshole. She learned this from an old woman in Moturiki and once she learned, it became the cure for all ailments, from the common flu to diarrhoea, and even depression.

She probably would have done the same to Jona. The young man who was her grandson. The young man she never met.

III

Peter Abraham Stanhope is a reasonable man. He is a man of sober habits. He raises a daughter and a son. Caroline, his daughter, looks very Indian. She looks just like her mother and, with a liking for tamarind and coconut in fish curries, Madrasi. His daughter's al-most-charcoal skin is a fascination to him—from birth at the

Levuka Hospital to the days before his dying, when receiving photographs from America. She is so black beside the white man she has married. Under her Patagonia™ parka, he can feel her subdued, quietened spirit.

For the first few years he convinced himself he was imagining it. But the feeling never left and his angst built on his growing distaste for his white son-in-law. He started praying again because he worried Caroline may be facing problems with her in-laws. After all, she was black, a sweet black, but white Americans were not likely to notice her sweetness. Or the fact that she was a good baker and had won a baking contest in Suva, under a cultural programme of the American Embassy. He was convinced that, to Americans, his daughter was just another black woman. Someone who could easily be shot while walking to a bakery, or while rummaging through a yard sale for old music records. In the early years, he had kept tabs on the time difference between Fiji and Maine, called her at 5am Maine time, reminding her not to attend any auction or yard sale, not to walk to little stores.

'Pa,' Caroline said from across several American states and an ocean, 'I'm in bed. And I have no interest in yard sales.'

Jona was a quiet child. The only one eager for Saturdays so he could wipe the old family photographs. Hook them up again in the living room, the dining room, and the bedrooms. Jona knew every person on the tree. Every story. Every piece of Stanhope furniture, cutlery, and book. He finished secondary school at Levuka Public School and went to Suva for a diploma in plumbing.

It therefore came as a shock to Peter Abraham Stanhope that his son was implicated in a bank robbery. He had put the telephone down that morning and sat at the kitchen table. He did not finish peeling the potatoes. For the first time in his life, he had left a piece of lamb defrosting an entire night. He did not put the lights on that night. He sat very still in the gathering darkness and watched the lights of the old capital come on. Oblivious to the cloud of mosquitoes rising in the falling dusk.

He remembered how his own father had sat at the same kitchen table and argued he would write to the Queen to intervene on a matter of land. 'The queen don't care about us,' his father ended up saying, 'Britain don't know we here or their blood in us. We fucked, man!'

Peter Abraham Stanhope contemplated writing to the Queen. He did not sleep that night. He began his letter the next morning. Jona was in police custody in Suva. But of late, young boys had died during questioning. He did not sleep.

The next day, he received word his son had died during the night. The police had taken him to the Colonial War Memorial Hospital but he had died before arrival. Jona made the return boat trip to Levuka, the town of his birth, the home of his ancestors, in a sealed coffin. The autopsy report talked of his broken bones, his collapsed lung, his crushed eyeballs, his rectum utterly unrecognisable. He knew that not all policemen were violent or brutal. There were good men and women in the force. He sat in his pitch-dark house and watched the lights at the Levuka Police Station a soft yellow. No, he told himself, not every police officer is the same. He sat up all night until the horizon turned a soft purple then pink, before the sun rose behind Wakaya.

He did not attend his son's funeral. He had the coffin brought home to sleep the night. He did not allow anyone to come to the house that night. His son lay on a mat and a *masi*⁴ barkcloth strip. The Wesleyan Chapel took Jona down in the morning. They buried him in the Stanhope lot in Draiba Cemetery. He did not have money to hire a lawyer.

Mac alone walked up the steps to him. All one hundred and ninety-nine steps. Mac did not speak at all. He brought a bottle of whiskey with him. Went into the kitchen to bring two glass tumblers. Mac put the lights out that night and lit two mosquito coils. They watched Wakaya and Makogai go blue, then black in the horizon.

They drank quietly.

'You know,' Mac said as the streetlights came on in the town be-low them, 'you gonna promise me you gonna get a cat. And you gonna guess rightly if she boy or girl. If you wrong, you gonna call it Sona. Every time, I gonna ask about the cat, I gonna get to ask about your arsehole.'

Mac did not know about the medical report.

Peter Abraham Stanhope laughed and wept in the darkness. Yes, he told Mac. I gonna get the cat. I gonna get the bastard cat.

They sat silent the rest of the night.

Synkrētic

Notes

These notes are provided by Synkrētic to clarify references and other details of interest.

1   Cassava (*Manihot esculenta*), also called manioc or yuca, is a starchy tuberous root common to many Pacific cuisines.

2   FEA, the Fiji Electricity Authority, was a majority government-owned Fijian power company established in 1966. In 2018, it became known as Energy Fiji Limited (EFL).

3   Public Works Department (PWD) is part of the Fijian Ministry of Public Utilities, Transport, Works and Energy.

4   *Masi* is the Fijian name for a decorative tapa cloth. It is made from paper mulberry and found across the Pacific.

The seven lives of Lapérouse*

Alex François,[†] *Teliki Thomas, Rubenson Lono,*
Emele Mamuli, Kaspa Niu Maketi, Willy Usao

TRANSLATED BY *Daryl Morini*[‡]

Introduction

'Any news from Mr Lapérouse?' Louis XVI famously asked the morning of his execution.[1]

While navigator Count of Lapérouse or Jean-François de Galaup (1741-1788) lived a legendary life which French children study at school, the circumstances of his death have long been a mystery.

A naval officer famed for his daring military feats against the British in the Americas, it was as a navigator that Lapérouse's name entered world history. In 1785, King Louis XVI ordered him to complete the Pacific discoveries of his British hero, James Cook.

---

* These stories were collected, transcribed, interpreted, and translated into French by Alex François from the original Teanu, Lovono, Tanema, and Tikopia languages in April-May 2005. Individual references are provided in the *Notes*. These seven stories appear here in English translation for the first time. Permission was graciously given by Dr Alexandre François and *de Conti/MkF éditions*, the publisher of story VII, Willy Usao, *How Lapérouse got away*.

† Alex François is Senior Research Fellow at LaTTiCe (CNRS, ENS, Sorbonne) and Honorary Associate Professor at ANU's School of Culture, History & Language. He holds a PhD from the Sorbonne. He lives in Paris, France.

‡ Daryl Morini is editor of *Synkrētic* and Pacific Research Fellow at ANU's Department of Pacific Affairs. He holds a PhD in International Relations from the University of Queensland. He is based in Canberra, Australia.

His political objective was to reconnoitre the region's islands and identify those with the potential to host French colonies.

Lapérouse and his 220-man crew spent the next four years at sea battling scurvy, storms, and slings and arrows. Their voyage was in the shape of a bowtie stretching across the Pacific.

The right-hand loop ran from South America's serrated tip up to Hawaii, touched Alaska, then glided down North America's western seaboard. The left-hand loop included stops in Macao, Taiwan, the Philippines, South Korea, Japan, and Russia's Kamchatka peninsula, where Lapérouse received fresh orders to set sail for Botany Bay, modern Australia. The British were up to no good.

On 11 December 1787, Lapérouse dropped anchor at Tutuila Island, modern American Samoa. Hundreds of Āsu villagers were waiting on the beach upon arrival. They gifted the crew five hundred pigs, pigeons, fruit, and two 'very tasty' dogs. The French paid with glass beads, which were more popular than their iron tools.[2]

One of Lapérouse's commanders, Captain de Langle, convinced him against his better instincts to send a party of sailors ashore for fresh water to stop scurvy from spreading. Setting out at low tide, their two long boats quickly beached. Confusion broke out. Hundreds of locals began pelting the French with stones, waded knee-deep into the water and clubbed de Langle and eleven crew to death. Thirty Samoans died in the fighting.[3]

The official French account claims the incident broke out because giving out the glass beads stoked the islanders' envy. Other sources blamed women's sexual advances for setting off the fight. 'Frenchmen have no weapons against such attacks,' Lapérouse wrote.[4]

Another theory suggests the French may have been mistaken for *aitu*, spirits or minor gods. Violence against gods was justified to snatch their gifts like glass beads. Only, real gods didn't usually die.

One oral account suggests a more secular explanation: Lapérouse may have unwittingly declared war by striking a chief and rejecting his offering of a pig.[5]

A month later, Lapérouse sailed into Botany Bay. He arrived six days after the First Fleet; three before the Union Jack was raised in

Sydney. Under strict orders not to mention the colony, British officers acted awkwardly around their unexpected French guests. Soon enough, Lapérouse was regaling Red Coats at *soirées* aboard his ship, charming them with his love of James Cook.[6]

Despite his 'most pleasant' time with the British, Lapérouse was in a dark mood.[7] A letter from Botany Bay shows his mind was still afflicted by the violence off Tutuila Island. While still glad he didn't launch a 'barbaric' retaliatory strike, as his crew had demanded, he also writes: 'I constantly mull over these events and can barely stop.'[8] Lapérouse 'always had a sort of secret foreboding' of the disasters awaiting him.[9]

A ship from the First Fleet, under the ensign of the enemy against whom he had fought gallantly in the Seven Years' War, dutifully carried his last letter to Europe. Once they had slipped over the horizon's edge, *La Boussole* and *L'Astrolabe* weren't seen again.

The sea kept their fate secret until 1826, when Captain Peter Dillon found artifacts belonging to *L'Astrolabe* on Vanikoro Island, modern Solomon Islands.

By interviewing locals, Dillon learned that local oral history preserved detailed stories of ships like Lapérouse's meeting their end on the island. French sailors were remembered for their enormous noses jutting out a foot from their foreheads. Such was the shape of their *tricorne* hats.[10]

One account collected in 1826 had Lapérouse's ships moored off Whanoo and Paiou villages (two coastal villages now known as Lovono and Paiu). Violent winds then picked up and blew them to shore. The first ship off Whanoo was dashed to pieces upon rocks. Most of the crew drowned. The few who swam ashore were clubbed, stoned, and shot with arrows. Dillon heard that 'not a single soul escaped out of this vessel.'[11]

The second ship off Paiou became beached. The survivors were captured and, because they didn't resist, then freed. They were allowed to build an emergency boat from the wreckage. When they could, a party of French sailors sailed away in this craft. A second group spent the rest of their lives on the island.

Locals said they had believed the French to be spirits, suggesting that violence could have broken out for the same reason as on Tutuila Island. Lapérouse had been shocked to see islanders who had killed his men glide up to his ship to trade with the surviving crew. This had also occurred after Captain Cook's death in Hawaii. Those who killed him also rowed up to his ship and asked to visit the god.[12] Had Lapérouse been mistaken for an evil spirit like his hero?

Promising clues surfaced in the 1960s. As predicted by oral historians, the *Boussole*'s wreck was discovered off Vanikoro island. In 2005, a French expedition confirmed the *Boussole*'s location on the seafloor and recovered its sextant.[13]

During this expedition, French linguist Dr Alex François found answers to the question of how Lapérouse died. While recording stories in the Teanu, Lovono, Tanema, and Tikopia languages, he found that Lapérouse had entered local lore.

'While Vanikoro island has many other wonders,' François writes, 'the most intense experience is surely to be able to hear the Elders recount the legend of Lapérouse to their grandchildren some nine to ten generations after the events of 1788.'[14]

Dr François' translations offer seven accounts of the last days of Lapérouse. They are translated into English and published here for the first time. In some stories, the navigator comes ashore to bury treasure, leave hidden messages, or build a boat to escape. Others have darker endings for Lapérouse.

How true are these stories? Aristotle, the minor god of logic in the Western pantheon, might insist that Lapérouse either died or survived the shipwreck. This law of non-contradiction, he writes, is the 'most secure' thing we can believe.[15]

This is the wrong attitude to take towards oral history, a mode in which fact and fiction, science and sorcery, memory and myth are not sharply distinguished. In Melanesian stories, the laws of logic are as yielding as the green coconut's gelatinous flesh. Oral historians seek a truth that isn't exhausted by the formal rules of thought, as it is for Aristotle.

'By being sublimated from history into myth,' François notes, the 'Lapérouse myth experienced the same alchemy that saw the Trojan War give birth to the *Iliad* and the *Odyssey*.'[16] Myth also has practical value. As François notes, studying Homer's verse helped archæologists track down the lost city of Troy.

The seven stories translated here, retold thousands of times over 217 years, might best be approached as one continuous, creative block of inter-generational memories. Each story could contain key facts from the original story. But the historical and cultural value of these stories is greater than the sum of their parts.

They are useful for shedding light on the tantalising "What if?" questions around Lapérouse's tragic end. One school of thought speculates that, had he escaped from the island, South Australia might today have been French speaking, something like Australia's Québec. Had he followed his itinerary, Lapérouse might have beaten British expeditions that led to southern Australia's settlement.[17]

Another counterfactual is even more striking. Among the men lining up to join Lapérouse's ship was an 'ambitious and energetic Corsican lad', one Napoléon Bonaparte.[18] Lapérouse, it's unclear why, rejected his application. History could have been knocked off course, hundreds of thousands saved, if the future French emperor had spent his last days on Vanikoro and not Saint Helena.[19] Would oral stories now feature a long-nosed Corsican rowing back to France in his single canoe?

But these stories speak to events far more traumatic to the community than the hundreds of drowned Frenchmen washing up on their beach. A few accounts describe Lapérouse's as blackbirding ships, which raided Pacific islands, abducting men to work on Queensland's sugar plantations. This isn't possible.[20] Blackbirding began a hundred years later. Queensland and its sugar plantations did not exist in his lifetime. Part of these stories' great cultural value is that they so movingly absorbed into their dramatic fabric the terror villagers felt when Europeans took their men away—often forever.

Accomplishing a greater feat than accuracy, these stories 'make the past reappear while keeping its emotional power intact,' as François writes.[21] A great debt of thanks is owed to Dr Alex François and to each storyteller for sharing the history of their village and island, and for finally giving us news of Lapérouse.

160

Synkrētic

I

The message left by Lapérouse[22]

Teliki Thomas (†2009) narrated this story in the Teanu language on 27 April 2005.

A group of sailors had sheltered over there, down by the *Paiu*[23] river, in the hope of making a boat.

They'd go off to chop mangrove wood out near the ancient village of Kama. Then they'd bring it back here, where they'd cut it into planks to build their boat. They worked away at their boat— like a smaller ship—for about two months. And once it was done, they got ready to go back to their country.

They took to sea and got just past the reef over there. It was there, out in the open sea, that their boat broke down, such that they found themselves adrift in the lagoon.

Now, just as they were leaving, Lapérouse was up there, up on the crest of that hill you can see just up there, not far from where the village chief out that way lives. He was in a little clearing up there. Lapérouse surveyed the sea in search of the boat, hoping to catch a glimpse of it making it ashore.

Suddenly gripped with anxiety about [*the fate of*][24] his men, *and maybe to get a better look*, he darted off and clambered up that peak, up there.

At this point, he wrote a message on a strip of metal. He then concealed the metal strip up there, in the clearing where he stood. He buried it in the ground, covering it with a pile of rocks so that no one else would ever discover or take it.

This metal plate has remained here to this day, [*which we know*] because it was never found. It's not clear to me, personally, whether we'll ever find what Lapérouse inscribed [*on the metal plate*], which he wrote and hid somewhere up in that clearing just above. Because, to this day, we search in vain.

II

The chest Lapérouse buried[25]

Teliki Thomas narrated this story in the Teanu language on 27 April 2005.

The chest that I mentioned is found over there, to your left, beneath the roots of the big chestnut tree you can see overhanging the beach.

So, as I was saying, the day Lapérouse landed here with his men, just as their ship was wrecked, well, on the same day, a little girl was in her house.

The adults [*from her village*] were either out bush or fishing. Which is why, as they came ashore, the men closed in on this house and found the little girl inside. They asked her, 'Where did the grown-ups go? Your mummy and daddy, where are they?'

'They're not here!' she answered. 'My mummy and daddy are gone. They went to the garden!'

'Don't be scared,' they told her. 'You've got nothing to fear.'

And since she was about to start crying, they repeated: 'No, no, don't be scared! Look, we came here with a little chest, and we'd like it to stay here, in this village, and we'd like you to be the one to look after it.'

Gently, they set about digging a hole in the ground and lowered the object to the bottom. Finally, they gave her their instructions: 'Very well. Looking after this chest will be your responsibility. When your mother is back, be sure to tell her to keep this secret, to tell no one about it: this is how you'll ensure you keep it with you. Maybe we'll come back to get it one day.'

They left the area soon after, leaving her with the chest.

When she saw her mother come home that night, the little girl said to her, 'Mummy, the Frenchmen came and they hid a chest here. They told me we shouldn't tell anyone about it, that this chest belongs to them, and that we have to look after it. Maybe they'll come back for it one day.'

This very chest still exists in our day, it's around here somewhere.

Synkrētic

III

Why our gods killed Lapérouse[26]

Rubenson Lono (1933–2020) narrated this story in the Lovono language on 2 May 2005.

Back in the day, white-skinned men would land on our island to recruit men. The French would come recruit men they'd take far away, whom they'd put to work for them.

Later on, they'd sometimes bring these men home, those they took away. But it wasn't always the case. Sometimes a man would just leave for good. When they took him, they took him for good! They took some to Fiji, some to Queensland.

They were men from the Ngama or the Lovono villages—yes, it was mainly those guys they took. And it's mainly those guys that never came back.

One day, the Lovono and Ngama villagers *gathered together.*

'Listen up,' one of them said. 'One of those ships that take our men just came back. You know, the ones that recruit people but never bring them back! Well, there's one just like that approaching now. O, Heavens, what will we do about this ship?'

So, they decided to gather their sacred money. When they had enough, they invoked their god, asking it to destroy Lapérouse's *ship.*

At once, they saw a great, black cloud descend to fill the heavens. The cloud descended so relentlessly that it crushed the ship, which immediately sank into the deep.

Some sailors survived the shipwreck, others on the other hand perished in it. But despite losing many men, some sailors did make it ashore and sheltered on the island.

To be honest, I'm not quite sure what happened to the survivors who made it to the island, or how they finally made it back to their country.

But for most sailors, it was all over—they had perished in the shipwreck.

IV

How our gods killed Lapérouse[27]

Rubenson Lono narrated this story in the Lovono language on 2 May 2005.

As I was saying, they'd gathered their ritual money and invoked their god.

This god was called Tornado *or Fisipure.*[28] Tornado got up, and we saw huge, dark clouds approaching which soon covered the whole sky. Suddenly, a tornado began to twist in the sky. It went round, and round, and round, and finally hit Lapérouse's ship, splitting it in half.

Some sailors perished as soon as the ship split asunder, while others were able to make it to the main island. The survivors thus found refuge on the island. But we don't know how they could have left.

Did a new ship come to pick them up? That, we don't know. That's it, the end.

V

Why the French are so proud[29]

Emele Mamuli (†) narrated this story in the Tanema language on 7 May 2005.

In the beginning, it was little ships that had grown accustomed to landing on our shores.

They didn't stay long: we traded goods and off they went to sea again. When this little boat was gone, another would come again. It bought a few things from us, then it too would leave again.

Among them there was a specific ship which, unlike many others, knew the way to our island very well. This boat, which had discovered our country, would come to buy trocas[30] from us. It bought trocas from us, then it would leave. On other days, it bought *bêches-de-mer*[31] from us. It was my father who ran that business; my father looked after it.

One day, Lapérouse's ship approached our shores. Our ancestors invoked their god, Tornado: 'Here's a ship for you. Destroy him!'

No sooner had they spoken than the god fell upon the ship. The two hulls cracked apart violently, the one drifting off, the other staying in place.

These islands where we are, it's the French who discovered them; no other whites had come before them.[32] And when the French came here, they carved their names into the dead trees. When they cut down a tree, they'd make use of one side while carving their name into the other.

They came back here later on because they saw this big island as their own. The French are proud because it was France that discovered our island.

This very island, where we stand, they're the ones who discovered it before all the other whites. That's all.

VI

The killing of Lapérouse[33]

Kaspa Niu Maketi[34] narrated this story in the Tikopia language on 10 May 2005.

Here, let me tell you the story of Lapérouse.

This story about Lapérouse relates to [*a certain*] Taureperangi Terua Matakai,[35] who was chief of Taumako village. This man had met Lapérouse in person, right here on this island of Vanikoro.

He's the one who beheaded Lapérouse. They'd worked together for five days before he beheaded Lapérouse. That's right, for five days he worked with him. But at nightfall on the sixth day, the chief began to pray according to his rituals. He prayed in this way while the sailors slept.

He stood up suddenly and slit their throats. He killed all of them. Then he took their bodies to bury them a little further inland, in a village by the name of Taumako. That's right, he buried them in Taumako.

Then he took his canoe to go see the place where the ship had sunk, right in front of Paiu. This is when he spotted several people who'd stayed on the ship. Again, he conducted his rituals and set fire to the ship, which burned to ashes. The men on board were also burned [*alive*] along with the ship.

This was the story of the Taumako chief, and Lapérouse too. He's clearly the one who wrecked the ship. This is the story of Chief of Taumako from Tikopia.

Afterwards, he gathered all the things *from the shipwreck* and took them back to Tikopia island. Saucepans, plates, and other objects, all these things he took there.[36]

That's where they stayed down to Peter Dillon's day.[37] Those are the very things Peter Dillon found in the end *in Tikopia*. Some of these objects were later returned [*to us*] here. Dillon and his men were the ones to repatriate some of the objects they found in Tikopia.

Finally, [*local inhabitants*] Pū Rātia and Meone explained to Peter Dillon that it was this very ship that Lapérouse ran aground off Paiu[38] on Vanikoro island.

This, then, is the story of Lapérouse in Vanikoro. I, Kaspa Niu Maketi, have just told it here, in the village of Paiu.

VII

How Lapérouse got away[39]

Chief Willy Usao (†2017) narrated this story in the Teanu language on 6 May 2005.

In olden times, some ships had grown used to coming here to re-cruit men. They took them to work down south, towards Santo.[40]

At times, the locals here would watch ships sail away but, for years on end, never saw them return.

Things went on like this until it was the turn of a great navigator by the name of Lapérouse. This man sailed in a huge canoe, of the kind we call a *tepakare*,[41] that is a two-hulled boat. This double-canoe was sailing straight for our island and it entered Paiu Bay.

Within moments, the whole island's population was in a state of alert, in Paiu as much as in Tanema, in Lovono, in Lale. The alarm was sounded everywhere 'Help! Here comes another one of those ships to again take our men away! This boat is so massive! It's the end of us!'

In this way, people hastened from every corner of the island, from the Lale region, from Ngama, from Lovono. The men held a council and resolved to invoke their gods.

'Hark, dear friends! The French are back, they come to take our men away! They will once again kidnap them and never bring them back to this land. This is the end of our people! O, mighty Filisao, god of arrows and tornadoes![42] Inflict on this vessel what it deserves! May it break, may it run aground at the mouth of this channel! Crush it, that it may sink deep into the sea!

Two tornadoes suddenly shot up: one black, the other white. They rose up in the sky all at once, before falling inexorably upon the ship, which they slammed into and broke in half, pulling its hulls apart.

One of the two tornadoes collided with the first hull, which was marooned out in the Ngambe Passage, in the very spot where objects are discovered in the present day.

The second hull drifted away a little, getting swept out to sea, where it was finally engulfed by the waves, out near the open sea.

Well, that's what my grandfather told me. I'm telling you the story just as he told me.

What became of the sailors on board this ship and of their captain? Well, their great chief Lapérouse and a handful of the young men under his command managed to get to shore along the coast of Paiu, to shelter on the island.

As soon they got there, they searched for a spot to hide, a temporary hide-out. That's when they dug in on—what's it called again? That's right! Filimoe island.[43]

While staying there, they got to work building a new boat in Paiu, on the banks of the Paiu river. They were rebuilding their ship in the form of our *tepakare* canoe, you see? Anyway, that's what I was told.

But the boat probably wasn't big enough to sail out in high seas. When their workday was over, off they'd go to hide out in their secret camp site on Filimoe island. And off they went again to work on their boat the next day. All their work they conducted in Paiu. It went on like that for a while.

Their work bore fruit because, in the end, they were able to get off the island and out to sea thanks to their makeshift canoe. They only ditched their boat when they'd made it on board a much bigger ship and got away safe and sound.

I've personally never heard [*anyone say*] that one or two men stayed behind in Vanikoro. Everyone knows that, had they stayed, the locals would have slaughtered them.

There you are. That's all. Thanks for listening to me, dear sir.

Notes

1   Louis XVI, '*A-t-on des nouvelles de M. de Lapérouse?*' Cited in Jean-Dominique Bourzat, *Les après-midi de Louis XVI* (Brédys: La Compagnie Littéraire, 2008), 1990.

2   Serge Tcherkézoff, *"First Contacts" in Polynesia: The Samoan Case (1722-1848): Western Misunderstandings about Sexuality and Divinity* (Canberra: ANU E Press, 2004), 53.

3   Tcherkézoff, *"First Contacts" in Polynesia*, 58.

4   Tcherkézoff, *"First Contacts" in Polynesia*, 54.

5   Tcherkézoff, *"First Contacts" in Polynesia*, 62.

6   The British were pleased to hear a Frenchman say (in French) that 'Mr Cook has done so much that he has left me nothing to do but to admire his works.' Cited in Ernest Scott, *Lapérouse* (Sydney: Angus & Robertson Ltd, 1913), 76.

7   Scott, *Lapérouse*, 73.

8   '*...vous voyez mon cher ami que je suis encore affecté par les événements, j'y reviens sans cesse et presque malgré moi.*' Lapérouse, Letter to Claret de Fleurieu, Botany Bay, 7 February 1788.

9   '*...des malheurs...dont j'ai toujours eu, en quelque sorte, un secret pressentiment.*' Lapérouse, Fleurieu letter, 7 February 1788.

10 Scott, *Lapérouse*, 95.

11 Scott, *Lapérouse*, 94.

12 Tcherkézoff, *"First Contacts" in Polynesia*, 59.

13 CNN, 'French explorer's shipwreck found', 10 May 2005, available at: <http://edition.cnn.com/2005/WORLD/asiapcf/05/10/laperouse.wrecked/>.

14 Alexandre François, 'Mystère des langues, magie des légendes', in Association Salomon (ed.), *Le mystère Lapérouse ou le rêve inachevé d'un roi* (Paris: de Conti, Musée national de la Marine, 2008), 230.

15 'The most secure of all beliefs is that mutually contradictory statements cannot be jointly true.' Aristotle, *The Metaphysics* (London: Penguin, 2004), 105-107 (1011b13-14).

16 François, 'Mystère des langues', 232.

17 Scott, *Lapérouse*, 46.

18 Robert W. Kirk, *Paradise Past: The Transformation of the South Pacific, 1520–1929* (Jefferson, North Carolina: McFarland & Company, Inc., 2012), 206.

19 Kirk, *Paradise Past*, 206.

20 François, 'Mystère des langues', 232.

21 François, 'Mystère des langues', 232.

22 Teliki Thomas, 'The message left by Lapérouse', 27 April 2005, in Alexandre François, *Field archives from the Solomon Islands*. Pangloss Collection, CNRS. Available at: <https://doi.org/10.24397/pangloss-0002605>.

23 *Italicised* words are those which the French translator, Alexandre François, inserted into the text inside brackets.

24 [*Italicised and bracketed*] words are those which the English translator, Daryl Morini, inserted into the text for clarity.

25 Teliki Thomas, 'The chest left by Lapérouse', 27 April 2005, in Alexandre François, *Field archives from the Solomon Islands*. Pangloss Collection, CNRS. Available at: <https://doi.org/10.24397/pangloss-0002604>.

26 Rubenson Lono, 'The story of Lapérouse', 2 May 2005, in Alexandre François, *Field archives from the Solomon Islands*. Pangloss Collection, CNRS. Available at: <https://doi.org/10.24397/pangloss-0002651>.

27 Rubenson Lono, 'Conversation about "The story of Lapérouse"', 2 May 2005, in Alexandre François, *Field archives from the Solomon Islands*. Pangloss Collection, CNRS. Available at: < https://doi.org/10.24397/pangloss-0002652>.

28 *Fisipure* is the Lovono word for the god known as *Vilisao* in the Teanu language. See VII, Willy Usao, *How Lapérouse got away*. See Alexandre François, *Teanu Dictionary (Solomon Islands)*, 2021, *Dictionaria* 15, 1-1877. Available at: <https://dictionaria.clld.org/sentences/teanu-XV001173>.

29 Emele Mamuli, 'The story of Lapérouse (3)', 7 May 2005, in Alexandre François, *Field archives from the Solomon Islands*. Pangloss Collection, CNRS. Available at: <https://doi.org/10.24397/pangloss-0002685>.

30 *Trocas* (*Tectus niloticus*) are a type of sea snail harvested across the Pacific and valued for its nacreous shell and meat.

31 *Bêches-de-mer* (*Holothuroidea*), a.k.a. sea cucumbers or trepang, are harvested in the Pacific and a delicacy in Asia.

32 The first Europeans to sight Vanikoro Island from afar were on board Spanish captain Álvaro de Mendaña's ship in 1595, two centuries before Lapérouse. Locals may not have seen them. The French were likely the first on shore.

33 Kaspa Niu Maketi, 'The story of Lapérouse', 10 May 2005, in Alexandre François, *Field archives from the Solomon Islands*. Pangloss Collection, CNRS. Available at: <https://doi.org/10.24397/pangloss-0002687>.

34 At the time of recording, Kaspa Niu Maketi was a leader of the Polynesian community established on Vanikoro island. That community, tied to the island of Tikopia further east, settled on Vanikoro's southern shores several centuries ago, and was thus present on the island at the time of Lapérouse.

35 *Taureperangi Terua Matakai*: presumably a 19th century Tikopia chief. No further written information is available.

36 As described in this story, Captain Peter Dillon's expedition found such artefacts on the island of Tikopia in 1826.

37 *Peter Dillon* was the captain who found remnants of the Lapérouse shipwreck in 1826. See *Translator's Introduction*.

38 A century earlier, oral history correctly designated *Paiu* (*Païou* in François' usage) as a site of one of the two shipwrecks.

39   Cited in Alexandre François, 'Mystère des langues, magie des légendes', in *Association Salomon, Le mystère Lapérouse ou le rêve inachevé d'un roi* (Paris: de Conti, Musée national de la Marine, 2008), 230-233.

40   *Espiritu Santo* in modern Vanuatu was colonised by the French. Like Vanikoro, Santo was targeted by the Queensland blackbirding trade. In one 1880s incident, local Santo residents fought back against HMS Cormorant, killing one of its officers with rifle fire. At the time, Royal Navy ships based in Australia protected the blackbirders and were tasked with crushing such acts of resistance with violent punitive expeditions—including in Espiritu Santo.

41   *Tepakare* is the name of a large double-hulled, catamaran-like canoe used by Polynesians. See entry *'Tepakare'* in François' dictionary. Available at: < https:// dictionaria.clld.org/units/teanu-tepakare_1>.

42   *Filisao,* or *Vilisao,* the god of tornadoes, is named after the Teanu word for "tornado", also *vilisao.* See Alexandre François, *Teanu Dictionary*, 2021, available at: <https://dictionaria.clld.org/units/teanu-vilisao_1>.

43   *Filimoe* is an ancient, submerged atoll on the west coast of Banie island, near Lale. Alexandre François, 'Vilimoe', *Teanu Dictionary*, 2021, available at: https:// dictionaria.clld.org/units/teanu-Vilimoe_1.

A cunning invasion*

Georges Baudoux†

TRANSLATED BY *Daryl Morini*‡

Clearly intent on defending his people's honour, the gentle Dalaï responded to my taunts with: 'The Kanaks[1] aren't to blame for that one. Just you wait, I'll tell you one of the elders' stories. Then you'll see.'

What follows reflects his state of mind.[2]

Obviously, this happened a long, long time ago. *Pirogues*[3] with men from the mainland had sailed to Yandé, Baaba, Tanlo,[4] and all the Nénéma islands[5] to say that the Pouébo tribe was preparing a great *pilou*[6] starting three nights from now, and that we, all us men, women, and girls, should come to Pouébo for the Chief's[7] great *pilou*.

---

*   This is the first English translation of Georges Baudoux's 'A cunning invasion' (*L'invasion sournoise*, 1938), a short story based on the oral history of the Pouébo people, an Indigenous Kanak tribe of New Caledonia. Sources and discussion are included in the *Notes* section below. This is a translation of Georges Baudoux, *Légendes Canaques II: Ils Avaient vu des Hommes Blancs* (Paris: Nouvelles Éditions Latines, 1952). This work is in the public domain.

†   Georges Baudoux (1870-1949) was the first New Caledonian novelist. He worked as a cobalt and nickel miner in the northwest of the main island, where he collected Kanak oral history. He lived in Nouméa, Koumac, and Koné.

‡   Daryl Morini is Editor of *Synkrētic* and a Pacific Research Fellow at ANU's Department of Pacific Affairs. He holds a PhD in International Relations from the University of Queensland. He is based in Canberra, Australia.

Now that, my friend, was a party. All were merry and got to work doing things they knew. The women wove pandanus-leaf mats with long strips on each end to stop mosquitoes. They braided tapa belts[8] from bleached cane they beat against the water, and made soft tapa from the banyan tree's fibres.

Men carved and hardened spears[9] with fire and shaved their tips sharp; they tied strips of bat's fur adorned with tiny shells around them. With shards of rock and cutting shells, they scraped head-breakers out of wood.[10] They rubbed, polished, and buffed their blue serpentine, round, and triangular axes, as well as sling-bullets. These were all intended as gifts to be presented at the *pilou*, over there in Pouébo.[11]

They fashioned huge, hulking pots by kneading clay and fine gravel into thin sausages, which they stacked on top of the other in a circular motion, much as wasps make their nests. Now those were hard to do, pots. Many would crack when cooking over large fires. The elders knew how to make pots. We've forgotten how, in our day.[12]

The elders took care of the money made of seashell tips scraped against stone, which the Chiefs kept. The young did nothing at all. They always mucked around.

Impatient was the moon that crept forward while the Indigenous people made their sumptuous gifts on the islands. Chiefs and dignitaries met in a great council to decide on the departure date and journey's legs.

The *pirogues*, both the big tandem boats and smaller ones, were packed with food rations and lavish gifts.

Then, one after the other, they took off with the early southern breeze to assemble and wait on a sand island at the mouth of the Balabio channel.

Though they had been warmly invited and promised wonderful things, their minds would not leave them in peace. Entering a stranger's house with strength of numbers was sound policy.

The *pirogues* met on the island that would later be named Saint-Phalle, in memory of a dozen navy hydrographers massacred there.[13] While waiting, the Kanaks rested and caught the most in-

173

credible fish. The biggest were browned with smoke to preserve them for days.

Headwinds always pick up as you approach Pouébo. You constantly tack, and then tack some more. The *pirogues* drift off to the sides, almost going sideways like crabs. Even when sailing into the wind, the destination is reached in the end. But the work is so relentless that one's muscles are sore on arrival. Far better to travel by land breeze at night.

Before daybreak, long before even birds awaken, around the time when the morning star shimmers above the sea out beyond the surf-swept reef, the Kanak clan stirred to life when puffs of wind from the valley blew through a fire's embers and carried off the sparks.

Dry wood is a precious resource that should always be preserved. It's worth the effort of gathering and carrying around.

Making whining noises and rubbing their skin with saliva,[14] the Kanak clan stretched and sat back down in their *pirogues*. As lateen sails unfurled like fans, the square sails snapped so tight as to almost rip. Once again, the flotilla with braided wings glided off in silence, stirring up phosphorescent sea creatures' lights as it went. They flew, how they flew!

It's always cold at night with the land breeze up and as fog creeps between the valley floors. It stings the skin. The women lay on the ground huddled together under an old, saggy woven mat grown soft with use. They kept warm. Because the men are tougher than the women, they tried to stay warm as best they could without letting on that they felt cold.

The headwinds blew while the sun hung low. The *pirogues* now made for the coast, clinging to the reef that lines the coast opposite Amos. Since the *pirogues* still had water under their bellies, the men and women used poles to push against the seabed. In this way, they kept going, kept going towards Pouébo.

But the falling tide gradually beached the *pirogues*, which now scraped the bottom. To avoid splitting up the party, the smaller *pirogues* were stopped too. The whole flotilla rested there, strewn along the sand, not far from mangroves that dot the coast.

Synkrētic

Despite seeing coconut trees and several huts from the shore, no islander from Nénéma tried to contact the mainlanders. They knew these were friends, that there was nothing to fear. But the deep distrust that keeps men alive was at work. No risk would be taken without good reason. Some passed the time fishing near the *pirogues*, planning to seek shelter in them if the alarm were sounded. Those overcome by it gave in to sweet sleep.

The *pirogues* floated again before the sun had fallen behind the mountains. The Nénéma squadron soon bristled with poles all pushing against the sea floor. In this manœuvre, they showed all the skill and endurance that heredity passed down to them.

They reached their objective in the dead of night. The flotilla was tied in place by driving hard poles into the coral.

But it wasn't the right time to go ashore. Protocols established by ancestral custom had to be observed. As they awaited dawn, fires were lit on purpose-built mounds of sand from materials stored aboard their *pirogues*, so that they might sleep soundly around cosy hearths that drive away the dew.

Gentle was the night they spent beneath the radiant stars as dampened sounds wafted in from land. The jittery cricket's hum. The screech of squabbling bats. A prowling heron's raspy call.

In the morning, a delegation of Nénéma islanders stepped onto the beach in full daylight. It was led by a Chief wearing vine around his waist and a ceremonial loincloth with seashells.[15] Four diplomats followed him. Each wore the same clothes and clutched bird-shaped head-breakers. Slingshot pellets hung from their ears. They were off to make contact with the great Chief of Pouébo.

A coterie of guards and advisers surrounded the Pouébo Chief while he awaited this delegation. When it had arrived within ten paces, the islanders froze in place. The Chief of their Yandé tribe spoke first.

'Great Chief of Pouébo, you invited us to your *pilou*. We come to enjoy your hospitality and bring you entrails from our island fish.'

The Chief of Pouébo responded:

'We're friends who go way back. You are guests of the Pouébo tribe. You'll eat our yams, taro, bananas, and our *pilou* you will dance. We'll show you to the huts in which you'll sleep.'

The Chief of Yandé stepped forward, holding out in his finger-tips a finely bound package of white-banyan bark, which he handed over with these words: 'Great Chief of Pouébo, I give you our fish entrails. They are yours.'

The connection was established once the Pouébo Chief received these gifts. Without breaking the reserve proper to the solemn character of the ceremony, the advisers exchanged a few words.

As the two chiefs met, most likely to discuss matters of state, a man went to great pains to carefully unwrap the soft banyan bark around the precious gift. Once he had opened it, he presented it to his Chief with an air of utmost deference, as was required.

Strings of nacreous shell shards tied off with bat's fur tassels on each end lay inside. There were also *ouacici*[16] necklaces and bracelets made from rare shells' whorls.

This Kanak money was a currency. It facilitated such encounters. Its value was calculated from the work, skill, and patience it took to make. Once the wealth of these gifts was appraised, and with no word of thanks going unnoticed, the Chiefs retired to the area reserved for guests.

The Nénéma people performed various rituals to accept gifts of huts and cooking pots from their hosts, the latter gift being a symbol of the Kanak family.

All the Pouébo people withdrew discreetly to avoid gawking out of idle curiosity, which could put them at a disadvantage in the strangers' eyes. They let the Nénéma people get ready.

As soon as the rising tide allowed them to float, the *pirogues* were beached in front of the huts. They unloaded much-depleted linen stocks, with clothing among it.

The gifts they made were carefully stored away from sun and rain, to keep them from fading.

While the Nénéma built makeshift dwellings, and not failing to show deference to the round, high-peaked huts reserved for dignitaries, the Pouébo women,[17] hunched under loads tethered to their shoulders with straw straps, lugged over and dropped off yams, taro, and all kinds of edible plants courtesy of the Pouébo tribe.

Giving themselves haughty airs, the men pretended not to have seen the women and stepped out of their way. This was their way of letting women take care of the logistics, the giving and taking of supplies. Men were supposed to stand above such trifling domestic chores.

Should a man more prideful than the others block their way, the women walking past him would bow deeply out of humility ingrained over millennia. They would almost be crawling on all fours.

The Nénéma people barely left their living quarters while waiting for the *pilou* to start. Casting a suspicious eye over their hosts, they felt no urge, since they had not been invited, to speak to acquaintances in whose company they felt ill at ease. They passed the time sleeping and eating to gather strength, and doing little else.

*
**

Reassured by how well the Nénéma were behaving on their land, the Pouébo tribe visibly warmed to their guests. They came over to see the Nénéma and told them of things strange, things utterly unknown, which to them had been revelations.

They told a story, whose details changed to fit the listener's views, about two huge *pirogues* with no outriggers, their masts a pine tree high and sails pulled tight every which way, whose crews had alighted here in Pouébo.[18] Instead of lowering a heavy rock tied to a vine, these *pirogues* latched onto the seafloor with hooks and ropes thrown in the water. *Splash.*

Men had come ashore on two lighter craft, these bulky *pirogues* without outriggers that moved by picking up water in their long legs. Not knowing who they were, the Kanaks watched on while hiding behind bushes. There was no doubt about it. These men were white. There were red ones, too. These men looked nothing like Kanak albinos.

A few of these white men came ashore and walked across the beach. Their heavy, bark-girt footsteps crushed the rocks. The many other white men stayed in their *pirogues*. Those Kanaks who know things well saw neither dread nor anger in these men.

Their fears waning, the more daring Kanaks, who wielded spears, slings, and head-breakers, showed themselves to the white men. They sought explanations for this unannounced landing.

The white men, from whose bodies hung all sorts of things that must have been weaponry, advanced on the Kanaks. They gestured, spoke, and laughed.

The Kanaks hesitated, watching them closely. Should they attack? Or should they wait? When they saw white men wrapped in strips of skin, or maybe soft woven mat, down to their legs for warmth and wearing baskets on their heads with hair as stiff as banyan beards,[19] the Kanaks also laughed and gave no more thought to attacking.

Upon reaching the Kanaks, the white men took them gently by the hand and smacked them on the shoulder. They spoke so quickly in a language no Kanak could speak.

The white men and Pouébo Kanaks made friends by means of exaggerated gestures, modulating their meanings with subtle signs, and used their bodies to communicate.

Without letting go of their instinctive distrust, the black and white men sat on coconut tree trunks lying in the dirt.

The other white men stayed seated in rows in their *pirogue*. Pressed between their hands and knees, they held long sticks with pointy ends and very broad bases. They glistened like the morning dew. The Kanaks had never seen such weapons: spear on one end, head-breaker on the other.

Two white men, who were sitting on a coconut tree trunk, took out little pieces of wood which they filled with dried, finely chopped herbs. Next, they sucked the ends of the wooden pieces and blew out smoke from their mouths. It smelled nice.

While the two white men ate smoke, the Chief arrived with his sorcerer and the all-knowing elders.

The great Chief, the white men, the sorcerer, and elders all spoke in turn. In the end, each understood that the white men wanted to take back fresh drinking water and wood to make fire aboard their great *pirogues*.

The whole tribe, usually apathetic, was struck by this strangest of sights and gathered around where the men not quite like the others had disembarked. They stood a hundred paces from the delegation of diplomats, whom they surrounded in the shape of a semi-circle that spilled onto the beach.

For a long, long time, the Pouébo Chief, his advisers, and the sorcerer, who was growing violently animated, talked and talked. This was a serious matter; it upset all customs. The white men awaited a response. But, still, the Kanaks talked and talked.

A white man, probably a chief, who was sick of waiting handed the Pouébo Chief an object as round and flat as a river rock. It was the colour of those rocks that poison the water.[20] A man's head was displayed on one side, tree branches on the other.

The Pouébo Chief grabbed the rock that looked like it might be a shell's operculum[21] or the seed of a tree. Joined by his sorcerer, they studied it a long time and deliberated.

When they had finished conversing, the Pouébo Chief told the white men that they could take river water with them, but that the wood was taboo.[22] Speaking very loudly, he also told the white men that they would need to go back to their country after they had taken the water. Then the white men, who didn't want to stay stranded without a single drop of water, went back to their great *pirogues*.

The next morning, three *pirogues* carrying many men came ashore with the rising tide. One of them stayed on the water's edge. Two *pirogues* slipped between mangroves to enter the river, where they filled up their bellies with fresh water.

They left to empty themselves into the great *pirogues*, coming back to take in more water.

The *pirogue* on the water's edge did not budge while this was occurring. A couple of men lay down in the shade and fell asleep. The others remained standing and didn't let go of their weapons. The Kanaks understood at once that these men provided security for the whole group. These white men were shrewd. Surprising them would be impossible. They wouldn't let themselves be eaten like mere dugongs.

One of the white men spoke to a Kanak, whom he beckoned over with a hand signal. Miming the activity with vivid gestures, the white man got across to the bewildered Kanak that he wanted a woman. The Kanak shook his head and clicked his tongue to convey that he couldn't, and that this was a bad thing.

To sway the Kanak, the white man gave him a thing as long and straight as the sea urchin's spike but that was firmer than rocks. The white man showed him that this particular spine could penetrate wood when driven in with a stone.

This Kanak's name was Timoin; he was the guy who lived in a hut at the base of the mountain. Timoin said yes. He made off with the spike that knew how to pierce wood. Timoin never came back with a woman.

The white men's two great *pirogues* stayed in Pouébo for three days. The white men went across to Poudioué island[23] to cut and steal wood. The Chief hadn't cursed the wood on that island.

The white men's *pirogues* were big, so big, they carried many men. The Kanak *pirogues* looked tiny beside them. The sorcerer had said that there lurked inside these great *pirogues* some white devils that could walk on water. After hesitating a long time, the Kanaks decided not to engage in a naval battle.

A morning came when the white people's great *pirogues* raised all their sails in the air. They lifted their hooks from the bottom of the sea while performing a *pilou* dance. And they went far away, beyond the big reefs. By night-time, they could no longer be seen from the mountain top.

This is what the Kanaks from Pouébo told their friends from Nénéma beneath coastal banyans as they awaited the great *pilou*.

*
**

With his cigarette finished, Dalaï picked up his story's thread, which plunged his tradition-steeped soul back into his ancestors' lives as he narrated it.

Synkrētic

The big *pilou* at Pouébo isn't worth narrating; all big ones are the same. And yet, this one was not quite like the others. The Chief introduced into it a ceremony that the Kanak elders hadn't expected.

After a rousing speech by the tribe orator and the warriors' fierce dancing and leaping to and fro in simulated fights, the Great Chief of Pouébo appeared at the foot of a tree that doubled as his rostrum. From here, he called forward all adults, parading before them the gift that the chief of the white men from the strange country had given him.

It was a large bronze medallion with Britannia on one side, and symbolic palms and a date on the other. Never had any Kanak seen a *baoui*[24] like this one.

But this was nothing. After the procession had passed the Chief, it was then made to parade before the Kanak called Timoin, whom the course of events had made into an exhibitor.

A nail dangled from a long piece of string hung around his neck, a thick iron nail from a navy ship. Now, this was a wonderful thing. The Kanaks touched the nail, feeling its square angles and rounded head. They chipped their teeth against it to test its strength. They dreamed of the many uses that could be made of this hardy spike.

Though not the arrogant type, Timoin still felt proud to be the owner of this unknown tool, useful in all things, which he had bought only with the subtle act of tricking a white man who had wanted a woman. The whole tribe had laughed about it.

But glory comes with a price. As the legitimate owner of the hard, pointy object forged from an unimagined material, he no doubt gained in prestige but also aroused envy in others, exciting their covetous thoughts. Every Kanak would have liked to own that nail. Timoin knew this and grew worried.

The talk was that the Chief's non-perforated medal was hardly a catch. It couldn't be threaded with string to be worn as an adornment. Timoin's nail, meanwhile, was a precious tool that was also an elegant jewel when he slid it into the lobe of his ever-pierced ear.

After seeing the things that white men brought, and with the *pilou* officially opened, the Kanaks, men and women, returned to their huts before nightfall to gorge themselves, as was tradition.

As soon as the heavy blows of the fig-bark paddles, the muffled pounding of the bamboo echoing in the earth, the precise rhythm of dry wood struck in time sounded into the black night, the whole Kanak race rushed to the *pilou*.

This is when the real party began. The whole crowd pivoted in the dark around the main pole. The whole crowd gestured, pounded their feet, stomping the ground rhythmically. The whole crowd rubbed, felt, and stepped forward as one.

When, in thrall to the rhythm, they had rubbed against each other, inhaling the scent of man's animal passions, a sort of collective hint arose, a feverish lust taking hold of the gyrating mass of human flesh.

The expected occurred. The women's rolling hips captivated the men; the men fervently pressed against the women, who were tireless. The party reached its apogee. Dawn's first light put an end to the frolicking.[25]

The Nénéma islanders slept like logs. Some lay heavily slumped on straw, others on mats. Some were in the open air, others in tall, peaked huts, dark from being sealed shut. All were blissfully unaware of a devilish threat slowly enveloping them.

The *pilou* party lasted four days. At night they danced, they stomped the earth, without any break besides tiring interludes. In the daytime they slept, ate, and slept again. The tiredness that dulls the senses prevented the Nénéma from feeling the first, faint attacks of which they were the hapless victims. Only three old women with saggy skin whom the men neglected in the *pilou*, who only felt things dully and mostly felt regret, had noticed the cunning manœuvres targeting the Nénéma. They saw it, the old women did, but they didn't feel it and didn't speak.

The *pilou* celebrations ended for the good reason that the hosting tribe had run out of food. As was customary, after endless feasting it was time to chew the gooey bark of the *bourao* trees.[26]

Synkrētic

The departure was brought forward to avoid a famine. The women got to work picking up the tools, rolling up the mats, and loading all the supplies on the *pirogues*.

The three old women who knew but didn't speak gently lifted their mats from each corner, closing them with great care, picking up their fringes to avoid losing their contents. Rather than rolling them up as usual, these mats were carefully folded and tied up with vines. And these old women placed these packages into selected areas at the bottom of the *pirogues*.

The trip goes by quickly with tailwinds. The *pirogues* were already far away by the time their sails were fully deployed. At night, the squadron stayed on Baaba island. The next day, the Nénéma Kanaks split up, each group heading back to its own island.

And life resumed its gentle, leisurely course without a care for the days to come. Planting was easy and fun for everyone, fishing was a real treat.

But since coming home, a torment had befallen their homes. It even hung around their huts and under the shade of the guardian-trees under which people lay.

No one was at ease anymore. It stung, it itched, they had to rub themselves everywhere, by day, by night, even in sleep. One was still sore upon waking up. And the more time passed, the worse it became.

The most tortured men and women, who were sick of rubbing their skin raw, dove headfirst into the sea. That felt nice, but you couldn't live there forever. They had no choice but to go home, and again the itching would come back.

What sickness was this? The fish itch,[27] the Acajou tree inflammation,[28] the leaves that burn your skin like nettle.[29] No, it wasn't. And still, they searched and searched.

By applying all their skill to the problem, the brightest researchers had concluded that this kind of itch was caused by the changing appetites of tiny animals as fine as grains of sand that jumped, and bit, and hid in the dust.

It was only learned much later that the ever-nosy old women, who picked up and by nature hoarded all they found, had also wanted a turn at keeping something from the white men.[30]

With these words, Dalaï cracked up triumphantly and declared:

'You see? You'll never again complain that I have little critters around my hut. It's the first white men who came to Pouébo that brought fleas to our country. We had none before them.'

What can you say? This idea, handed down by the ancestors, was deeply entrenched in his brain. It would have been impossible to prove the contrary. Were there or were there not fleas?[31] Now, that is the question.

Notes

These are not the author's notes. They are provided by Synkrētic to clarify references and other details of interest. Initial page numbers (e.g. P. 9) refer to the original French text cited on p. 172.

1   P. 9: Boudoux's *Canaques* is an antiquated form of *Kanak*, the Indigenous Melanesian people of New Caledonia.

2   P. 9: Baudoux is signposting that his story, as with many of his others, is claimed to be based on the oral history narrated to him by local sources, in this case a Kanak called Dalaï, who thereby becomes the implied narrator.

3   P. 9: *Pirogue* is the French word for Kanak sailboats made from timber canoes, stabilised either using an outrigger or in some cases a second hull connected by a deck, and with one or two triangle-shaped sails like the modern sloop.

4   P. 9: The Yandé/Yade, Baaba/Paava, and Taanlo/Tâânlô/Taalo islands are clustered around the northern tip of New Caledonia's mainland. Today, they are part of the independentist-run Northern Province's Poum district.

5   P. 9: The Nénéma people live in the tribe of Titch/Thiic, on the above islands, and on Néba/Nééva/Yaba, Tiabet/Cavet, Tié/Ce, and Yenghébane/Yenjevan islands. Their Nêlêmwa-Nixumwak or Kumak language was spoken by over 1,100 people at the 2009 census. The Nénéma are part of the Hoot Ma Waap customary area.

6   P. 9: A *pilou* (or *pilou-pilou*), from the Nyelâyu language's *pilu* meaning 'to dance', is a traditional Kanak ceremony. It tended to involve group dancing by night in a circular motion around a pole for hours, as in this story. Colonial authorities began banning the *pilou* in 1854, fearing the war-like trances of the dancers. Referring to the same Hoot Ma Waap region, Denis Monnerie notes that the term *pilou* tends to be misapplied to other Kanak ceremonies, such as the welcoming ceremony that Baudoux also describes. See Denis Monnerie, *La Parole de notre Maison: Discours et cérémonies kanak d'aujourd'hui (Nouvelle-Calédonie)* (Paris: Éditions de la Maison des Sciences de l'Homme, 1993), 82.

7   P. 9: A *chef de tribu*, also known as a *grand chef*, is the sovereign of a tribe, a key unit in Kanak political life.

8   P. 10: In the Pacific, tapa belts were made from the inner bark of the banian and other trees, and here out of cane.

9   P. 10: *Sagaïe* are short, hard-wood spears with a range of 100 metres or more when thrown with a strap.

10   P. 10: *Casse-têtes* ("head-breakers") are clubs with heads carved into bird beaks, phalluses, and other shapes.

11   P. 10: Pouébo (*Pweevo*) is on the northeast coast of New Caledonia's main island. James Cook alighted just north of Pouébo in 1774, in the first recorded contact between European and Kanak people. The 100km trip to the other side of the island that the protagonist tribes in the story undertake by *pirogue* is historically plausible. Records suggest the Nénéma islanders were valued as allies for their naval skill. In October 1855-January 1856, Nénéma islanders threw their support

behind Pouébo in battles against the Hienghène people. At the time of the story, they are implied to be allies. Other sources speak of the allies being at war at a different time. See the chronololoy of the Roman Catholic Archdiocese of Nouméa, *Éphémérides de la Nouvelle-Calédonie*, in Georges Coquilhat, *Ma Nouvelle Calédonie*, available at: <https://gnc.jimdofree.com/nouvelle-cal%C3%A9donie-eph-emerides-1853-1862/>

12   P. 10: Baudoux describes part of the process of making the ceramic *marmite canaque*, as Europeans described it. The making of this utensil, formally known as the tradition of Oundjo pottery, emerged a number of centuries before colonisation. It did fall out of use in the early 20th century when Baudoux was writing, reportedly because of the growing availability of European cooking utensils. Maurice Leenhardt dated 1906 as the end of this style of Kanak pottery. See Isabelle Leblic, Françoise Cayrol-Baudrillat and Jean-Yves Wédoye, *Étude ethno-archéologique de quelques sociétés de potiers kanak (Ponérihouen et région de Hienghène)* (Paris: Ministère de la Culture, 1996), 9-10.

13   P. 11: Xavier de Saint-Phalle (1831-1850) was a naval officer cadet who died in a major battle between the people of Yenghébane and a French corvette. On 1 December 1850, the corvette *L'Acmède*, crewed by 248 sailors, is reconnoitring northern New Caledonia for its potential as a settler colony. Fifteen men take a tender boat to Yenghébane Island. Coconuts and biscuits are exchanged. The next night, Chief Dindi and the tribe's sorcerer decide to kill the French because, according to one version of events, they feared the white men would offer gifts to their enemies on the mainland. Hundreds of Nénéma and Daye fighters kill all but three of the sailors; the tribe adopts the three, one of whom is rescued. The ship's commander orders a punitive raid weeks later in which the Pouébo Kanaks reportedly take part, killing 24 Kanaks and destroying three villages. This incident, coupled with *L'Acmède*'s recommendation that a penal colony be set up, reportedly impels Napoleon III to seize the islands in 1853. See Sylvain Joualt, *Monographie historique de la compagnie de gendarmerie territoriale de Koné et de sa circonscription* (Koné: Gendarmerie Nationale, 2018), 12-13; Bernard Brou, *Memento d'histoire de la Nouvelle-Calédonie les temps modernes, 1774 1925* (Nouméa: Editions le Santal, 1973), 43; *Bulletin scientifique de la Société d'études historiques*, Issue 79 (1989): 19.

14   P. 12: No explanation is given for why the sailors rub saliva on their skin. Baudoux describes a similar scene on land in a different story, where, on waking up, Kanak characters clean their skin and warm their muscles in this way. The implicit claim is that it is a morning ritual. See Georges Baudoux, 'Kaavo', in *Légendes Canaques I*, 18.

15   P. 15: The *bagayou* or *baguiyou*, supposedly from the Iaai language's *baga* for 'man' or 'male sex', was a penis-sheath.

16   P. 16: The *ouacici* is the small white shell of the *ovula ovum*, a cowrie shell used for necklaces. The word is common to at least ten Kanak languages, with slight variations. See Jean Mariotti, Mireille Soury-Lavergne, Bernard Gasser, *Nouveaux contes de Poindi* (Nouméa: Grain de Sable, 2002), 183.

17   P. 17: *Pouébo women*: Baudoux uses the word *popinée* throughout this story, a dated word used for Kanak women.

18 P. 19: Some local scholars see this story as evidence that Lapérouse's ships first visited Pouébo, and that the white men described in this story are Lapérouse's crew, as preserved in the local oral history of the Pouébo people. See Georges Baudoux, *Jean M'Barai The Trepang Fisherman*, transl. Karin Speedy (Sydney: UTS ePRESS, 2007), 25.

19 P. 20: 'Banyan beard' (*barbes de banian*) likely refers to the *ficus prolixa*'s aerial roots that hang down like long beards.

20 P. 22: 'That poison the water' (*cailloux qui empoisonnent l'eau*) is a probable reference to a sorcerer's curse or *tabou*.

21 P. 22: The operculum is the retracting disc in sea snails and gastropods, coveted in Asia as a source of incense.

22 P. 22: The placing of a *tabou* on the wood implies a protective curse had been placed on it if used by outsiders.

23 P. 24: Poudioué/Poudiou island, 10 nautical miles north of Pouébo. In 1774, James Cook passed the island on his second Pacific voyage, during which his scientist Johann Forster observed an eclipse. In 1793, French naval officer Jean-Michel Huon de Kermadec, who was searching for the Lapérouse expedition, would be buried on the island.

24 P. 26: *Baoui* appears to be a synonym for a *ouacici* shell (note 16). See Jean Mariotti, *Takata D'Aïmos* (Nouméa: Grain de Sable, 1999), 16; and 'Proceedings of the Linguistic Society of New Zealand, *Te Reo*, Vol. 1-7 (1958): 7.

25 P. 28: The earliest colonial accounts of the *pilou* insinuated that it always led to debauchery. As Christine Salomon explains, they were an opportunity for unmarried men and women to meet during the dance and arrange to meet again later. Some fights might break out. Salomon analyses the power differential between male and female dancers. See Christine Salomon, 'Hommes et femmes: harmonie d'ensemble ou antagonisme sourd ?', in *En Pays Kanak*, Alban Bensa and Isabelle Leblic (Paris: Éditions de la Maison des sciences de l'homme, 2000), 322.

26 P. 29: *Bourao* trees (*Hibiscus tiliaceus*), found on the coast and some inland, are used in traditional Kanak medicine. The leaves are chewed and served as tea to heal the liver or for relaxation. The leaves' sap is also applied to wounds.

27 P. 31: 'Fish itch' (*gratte de poisson* or *la grate*) is a local term for ciguatera fish poisoning, typically caused by consuming a fish that ate the reef organism *Gambierdiscus toxicus*, whose toxins cause the skin to itch painfully.

28 P. 31: The *Acajou* or *Goudronnier* tree (*Semecarpus vitiensis*) is widespread on the mainland's west coast. Its fruit contains a resinous vesicant that can cause swelling and hard-to-treat ulcers. Though toxic when raw, the fruit's kernel can be eaten cooked. Jean Rageau, *Les Plantes Médicinales de la Nouvelle-Calédonie* (Paris: ORSTOM, 1973), 61.

29 P. 31: 'Like nettle' (*comme les orties*) may refer to an endemic plant some accounts call 'Kanak nettle' (*orties canaques*), possibly a species of endogenous *Urticaceae* in the nettle family which have stinging hair.

30 P. 31: This detail, according to which Kanak grandmothers brought back fleas from a Pouébo *pilou*, is supported in oral history from the same region. This confirms

that Baudoux built his narrative on local Kanak oral history. Cited in *Etudes mélanési-ennes: Bulletin périodique de la Société d'études mélanésiennes*, No. 10-11 (1958): 144.

31 There is evidence that some species of ticks may have been introduced to New Caledonia by the first European ships. Local oral history supports the claim that 'the first two boats to stop in Pouebo, probably with La Pérouse, introduced ticks and a new disease.' Christopher Sand, Jacques Bole, A. Ouetcho, 'What Were the Real Numbers? The Question of Pre-Contact Population Densities in New Caledonia', in *The Growth and Collapse of Pacific Island Societies*, eds. Patrick V. Kirch, Jean-Louis Rallu (Hononlulu: University of Hawai'i Press, 2007), 318.

Io of the hidden face

H.T. Whatahoro,* Te Mātorohanga,† Nēpia Pōhūhū,‡
Aporo Te Kumeroa,§ Percy Smith,** et al.

I

H.T. Whatahoro, 'Philosophy of the *whare-wānanga*' (1913)††

'Now I, Te Mātorohanga, have another word to say so you may be clear on this subject. Be very careful in reciting these valuable teachings that your ancestors collected over past generations.

The teachings of the *whare-wānanga* are now mere shreds since they are no longer combined. Some remain while others are lost. Some parts diverge from the originals and additions have been made to others.

---

* Hoani Te Whatahoro Jury (1841-1923) recorded this story in 1865. He wrote on Māori traditions in *The Journal of the Polynesian Society*. Of the Ngāti Kahungunu tribe (henceforth *iwi*), he was from Rakaukaka, Aotearoa New Zealand.

† Te Mātorohanga (c. 1836-1876) is the speaker in this text. He was a priest trained in a traditional Māori school or *whare-wānanga*. Of the Ngāti Kahungunu *iwi*, he was from Te Ewe-o-Tiina, Wairarapa, Aotearoa New Zealand.

‡ Nēpia Pōhūhū (fl. 1860s) was a priest, who has been cited as another source of this material.

§ Aporo Te Kumeroa (fl. 1890s) assisted H.T. Whatahoro as another scribe for this project. He was a chief and corresponding member of the Polynesian Society. He lived in Wairarapa, Aotearoa New Zealand.

** Stephenson Percy Smith (1840-1922) is the editor and translator of this text. He was an ethnologist and a founding editor of *The Journal of the Polynesian Society*. He lived in New Plymouth, Aotearoa New Zealand.

†† This is an edited extract of Chapter 2, 'The philosophy of the Whare-wānanga—the nature of matter, etc.', of H.T. Whatahoro, *The Lore of the Whare-wānanga: Or, teachings*

189

This happened due to the decaying power, authority, and prestige of rituals, abrogation of *tapu*,[1] and unbelief in gods. So that, at present, we have none of the ancient *mana* or power left. All things have changed. The *tapu* has ended. The true teaching was lost. As are the *karakias*, incantations whose meaning few people now know.

The *tapu* was all important, the first of things. Without it, the gods are powerless. And without the help of the gods, things are without authority and ineffectual.[2] Man's mind is cast in a state of confusion, like a whirlwind, as are all his deeds.

It is the same with the land. The *whare-wānangas*, the *karakias*, the *tuāhus* or altars, the *pures* or ways of sanctifying man, the baptising of men with water are all abandoned. So are the powers to attract fish and birds,[3] to influence the growth of edible plants. Nowadays, people use different *karakias*, methods, and *tapus*. It's as if they spoke a different language. That's how much modern teachings diverge from those of the old priests.

I stress the way things were so that you may be clear-headed about why the divine powers, the *mana atua*, have declined. Even Io was affected by this, as were his *whatukura*[4] and *mareikura* guardians,[5] the *Apas* who relay the gods' messages, down to the forest-dwelling *patupaiarehe*[6] and the *Tūrehu* fairies.[7] Nowadays, those kinds of gods no longer exist. The present gods have been reduced to being reptiles, stones, and trees. Meanwhile, the original reptile, stone, and tree gods no longer exist.

Men now live in a wilderness. They are careless of these things, as of all things. That's why you'll no longer find any *mana*, the power to make use of this knowledge. Bear in mind, then, that what you are writing from my dictation are mere crumbs of truth, fragments of the sacred things. The anciently established and true teaching is

of the Maori College on religion, cosmogony, and history, written down by H.T. Whatahoro from the teachings of Te Matorohanga and Nepia Pohuhu, priests of the Whare-wānanga of the East Coast, New Zealand, Part I. 'Things Celestial', transl. S. Percy Smith (New Plymouth: N.Z., 1913), 104-114. The text has been modernised. Paragraphs from section 'Io-Matua, the Supreme God' are included. This work is in the public domain.

now erased. So is the science of the *tapu*, as are the true god-like powers that came from Io-the-great, Io-the-parentless. But enough of these words.

Now, you must clearly grasp the roles played by Tama-nui-te-rā our sun, Te Marama-i-whanake the waxing moon, and their younger brethren the stars. All worlds have their own earths and waters, rocks and trees, plains and mountains. The *hau*,[8] the air, complements all things, be it the earth, heavens, sun, moon, or stars.

These things, four in all, give and sustain all life. With the earth, ocean, fire, or air alone, nothing would exist nor have shape or growth. Nothing would have life. Be clear about this: things only gain form and life by combining earth, water, fire, and air.[9] The origin of all things is Io, who lives in the upmost of all the heavens. It is he who gained universal knowledge of the heavens.[10]

There is a reason for each of Io's names.

Io is his name for short, but we also say *Io-nui*[11] for he is god of all gods. He is *Io-matua*[12] the parent of all things, *Io-te-wānanga*[13] who knows all things, *Io-tikitiki*[14] whose name is exalted on earth, hell, and the heavens. He is *Io-mata-aho*[15] when he visits other worlds as a flash of light. He is *Io-matua-kore* the parentless.[16] Man never sees him for he is *Io-mata-ngaro*[17] of the unseen face. He is *Io-mata-putahi*[18] whose command all obey, the loving god *Io-mata-wai*,[19] *Io-te-hau-e-rangi*[20] the ruler of all heavens,[21] and *Io-tamaua-take*[22] whose decree is unchanging. This ends the subject.[23]

All matters of life and death come from Io of the hidden face. Nothing is outside or beyond him. All godships are his to decide. He appoints gods for the dead and the living. All things were created by this god. In every world and realm, each thing has its function. The smallest atoll, grain of dust, and pebble have their place, such as to hold the boundaries of the ocean.

You must also be clear on this fact: the god Io made nothing that will not end. Everything must end, whether from being injured by drought, fire, water, wind, land,[24] sun, or moon—leaving aside those deaths the god decreed should end in this and other worlds.'[25]

At this point of the audience, Rihari Tohī[26] exclaimed, 'O Sir! How did the things you are teaching become known? Perhaps they are only things that you priests think?'

Te Mātorohanga replied:

'I already told you that our knowledge of *wānanga* was brought down by Tāne-nui-a-rangi, the Great Tane of the Heavens. He begged that Io might give him the *wānanga* of Rangi-nui and Papa-tua-nuku, the Sky-father and Earth-mother. Io-the-father agreed, so this knowledge was brought down from heaven to earth. Enough already!

One thing do I ask of you: do not disclose these matters to strangers. Keep these words as a strengthening knowledge for you, your brethren, children, and grandchildren to hold your own in the *marae*[27] of strangers.

I would not disclose to you all the precious things of the *whare-wānanga* had you been a total stranger. But I see that you are bright and quick-witted, that you'll retain what is taught. I am very pleased that you are preserving these things in writing.

One more thing do I ask of you. Learn these precious things but do not gossip about your ancestors or the messengers of the gods. Do not defile these things, lest evil befall you. I warn you of this as I see that, in our day and age, houses are only used for food. Our ancestors' *tapu* houses have disappeared.'

II

Elsdon Best,* 'The cult of Io' (1913)†

Io's name was deemed so sacred that it was never uttered, even by high priests. It was repeated only in secluded spots like a forest, river, pond, or other sheet of water, where nothing man-made like

---

* Elsdon Best (1856-1931) was an ethnographer in the Dominion Museum. He was a founding member of the Polynesian Society and wrote for *The Journal of the Polynesian Society*. He lived in Wellington, Aotearoa New Zealand.

† Edited extract of Elsdon Best, 'The Cult of Io, the Concept of a Supreme Deity as Evolved by the Ancestors of the Polynesians', in *Man*, Vol. 13 (1913): 98-103. This work is in the public domain.

a roof separated speaker from the vault of heaven. At all other times, Io was alluded to as "the Beyond", "the High One", or some such term.

Before Io was invoked, the priest uttering the prayer entered the water nude and stood in it breast deep. He would then stoop to immerse his upper body in the water. In Percy Smith's translation, the priest's opening prayer to Io would say:

> Enter deeply, enter to the very origins,
> Into the very foundations of all knowledge,
> O, Io of the hidden face.
> Gather in, in the inner recesses of the ears,
> As also in the desire, and perseverance, of these thy offspring, thy sons.
> Descend on them thy memory, thy knowledge.
> Rest within the heart, within the roots of origin.
> O, Io the Learned,
> O, Io the Determined.
> O, Io the Self-Created.[28]

No prayers were made to Io on minor or trivial affairs, nor in connection with evil things like war.

No threat or form of punishment ever came from Io. He condemned none. The contest between good and evil was to be fought out in this world. No one was tortured in the afterlife, no soul rewarded for doing good.

'I think', an old Māori quaintly said to me, 'that if your missionaries had sympathised with our people and patiently studied the cult of Io, instead of despising and condemning our belief, that it would have been incorporated with your Bible.'[29]

A few months ago, I visited an elderly Māori[30] deeply versed in the occult lore. We chanced upon the topic of the origin of life, and of that of the spirit. I put this question to him: 'Do the lower animals, trees, and stones possess a *wairua* or soul?'

The old man picked up a stone from the ground, and replied: 'All things possess a *wairua*, otherwise they could not exist. Matter cannot exist without such a principle. This is undeniable. Were this stone not possessed of a *wairua*, then it could not be seen by you; it could not exist, it would disintegrate and disappear.'[31]

When the grey-haired old man stopped speaking, I looked up and saw before me a fair land teeming with the homes of an alien and intrusive people, my own, who discourse glibly of aeroplanes and race over the trails of neolithic man in flying motor cars. And yet I was talking to a man who had evolved these views ere Zenobia dwelt by the palm-lined city of the Orient, when Europe was held by savage tribes of bushmen.

Of what use to me was the cramped mind of the twentieth century for understanding this man's thought? Fifty centuries ago, we deserted the road he treads, long overgrown with the weeds of forgetfulness.

III

A.C. Haddon,* 'The hidden teachings of Māori' (1914)†

In the late 1850s, a great political rally of Māori was held in the Wairarapa district, North Island, when it was decided that instruction in the origin and history of their race should be given to the assembled tribes by three priests, whose words were to be taken down by two scribes, both educated in the mission schools.

One of the two, H.T. Whatahoro, carefully amplified his record subsequently from the dictation of certain learned men, who, in a building erected for the purpose, taught him the lore of the *wharewānanga*, and subjected him to all the ancient forms and rituals.

Till recently these ancient traditions were considered too sacred to be imparted to Europeans. For fifty years, they were jealously guarded, but at length the tribal committee allowed them to be

---

* Alfred Cort Haddon (1855-1940) was an influential British anthropologist. He held a PhD in science from Cambridge University. In 1898, he carried out a famous expedition to the Torres Strait. He lived in Cambridge, UK.

† Edited extract of A.C. Haddon, 'The hidden teaching of the Maori [Review: *The Lore of the Whare-wananga*]', in *The Journal of the Polynesian Society*, Vol. 23, No. 89 (March, 1914): 55-57. This work is in the public domain.

copied and made known. The author had access to the original folio volumes.

The author, Percy Smith, believes that Polynesians may be traced back to India. He even suggests tentatively that 'these Caucasian Polynesians are an early branch of the Proto-Aryan migration into India.'[32] This is, of course, mere hypothesis and will probably remain so.

Mr Smith's method of working is an excellent one: he gives first a transcription of Māori texts, which is followed by careful literal translations of these, with brief explanatory notes and interpolations. Centre and core of the whole religious teaching is the doctrine of Io, 'the supreme god, creator of all things, dwelling in the twelfth, or uppermost, Heaven, where no minor god might enter except by command.'[33]

After death souls go to Hawaiki, the temple situated in the Fatherland, where they are divided. Those who showed love for Io ascend, after purification, to the twelfth Heaven to live in everlasting peace with the god. Those who chose Whiro, the evil spirit, went to Hades, where Whiro reigns together with the god of eruptions and earthquakes and the Great-lady-of-night, who 'drags men down to death'.[34] There is no idea of judgment in the ultimate fate of souls. Rather, it is a matter of free choice during life.

There is abundant evidence that this high god is no modern introduction. The *karakias* or prayers to him contain many obsolete terms. There is a certain resemblance between Moses and the god Tāne, whom Io summons to give him the 'three branches of knowledge and the two sacred stones,'[35] but the author disclaims all leanings to lost-ten-tribe theories.[36]

In a passage of the book, the priest explains why his sacred knowledge was kept secret from Europeans, after whose arrival all became void of *tapu* and ancient teachings were lost. 'We never wished that these [sacred] things should fall into the white man's hands, lest our ancestors become a source of pecuniary benefit,' he says. 'All that the white man thinks of is money, and for these reasons this ancient knowledge of ours was never communicated to the Ministers and Bishops.'[37]

IV

Te Rangi Hīroa,* 'Creating the creators' (1949)†

The discovery of a supreme god named Io in New Zealand was a surprise to Māori and Pākehā alike. For years, we had accepted that gods were co-equal gods and looked after their own domains.

While the literature had mentioned Io, the extent of his claims was not fully realised until Percy Smith and Elsdon Best furnished an extraordinary amount of detail by publishing copious extracts. They both enthusiastically accepted the Io material. But many were doubtful. Io's separation of light from dark, division of the waters, and creation of the earth were too reminiscent of the first chapter of Genesis.

Doubts grew because the source of these claims, Te Mātoro-hanga, and his scribe H.T. Whatahoro, had been converted to Christianity before the detailed story of Io was written down. The discovery of a supreme creator in New Zealand led to a search for the same or similar ones in Polynesia. Incredibly, a mass of secret information allegedly locked up in the minds of cautious Christians was unloosed. The floodgates of memory broke open simply because they were asked about Io.

Io and his acolytes remained aloof from the masses. People had generally never heard of Io. The reason given was that the cult was supposedly too sacred for priests to divulge it to their own flock. The cult of Io did not interfere in any way with the popular religious system.

Unlike Whatahoro's manuscript, there is some authentic evidence in support of Io in a long poem attributed to Tuhoto-Ariki, whose translation I have altered:

---

* Te Rangi Hīroa (1877-1951), a.k.a. Sir Peter Henry Buck, was a prominent Māori politician and doctor. He held an MD from the University of Otago. Of the Ngāti Mutung *iwi*, he was from Urenui, Aotearoa New Zealand.

† Edited extract of Te Rangi Hīroa, Chapter 5, 'The Creation of Creators', *The Coming of the Maori* (Wellington: Māori Purposes Fund Board, 1949), 526-536. This piece is in the public domain.

Whakarongo mai e Tama!	Listen, O my Son!
Kotahi tonu te hiringa,	One only was the incentive,
I kake ai Tane ki,	Why Tane ascended to,
Tikitiki-o-Rangi,	The topmost-sky,
Ko te hiringa i te mahara,	It was the incentive of the thought,
Ka kitea i reira ko,	That there he would behold,
Io-matua-te-kore-anake,	Io-the-parentless,
I a ia te Toi-ariki,	With whom was source of regal might,
Te Toi-urutapu, te Toi-ururangi,	Of sacred and divine control,
Te Toi-uru-ora.	And power over life itself.[38]

The composer of this poem was clearly acquainted with ideas surrounding Io from after the creation periods.

But there is no authentic proof that the concept of a supreme creator named Io existed among central Polynesians before their dispersal to various islands. The Māori concept of Io was a local development in New Zealand. It appears to have originated with the Ngāti Kahungunu tribe, from which rumours of the cult spread to a few other tribes.

Details seem to have been added after the Europeans arrived, when Māori acquired knowledge of the biblical story of creation.

The Io myth, for example, speaks of a clearing house for the spirits of the dead at Hawaikinui. The righteous will go through the east door and ascend to the heavens. Sinners will enter the underworld through the south door. This is contrary to Māori concepts of the afterlife. It is too closely allied to Christian teachings of heaven and hell to have been taught before European contact.

V

Āpirana Ngata,* 'Io's only white adept' (1950)†

Casting doubt on the value of Whatahoro's work, some people have concluded that the cult of Io evolved in New Zealand rather than in the Pacific as he claimed. *I tupu ki konei.*[39] I agree, it evolved here.

---

* Sir Āpirana Turupa Ngata (1874-1950) was a Māori statesman. The first Māori to graduate university locally, he held an LLB from Auckland University. Of the Ngāti Porou *iwi*, he was from Te Araroa, Aotearoa New Zealand.

The evidence of the coverage of the cult of Io in New Zealand shows that it is not confined to one district like the Wairarapa or even the East Coast. The East Coast is fairly uniform in its Io tradition. You find it in the Wanganui River and at Thames. Remarkably from my point of view, you also find it on the East Coast at Tolaga Bay, in the Rakeiora *whare-wānanga*.

As a young man not long settled in the Hokianga and quite unaware of the *tapu* and prohibitions, Judge Maning[40] one day chased after his horse, which had strayed. Suddenly, he heard a voice intoning something. He began to follow the voice and broke in on an old chap stark naked up against a cliff intoning the Io prayer.[41] The old *tohunga* pulled himself up and spoke to the young Pākehā, saying: 'Oh well, you have only got the alternative of death or becoming an adept of this cult.'[42]

Maning chose to become an adept and he was the only Pākehā who made a complete study of the cult of Io. He absorbed it all, *karakia* and everything, and was even initiated in it. Well, in due course he had to go to London for medical advice. He had cancer and wrote down all this material while he was dying. Then his conscience began to prick him because one of the things that you do when you become initiated in the cult of Io is to swear secrecy, and he had taken the oath of secrecy.

Well now, would that obtain in the case of an oath made to a savage? He was arguing that point when he heard of Bishop W.L. Williams from Gisborne.[43] Williams was not a Bishop then but an Archdeacon. So, Maning sent for him and they discussed this question of conscience.

The Archdeacon said, 'Well, your duty is clear. It does not matter whether the oath is given to a heathen or otherwise. Once it is given it is binding on your conscience.' When the Archdeacon left, Maning ordered the housemaid to make a fire and he burned the manuscript.

------

† Edited extract of A.T. Ngata, 'The Io Cult - early migration - puzzle of the canoes', *The Journal of the Polynesian Society*, Vol. 59, No. 4 (1950): 335-346. This piece is in the public domain.

Synkrētic

Now, that story is well accredited. Bishop W.L. Williams told it to Bishop H. Williams,[44] who then told it to me. I said to Herbert, 'What would you have done?' 'Oh,' he said, 'I would have had the manuscript saved in the interest of science.'

A cult like this couldn't have continued to exist in seven different tribes if the secrecy around it had collapsed when the Pākehā came. But it didn't.[45]

VI

Jerry Flexer,* 'Out of many gods, one' (2015)[†]

The American mythology expert David A. Leeming recorded a version of Io's creation story. 'In the beginning,' it says, 'Io uttered words calling on darkness to become light-possessing darkness.'[46] And there was light.

The supreme god Io can perhaps be traced to New Zealand ethnographer Elsdon Best, whose primary source was H.T. Whatahoro's 1913 manuscript, itself based on the teachings of Māori priest Te Mātorohanga.

As a result, many now believe that, although the Māori pantheon contained many gods, Io rules over all as the uncreated creator of the minor gods, universe, and man.

There are obvious parallels between Genesis and the Io creation myth.[47] But, beyond this, Christian missionaries made a variety of religious material available to Māori from the 1830s. This included Māori versions of the Old Testament. Māori felt an affinity with Old Testament stories, studied them with enthusiasm, and often recited whole passages they saw as relevant to them.[48]

This casts some doubt on the idea of the Io creation myth being authentic and predating European contact.

---

* Jerry Flexer is a PhD candidate researching the life and works of Indian philosopher Jiddu Krishnamurti. He holds an MA in Pacific and Asian studies from the University of Victoria. He lives in Victoria, Canada.

† Edited extract of Jerry Flexer, 'From Many Gods to One God', *Online Academic Community*, 27 August 2015.

Te Ahukaramū Charles Royal writes that early Māori mythological material contains no reference to Io before the late 19th century. While some scholars argue that Io was invented to bring Māori beliefs more into line with Christianity, the Io tradition, says Royal, was accepted by many tribal elders. Consequently, as Royal writes, today almost all tribes have a view one way or the other on Io.[49]

Māori Christianity, another scholar suggests, absorbed the Io tradition in such a way that it now 'identifies the Hebrew Jehovah with Io, allowing the genealogies of both traditions to be aligned and providing Māoris with both traditional and Christian identity.'[50]

Regardless of whether the Io myth is a Māori tradition that existed before Europeans came to New Zealand or was invented later, it is a fascinating example of religious syncretism.

Elsdon Best seems to have wanted to use the Io myth to establish that Māori were capable of higher order thinking. At the time, Western scholars and Christian missionaries associated the concept of a supreme god with a high culture. Best believed that, if it had not been for the Io cult, Māori religion would be no more than shamanism.[51]

But for modern Māori, the question is moot. Many Māori tribes now accept Io as part of their traditional pantheon.

There is a lesson in all this for anthropology. As Allen Hanson writes, 'anthropologists too are inventors of culture' because 'ethnographic research and writing inevitably produce cultural inventions'.[52] Elsdon Best, in this case, seems to have been consciously trying to elevate Māori culture in the eyes of European colonisers.[53]

What he may not have foreseen, however, was that his work would catapult the idea of a supreme god into wider Māori culture. Nor could he have predicted that Io would become an umbilical cord connecting the old Māori gods to their adopted Christianity.

Notes

I

H.T. Whatahoro, 'Philosophy of the *whare-wānanga*' (1913)
(Notes by Percy Smith and *Synkrētic*)

1 *Synkrētic* – *Tapu* may refer to holy and sacred objects, religious prohibitions, rules, and restrictions in Māori culture. It is the origin of the English word "taboo".

2 *Waimeha*, without *mana*, powerless.

3 Many interesting *karakias* are still extant, the recitation of which with the proper ritual were held to have power to attract fish to the bait, birds to the snares, and other things, in which the old-time Māori had the firmest belief.

4 *Synkrētic* – *Whatukuras:* male guardian spirits in the twelfth heaven who serve Io as loyal attendants, messengers, etc.

5 *Synkrētic* – *Mareikuras:* female guardian spirits in the twelfth heaven who serve Io as loyal attendants, messengers, etc.

6 *Synkrētic* – *Patupaiarehe* are pale-skinned supernatural creatures who, on some accounts, are hostile to humans because Māori pushed them off their lands. A version of the word's etymology suggests that Māori who first saw Europeans mistook them for *patupaiarehe* (also *pakehakeha*), thus calling them *Pākehā*, the term for white New Zealanders. In modern writings, the *patupaiarehe* and *Tūrehu* are sometimes treated as synonyms for the same mythological creature.

7 All knowledge of these matters was brought from the highest Heaven by the god Tāne, and through him became known to mankind. The names mentioned are those of the male and female guardians, gods, and goddesses of the various Heavens, the two last being the so-called Fairies, the Apsaras of Sanskrit Holy Writ.

8 *Whakatutuki*, is the word in the original. It ordinarily means 'to bring to a finish,' 'to effectually complete'.

9 This idea of the four elements is not Polynesian alone. Among the beliefs of the Yezidi, a people living in the Mosul district of Asiatic Turkey, on the Tigris river, will be found this statement: 'I have created four elements of the earth to fulfil the needs of men, which are water, earth, wind and fire.' This is the second verse of Chapter IV of the Holy Book of the Yezidis, called *Jelwet*, and is supposed to have been written by their god. Also on the same page as above, being the last verse of Chapter IV, we find: 'Ye must not utter my name, nor speak of my shape, for if ye do it is a sin…' This, also, is exactly the doctrine of the cult of Io. His name was never mentioned outside the inner circle of priesthood. Of course, the idea of the four was the common belief of our ancestors at one time. Did the Polynesians evolve the idea from their own study of nature, or did they learn it from some other race or nation? See W.H. Heard, 'Notes on the Yezidis', *Journal of the Royal Anthropological Society*, Vol. XLI: 217.

10 *Synkrētic* – The following two paragraphs, beginning (1) *'There is a reason…'* and (2) *'All matters of life…'*, are drawn from the next section of the same chapter, which is entitled 'Io-Matua, the Supreme God' in the original. Because these paragraphs

extend the priest's definitions of Io, they are inserted here to maintain narrative flow and clarity.

11 *Io-nui*: Io-the-great-god-over-all.

12 *Io-matua:* Io-the-all-parent, the omniparent.

13 *Io-te-wānanga*: Io-of-all-knowledge, the omnierudite.

14 *Io-tikitiki(-o-rangi)*: Io-the-exalted-of-heaven.

15 *Io-mata-aho*: Io-only-seen-in-a-flash-of-light.

16 *Io-matua-kore*: Io-the-parentless, the self-created.

17 *Io-mata-ngaro*: Io-the-hidden-face.

18 *Io-mata-putahi*: Io-the-god-of-one-command.

19 *Io-mata-wai:* Io-god-of-love.

20 *Io-te-hau-e-rangi:* Io-presiding-in-all-heavens.

21 The Scribe informs me that the meaning of this is that Io's presence is in all winds or air, the word *hau* meaning wind, air. Hence, perhaps, the name is better translated as 'all pervading', 'omnipresent'. The idea of the Deity being present in the wind is common to all old Māoris. I have often in former days heard them say as the wind blew through their hair, that the *atua* (god) was there.

22 *Io-tamaua-take:* Io-the-immutable.

23 The name of Io was so sacred that it was rarely mentioned, and then only away from the contaminating influence of food and dwellings. The priests alone had a complete knowledge of him, and ordinary people knew nothing, or never heard his name, except when used in some rarely repeated *karakias*.

24 Unclear. Earthquakes, volcanoes, etc.

25 This is not very clear. Probably, the interruption following put the Sage off as he did not complete his explanation.

26 *Synkrētic* – Possibly an attendant to the priest, Rihari Tohī's identity is not clear from the text and remains unclear.

27 *Marae*, the courtyard or meeting place in a fort (*pa*), where speeches and ceremonies were held.

II

Elsdon Best, 'The cult of Io' (1913)

(Notes by *Synkrētic*)

28 Smith's translated prayer was inserted here, where it logically belongs, rather than at the very end of the article where Elsdon Best placed it in the original article.

29 No name or source has been given for this speaker.

30 No name or source has been given for this speaker.

31 Best clarifies this discussion on the nature of the soul or *wairua* with the following anecdote: 'Addressing his pupils, one teacher closed a session of the traditional Māori school or *whare-wānanga* with the same thought that all things possess a soul.

"There is but one parent of all things, one origin of all things, one god of all things, one lord of all things, one spirit of all things, one soul of all things," he said. "Therefore, O sons, all things are one. All things are one and emanated from Io the Eternal." This may explain why the term *toiora* only refers to the spark of the divine, the portion of the god's *wairua* that is in every man. It represents the spiritual and intellectual welfare of the *genus homo*, whose physical health or welfare is described by the common term *ora*.'

III
A.C. Haddon, 'The hidden teachings of Māori' (1914)
(Notes by *Synkrētic*)

32 Smith, cited in Whatahoro, *The Lore of the Whare-wānanga*, iv.

33 Smith, cited in Whatahoro, *The Lore of the Whare-wānanga*, xiv.

34 Smith, cited in Whatahoro, *The Lore of the Whare-wānanga*, xvi.

35 Smith, cited in Whatahoro, *The Lore of the Whare-wānanga*, x.

36 The author is referring to the theory, popular among missionaries, that Māori descended from the said Lost Tribes of Isræl. Some proponents described Māori as Semites. The theory was at times bundled with the Io myth.

37 Cited in Whatahoro, *The Lore of the Whare-wānanga*, 160.

IV
Te Rangi Hīroa, 'Creating the creators' (1949)
(Notes by author)

38 Tuhoto-Ariki, 'An Ancient Maori Poem', *The Journal of the Polynesian Society*, Vol. 16, No. 1 (1907): 43.

V
Āpirana Ngata's 'Io's only white adept' (1950)
(Notes by *Synkrētic*)

39 The original gives the English translation of these words in brackets as: 'It was evolved here.'

40 Frederick Edward Maning's (1812-1883) manuscript on Io has not been found or published. He had lived among Māori and written under the pen name "Pākehā-Māori". Some suggest he experienced mental breakdown, paranoid delusions, and became alienated from Māori friends and family in the three years leading to his death in London.

41 Ngata uses the term *karakia*, a prayer or incantation.

42 No name or source has been given for this speaker.

43 William Leonard Williams (1829-1916) was an Anglican bishop in the Diocese of Waiapu. He was a prominent scholar of the Māori language. From 1877-1894, he lived in Gisborne where he ran a Māori theological college.

44   Herbert William Williams (1860-1937), William L. Williams' son, was the Anglican bishop of Waiapu and a scholar of Māori. He campaigned with Sir Ngata for Māori to be a recognised academic subject in New Zealand universities.

45   This is an interpretation of Ngata's ambiguous: 'You can't have a cult obtaining amongst seven different tribes unless you were to say that the secrecy which hedged round it had collapsed when the Pakeha came. It did not.'

VI
Jerry Flexer, 'Out of many gods, one' (2015)
(Notes by author)

46   David Leeming, *Creation Myths of the World: An Encyclopedia.* (Santa Barbara, California: ABC–CLIO, 2010), 184.

47   Leeming's story reads as follows: 'In the beginning there was darkness and water, where Io lived alone and was inactive. In order to become active, Io uttered words calling on darkness to become light-possessing darkness. So came light…Day and night were born. Io continued creating with words, calling on the waters to separate and the heavens to be formed. Then Io became the gods. Most important, he created Sky Father and Earth Mother.'

Genesis is the first book in the Hebrew Old Testament, where we find the creation myth that forms the basis of the Judæo-Christian tradition. Genesis 1:1-2:4a reads: 'In the beginning God made heaven and earth. All was empty, chaotic and dark. And God's Spirit moved over the watery deep. God said, let light shine and it did. And God observed the light, and observed that it was good: And God separated the light from the dark…'

Cited in Leeming, *Creation Myths of the World*, 184-185.

48   Bronwyn Elsmore, *Like Them That Dream: The Maori and the Old Testament* (Auckland: Reed Publishing, 2000).

49   Charles Royal, *Māori Creation Traditions. Te Ara – The Encyclopedia of New Zealand*, 2012, available at: <http://www.TeAra.govt.nz/en/Māori-creation-traditions/ accessed June 19, 2015>.

50   Lynne Hume, 'Indigenous Traditions of Oceania and Australasia', in *The World's Religions: Continuities and Transformations*, eds. Peter Clarke and Peter Beyer (London: Routledge 2009), 290-302.

51   Elsdon Best, *Māori: Volume 1, Memoirs of the Polynesian Society* (Wellington, NZ: H.H. Tombs, 1924).

52   Allan Hanson, 'The Making of the Māori: culture invention and its logic', in *American Anthropologist*, Vol. 91, No. 4 (December 1989): 895.

53   James Cox, *The Invention of God in Indigenous Societies* (Durham: Acumen, 2014).

Nakaa and the forbidden tree*

Nei Tearia†
Arthur Grimble‡

This is a creation myth of the Banaban people from Banaba island, Kiribati, in Micronesia.

In the beginning were born Tabakea and his sister Tituabine from the rubbing together of heaven and earth. And as yet it was all a black darkness, for heaven and earth were not yet separated. From the overside of heaven, as it lay upon earth, sprang Banaba. This was the navel of *Tebongiro*, which is to say, the multitude of islands that were in the darkness of heaven and earth.

Then Tabakea lay with his sister Tituabine on Banaba, and she bore him children. Firstborn was a son, whose name was Nakaa the old one. After him were born many others, both men and women. They all lived on Banaba, and Nakaa was chief of them all, for he was the firstborn.

But in those days, the people were innocent. The men knew not the women. So, the brothers of Nakaa lived with him on the north-

---

*   This is a lightly edited version of Arthur Grimble, 'Myths from the Gilbert Islands, II', *I. The Myth of Nakaa and the Forbidden Tree (Nei Tearia of Banaba)*, published in *Folklore*, Vol. 34, No. 4 (Dec. 31, 1923): 370-372. It is reproduced in this form with the kind permission of The Folklore Society.

†   Nei Tearia (fl. 1920s) was a female elder from Tabiang village, Banaba. Lady Tearia is one of the main sources of Banaban oral history recorded in writings by Arthur Grimble, H.C. Maude, and *The Journal of the Polynesian Society*.

‡   Arthur Grimble (1888-1956) was a British administrator in the Gilbert and Ellice Islands (modern-day Kiribati and Tuvalu) and a scholar of Gilbertese culture. He lived in Banaba, Tarawa, Seychelles, Windward Islands, and London.

west side of Banaba, in the place called Bouru. And the women, their sisters, lived apart from the men, on the southeast side of Banaba.

In Bouru, the place of the men, there was a fish trap by the shore, where the fish might never be exhausted. And yet, there was but a single fish in the trap at a time. But, when it was taken out, another took its place right away. In Bouru, there also grew the coconut tree whose fruit was inexhaustible. Yet there grew but a single coconut on the tree at a time. But when it was plucked, another grew right away on the same stalk. The name of that tree was *Tarakaimaiu*, the Tree of Life.

In the place of the women on the southeast side of Banaba there also stood a Tree, whose name was *Karikibai*. That Tree was a woman, and all the brothers of Nakaa were forbidden to approach her.

One day, Nakaa said to his brothers, 'I go on a journey. See that ye pluck not the flowers of the woman called *Karikibai*.' So, he left them, and for a while they remembered his judgment. But the wind bore them the scent of the woman's flowers, and their hearts were full of desire. They said one to another, 'Let us go and see for ourselves; perchance some good thing may happen that Nakaa begrudges us.' So, they went and plucked the woman's flowers and disported themselves with her.

When Nakaa returned from his journey, he looked upon the faces of his brothers and knew that they were no longer children. He was aware of a sweet smell in the air, and knew that it was the smell of the woman's flowers in their hair. He seized hold of them one by one and searched the hairs of their heads. Behold, their hair was beginning to turn grey. And he went to the women of the Tree in the East, and it was the same with them.

So, Nakaa was full of anger and said, 'Fools, that could not abide my word! Old age and death are come among you!'

And he knew that their eyes were blinded, and their hearts darkened with unwisdom. So, he led them to the Tree of Life, and he led them again to the Tree of the Woman, saying, 'Choose, ye fools, between the two Trees, and I will take away with me the Tree that ye choose not.' This he did to try them. And lo, they chose the

Synkrētic

Tree of the Woman, that is also called *Tarakaimate*, the Tree of Death. And Nakaa arose to leave them, taking with him the Tree of Life.

But before he left them, he flung at them a handful of small insects that he had made, wrapped in the leaves of the pandanus tree. And the insects settled on the backs of their heads, and never again left them, nor their children, nor their children's children, until today. And they began to bore at the base of their skulls, until the life was eaten out. And so, men came by their death. And because of the pandanus leaves in which the death-insects were wrapped, we enshroud our dead in a winding-sheet of pandanus leaf matting even to this day.

As for Nakaa, he took away with him the Tree of Life and the fish trap that is never empty. He departed to the western horizon, and there he sits in the heavens awaiting the souls of dead mortals. He faces north, forever weaving nets. And when a soul comes to him, he catches it in the flying strand and laughs with scorn, saying, 'Child of the Woman, thou art come back to me, for my word was a hard word in Bouru.'

Then with jibing words he gazes upon the soul, and if it is of a comely appearance his heart is softened, and he says, 'Pass on to the Tree of Life.' But if the soul is of an unpleasant shape, he throws it into the midst of a struggling heap of souls that are condemned to writhe in everlasting entanglement. The name of that heap is *Te Rekerua*.

NOTES

The legendary David Unaipon's tale

Stephen Muecke *

Professor Muecke, you have researched Aboriginal storytelling since the 1970s and still write on it in your latest book.[1] What drew you to this field?

Back then, narratology was a trending field. And, after reading Tzvetan Todorov, Roland Barthes, Milman Parry and Albert Lord, I became interested in both narrative structure and the formulæ of oral composition.

    I had heard the Aboriginal Elder Paddy Roe tell stories about his fieldwork around Broome, North-West Australia. I'd later have the enormous pleasure and privilege of doing further work with him.[2]

    Aboriginal literature written in English was burgeoning at the time, and the idea of Aboriginal oral storytelling *as literature* was unheard of. Further to that, my training in sociolinguistics made it clear to me that non-standard varieties of language were just as valid and poetic as "the Queen's English".

Your book *Ancient & Modern* (2004) is one of the top Google results for "Aboriginal philosophy". In it, you parody the idea that Aboriginal thinkers need to be as detached as Western scholars to be true philosophers.[3] This made me think of the time Socrates'

---

* Stephen Muecke is Professor Emeritus of Ethnography at UNSW and Adjunct Professor at Notre Dame University. He holds a PhD in linguistics from the University of Western Australia. He lives in Adelaide, Australia.

wife emptied a chamber pot on his head to snap him out of a daydream.[4] Is Aboriginal thought about action?

Yes, I think there is a Western tradition fixated on cognition and interiority, as in the brain and the soul. But Aboriginal thought is externally oriented and, as you say, pragmatic. It has to be if it is to be situated in specific places, relating to multiple ontologies, and articulated with kinship.

If, as Aboriginal thinkers assert, Country is alive and specific places have power, then I think I am right to say that people *attend to* these powerful life forces. People don't have mastery over Country, its laws, and Dreamings.[5] Country will guide them. In this sense, Country is philosophising as well.

Aboriginal Dreamings point to a world rich in ontologies. Dreamings are as real as a snake, a tree, or a song.

Finally, kinship is reciprocal, situated, tying human beings to specific kinds of animals and plants, and to the wider seasons and patterns of this world.

Children learn their kinship rights and obligations from a young age, and much time is spent discussing this complex system. Intergenerational and multispecies kinship could be said to be a central topic in Aboriginal philosophy.

Ngarrindjeri man David Ngunaitponi (Unaipon), who is depicted on Australia's $50 bill, may be the first Aboriginal person to be called a philosopher.* Praised as a polymath, Leonardo-like, a Renaissance Man, some meant by this that an Aboriginal philosopher was 'a contradiction in human terms'.[6] Unaipon must have had a thick skin to write when he did.

Yes, he must have had amazing resilience and energy to be doing that intellectual work back in the 1920s, buffeted on all sides by en-

---

* See David Unaipon, 'How koalas lost their tails', *Synkrētic* №1 (Feb. 2022): 133-144.

trenched racisms, and condescension at best. I was attracted by the fact that this first great Aboriginal scholar was neglected.

I was interested in the emergence of Aboriginal literature in English, whose beginnings people often associate with Kath Walker (Oodgeroo), Jack Davis and Colin Johnson (Mudrooroo) writing in the 1960s. So, I was amazed by what Unaipon had done forty years earlier.

His personal qualities are unfortunately more elusive. His would-be biographers have come up against a scant archive. Hopefully his letters will be discovered some day.

Curiously, philosophers feature as protagonists in some of Unaipon's tales.* Was he using terms like "philosopher" to explain Aboriginal concepts?

Analogy is the key rhetorical term for him. I think his writings, lectures, and scientific demonstrations were performances designed to convince a sceptical audience that his people were "as good as" white people.

Because he used this trope, his writings about his own people weren't anthropologically realistic. The social sciences were in their infancy at the time and his was an insider account. He drew on whatever he could from his wide readings.

In one story,† Unaipon shows young Indigenous people having their flesh mortified as a rite of passage. This was also practised by the Stoics, Cynics, Buddhists, Hindus, and Christians. These traditions also share the idea that philosophy is a thing you physically *do*. Is Aboriginal thought like that?

I think you're right. The idea that knowledge comes as easily as reading books and remembering some of their content seems like a weak version of knowledge acquisition.

---

* See 'How Teddy lost his tail', 141-143.
† See 'Belief of the Aborigine in a Great Spirit', 134-137.

But when it comes to being initiated into knowledge, with the marks literally inscribed on one's body, and the knowledge becoming inalienable and repeatable, there is clearly an epistemological price to pay.

There may be something like this pain in the process of writing a PhD, but we moderns tend to downplay the ritual aspects of this transformation process—even though we dress in mediæval gowns for graduation ceremonies.

Right. I hadn't made the connection between ritual and learning before.

Pierre Hadot's *Philosophy as a Way of Life* speaks to this idea.[7] In my reading, a ritual substratum also runs through the Western Judæo-Christian tradition. But it has been supressed by the emphasis on the rational individual and on cognitivism.

Pragmatism is also evident, I think, in Aboriginal traditions, where learning by example is stressed. A boy follows his mother's brother in the pre-initiation journey. Rather than pestering him with questions, he learns to attend to what he does and how he does it.

Logos is perhaps not central to this tradition.

Western philosophy is often called a series of footnotes to Plato.[8] That's interesting when you consider that Plato wrote stories and myth. Is that to say that the European philosophical tradition, too, is rooted in myth?

This would be true for certain kinds of Western philosophical schools, those that read Michel Serres for instance.[9] Or those who agree with Wittgenstein that 'an entire mythology is stored within our language.'[10] I am sympathetic to this line of enquiry. I think it is richly poetic and describes the cosmos better than logical-symbolic formulæ ever will.

It's also true of Aboriginal traditions, in which storytelling facilitates intergenerational knowledge transfer. "Yarning"[11] is also a way to form a collective consensus. Stories can also illustrate traditional laws using myth.

Unaipon was the first Australian Aboriginal to write a book, publish it in English, research perpetual motion, design a helicopter, and invent mechanical sheep shears. But his biography is also a litany of injustices, among them that others profited from his shears. Most egregiously, until 2001, W. Ramsay Smith was credited as the author of a book actually written by Unaipon. How did this happen?

My co-author Adam and I recount the whole story in our introduction to *Legendary Tales of the Australian Aborigines*.[12] Very briefly, Unaipon was contracted to write the book but, when it was nearly finished, he missed a telegram relating to it.

The opportunistic Ramsay Smith intervened and secured the rights. Smith was the kind of guy who trafficked human remains back to England, so stealing Unaipon's IP would not have given him pause.

But we have to consider the historical context. An Aboriginal author in 1929 would have been an amazingly progressive move for a publisher, even though Unaipon had already published a few pamphlets.

The story of how Unaipon's rights were restored is incredible. I understand that you and your colleague Adam Shoemaker achieved this by re-editing *Legendary Tales*, and publishing it in David Unaipon's name for the first time. How did this happen, and how did it feel to right such a great wrong?

Well, we knew that the Mitchell Library in Sydney held the original manuscript. From there, it was only a matter of restoring it.

We collaborated with his descendant, Harold Kropinyeri, and met some of the other members of his family. We called our introduction 'Repatriating the Story' to symbolise the reversal of what Ramsay Smith had done.

And we made an occasion of it, bringing the book back and handing it over at a launching event at the Art Gallery of South

Australia. That felt good, as did the privilege of publishing with the prestigious Miegunyah imprint at Melbourne University Publishing.

In *Legendary Tales*, Unaipon looks forward to the day when 'Australian writers will use Aboriginal myths and weave literature from them,' just as they cite Græco-Roman myths.* There's a sad irony to this: the gift of his culture was stolen from his open hands. But his words are so full of hope.

Unaipon, like Paddy Roe, lived into his mid-nineties. These men saw massive changes, with their cultures taken to the brink of destruction, surrounded by insensitive invaders who treated their disappearance as inevitable. How could they have had any hope, one has to wonder.

Both men realised that white and black would have to live together, and Unaipon was a Christian who used writing and performance to forge a syncretic future for his culture. He avoided confrontation, seeking higher accomplishments in science, literature, and philosophy.

Are we getting close to realising Unaipon's vision for Australian culture?

No, Aboriginal myths have not yet displaced Græco-Roman ones in Australia.

I think we first have to get around monotheism to restore what the Græco-Roman and the Aboriginal share: the *paganism* of multiple spirits, with one for all significant landscape features like the winds, water, and home.

The singular god is too mobile and destructive, while spirits have to be respected and cared for in their places.

Unaipon says the Water Spirit 'is the most multiple Spirit of all,' and that 'Everything that exists has some life apart from itself.'[13] These are profound ecological insights that have nothing to do with Christian thought.

Gems like these are scattered throughout Unaipon's work.

---

* See 'Aboriginal folklore', 133-134.

Notes

1 Stephen Muecke and Paddy Roe, *The Children's Country: Creation of a Goolarabooloo Future in North-West Australia* (London: Rowman & Littlefield International, 2021).

2 Paddy Roe (c.1912-2001), also known as Lulu, was an Aboriginal Elder of the Goolarabooloo people, told the stories which Stephen Muecke transcribed in their ground-breaking collaboration, which was first published in 1983. See Paddy Roe, *Gularabulu: Stories from the West Kimberley*, ed. Stephen Muecke (Perth: UWA Publishing, 2016).

3 Stephen Muecke, *Ancient & Modern: Time, Culture and Indigenous Philosophy* (Sydney: NSW University Press, 2004), 111.

4 Diogenes Laërtius, *Lives of the Eminent Philosophers*, transl. Robert Drew Hicks (1929), Loeb Classical Library edition, Volume 1, published 1925, section 2.36-37.

5 *The Dreaming* or *Dreamtime* is a core concept in traditional Aboriginal cultures, one whose content varies across groups. R.M. Berndt defines it as a symbiotic view of life that places 'human beings within a preordained scheme or patterning symbolising a three-sided relationship between mythic beings, nature and people. Each was dependent on the others.' Cited in E.A. O'Keefe, 'Towards an Understanding of the Significance of "The Dreamtime" to Aboriginal People', *The Australian Journal of Indigenous Education*, Vol. 12, Issue 4 (September 1984): 50.

6 Barry Judd, Rachel Standfield, Katherine Ellinghaus, 'Unaipon: Behind the Da Vinci Comparisons', *Pursuit*, available at: <https://pursuit.unimelb.edu.au/articles/unaipon-behind-the-da-vinci-comparisons>.

7 See Pierre Hadot, *Philosophy as a Way of Life: Spiritual Exercises from Socrates to Foucault*, ed. Arnold Davidson, transl. Michael Chase (Hoboken, New Jersey: Wiley, 1995).

8 Alfred North Whitehead, *Process and Reality* (New York: Macmillan Company, 1969), 39.

9 French philosopher Michel Serres (1930-2019) described mythological figures like angels and Hermes as metaphorical concepts for communication. Michel Serres, *Angels, a Modern Myth* (Paris: Flammarion, 1995).

10 Duncan Richter, *Historical Dictionary of Wittgenstein's Philosophy* (Lanham, Maryland: Rowman & Littlefield Publishers, 2014), 145.

11 "To yarn", "to have a yarn", "to be yarning with" is an expression associated with Aboriginal English and rural Australians. It can mean to casually converse with a group, to have an intimate conversation with someone, or, especially in the Aboriginal context, to purposively strengthen social connections by telling and sharing stories.

12 David Unaipon, *Legendary Tales of the Australian Aborigines*, eds. Stephen Muecke and Adam Shoemaker (Melbourne: Melbourne University Press, 2001).

13 Unaipon, *Legendary Tales of the Australian Aborigines*, 53.

Pythagoras in India*

Voltaire†

All the world knows that Pythagoras, while he resided in India, attended the school of the Gymnosophists and learned the language of beasts and plants. One day, while he was walking in a meadow near the seashore he heard these words:

'How unfortunate that I was born an herb! I scarcely attain two inches in height, when a voracious monster, a horrid animal, tramples me under his large feet; his jaws are armed with rows of sharp scythes, by which he cuts, then grinds, and then swallows me. Men call this monster a sheep. I do not suppose there is in the whole creation a more detestable creature.'

Pythagoras proceeded a little way and found an oyster yawning on a small rock. He had not yet adopted that admirable law by which we are enjoined not to eat those animals which have a resemblance to us. He had scarcely taken up the oyster to swallow it, when it spoke these affecting words:

'O Nature, how happy is the herb, which is, as I am, thy work! Though it be cut down, it is regenerated and immortal, and we, poor oysters, in vain are defended by a double cuirass; villains eat us by

* Edited version of Voltaire, 'An Adventure in India', *The Works of Voltaire. A Contemporary Version. Romances*, Vol. III, ed. Tobias Smollett, transl. William F. Fleming (New York: E.R. DuMont, 1901). This work is in the public domain.

† François-Marie Arouet, a.k.a. Voltaire (1694-1778) is one of the most influential Enlightenment writers. He is famous for defending tolerance and attacking the abuses of power by church and state. He lived in Paris, France.

dozens at their breakfast, and all is over with us forever. What a horrible fate is that of an oyster, and how barbarous are men!'

Pythagoras shuddered; he felt the enormity of the crime he had nearly committed; he begged pardon of the oyster, with tears in his eyes, and replaced it very carefully on the rock. As he was returning to the city, profoundly meditating on this adventure, he saw spiders devouring flies, swallows eating spiders, and sparrowhawks eating swallows. 'None of these,' said he, 'are philosophers.'

On his entrance, Pythagoras was stunned, bruised, and thrown down by a rabble in ragged clothes who were running and crying: 'Well done, he fully deserved it.'

'Who? What?' said Pythagoras, as he was getting up.

The people continued running and crying: 'Oh, how delightful it will be to see them boiled!'

Pythagoras supposed they meant lentils or some other vegetables, but he was in error; they meant two poor Indians. 'Oh!' said Pythagoras, 'these Indians, without doubt, are two great philosophers weary of their lives; they are desirous of regenerating under other forms; it affords pleasure to a man to change his place of residence, though he may be but indifferently lodged; there is no disputing on taste.'

He proceeded with the mob to the public square, where he perceived a lighted pile of wood and a bench opposite to it, which was called a tribunal. On this bench judges were seated, each of whom had a cow's tail in his hand and a cap on his head, with ears resembling those of the animal which bore Silenus when he came into that country with Bacchus, after having crossed the Erythræan sea without wetting a foot, and stopping the sun and moon, as it is recorded with great fidelity by the Orphics.

Among these judges there was an honest man with whom Pythagoras was acquainted. The Indian sage explained to the sage of Samos the nature of that festival to be given to the people of India.

'These two Indians,' the sage said, 'have not the least desire to be committed to the flames. My grave brethren have adjudged them to be burnt; one for saying that the substance of Śākra[1] is not that of Brahma, and the other for supposing that the approbation of the

Supreme Being was to be obtained at the point of death without holding a cow by the tail.[2] "Because," one of the men reasoned, "we may be virtuous at all times, and we cannot always have a cow to lay hold of just when we may have occasion." The good women of the city were greatly terrified at two such heretical opinions; they would not allow the judges a moment's peace until they had ordered the execution of those unfortunate men.'

Pythagoras was convinced that, from the herb up to man, there were many causes of chagrin. However, he obliged the judges and even the devotees to listen to reason, which happened only at that time.

He went afterwards and preached toleration at Crotona,[3] but a bigot set fire to his house and he was burned to death—the man who had delivered the two Hindus from the flames! Let those save themselves who can!

Synkrētic

Notes

These notes are provided by Synkrētic to clarify references and other details of interest.

1   *Śākra:* Voltaire's *Xaca* is the French spelling for *Śakra* or *Sakka:* the ruler of the gods in the *trāyastriṃśa* heaven in Buddhism, and an epithet of the god Indra in Hinduism. Traditionally, Indra and Brahma jointly protected Buddha. The theological dispute Voltaire posits between the 'substance' of Śakra and Brahma is thus likely a nonsensical play on European debates on the nature of God for polemical reasons. Voltaire is using Hinduism as a vehicle to attack what he called *l'infâme*, that is religious obscurantism in Europe. See D.T. Devendra, 'Brahma and Indra with the Buddha', in *The Journal of the Ceylon Branch of the Royal Asiatic Society of Great Britain & Ireland*, Vol. 14 (1970): 55-57.

2   *Holding a cow by the tail:* A reference to a Hindu custom according to which a dying person held onto a cow's tail, which animal was believed to then guide the dead person's soul across the terrifying Vaitarani river. The belief is based on the following verses from a Hindu holy text: 'I have presented this to you, being desirous of crossing that river…Salutations to Vaitarani. O Cow, look upon me, for the sake of my passing through the gateway of Yama on the great path.' *Garuda Purana*, transl. Ernest Wood and S.V. Subrahmanyam (Allahabad: Panini Office, 1911), 71.

3   *Toleration at Crotona:* Regardless of whether the story of Pythagoras' visit to India is true, which scholars still debate, he did settle in Crotona where he founded a community. Pythagoras was driven out but perhaps not for preaching tolerance, as Voltaire imagines after his own image, so much as for being perceived as meddling in local politics. See George P. Conger, 'Did India Influence Early Greek Philosophies?', *Philosophy East and West*, Vol. 2, No. 2 (Jul. 1952): 116-117.

On learning to forgive*

Anshi Zhou[†]

TRANSLATED BY *Brian Chung*[‡]

The myriad teachings of the wise and sagely all encourage people to reflect on their own behaviour, and for those in whom the habit of self-reflection and improvement is cultivated, there can be no time to spare for blaming others. Offences done by accident are easy to forgive, but wilful wickedness is hard to forgive. However, those who wish to cultivate themselves must start by forgiving all that which is hardest to forgive. If even intentional mistakes can be forgiven, then all lesser offences can be easily forgotten. If the offences are grave to the point of being completely intolerable, they must still be tolerated, no matter how hard doing so is. How could we accomplish this level of forgiveness? There are three methods:

1. Recognise that the offender's actions are born out of their ignorance. It would be unreasonable to judge them in accordance with the standard of the sages, or to expect much from them. Our disappointment is due to our own excessive expectations, so the fault lies with us.

2. Pity the short lifespans of the offenders [*i.e. evil deeds karmically shorten a person's lifespan*]. Their human life passes as fast as a bolting steed, with the days decreasing constantly, like a condemned person being led step by step to the gallows. How could we not pity them?

3. Use them as medicine to heal ourselves. As our own faults are often unknown to us, we can only identify them by observing the wickedness of others, using them as a mirror to self-reflect. Therefore, as they are like our teachers, how could we not be grateful?

When our hearts were not at peace, we were afflicted by a field of thorns, and even little ants seemed like mighty obstacles. A heart at peace is as stable as a citadel.

---

* This is an edited extract of Brian Chung's translation of Upasaka Zhou Anshi's commentary on Wen Chang's Buddhist text *Yin Chih Wen (The Tract of the Quiet Way)*. Brian Chung released this translation into the public domain. See Brian By Sheng Chung, 'Why is it so hard for people to forgive?', in *Quora*, 15 October 2021, p. 88 of original.

† Zhou Mengyan (周夢顏) a.k.a. Zhou Anshi (1656-1739) was a Qing dynasty-era Chinese Buddhist lay writer.

‡ Brian Bye Sheng Chung is a translator of rare Pure Land Buddhist scriptures from the original Chinese texts.

Synkrētic
SUBMISSIONS

Australia and its place in the world continue to evolve. Now more than ever, we have to understand our region and our place in it. *Synkrētic* is an outlet for thought-provoking writing on philosophy, literature and cultures, from and about the Indo-Pacific. It aims to showcase the diverse traditions of thought, story-telling and expression which are woven into the living tapestry of this culturally, linguistically and politically complex region. We're looking above all for well-written and substantive pieces for publication in the following formats.

Essays	3000 - 6000 words
Stories	≤ 8000 words
Responses	800 - 1600 words
Translations	≤ 8000 words
Notes	300 - 3000 words

For details and guidelines:
synkretic.com

www.ingramcontent.com/pod-product-compliance
Lightning Source LLC
Chambersburg PA
CBHW032134020426
42334CB00016B/1156